The Trials of Frances

The Trials of Frances Howard

Fact and Fiction at the Court of King James

David Lindley

London and New York

First published 1993
First published in paperback 1996
by Routledge
11 New Fetter Lane, London EC4P 4EE

Simultaneously published in the USA and Canada
by Routledge
29 West 35th Street, New York, NY 10001

Routledge is an International Thomson Publishing company

© 1993, 1996 David Lindley

Typeset in 10 on 12 point Bembo by
Selwood Systems, Midsomer Norton
Printed and bound in Great Britain by
Biddles Ltd, Guildford and King's Lynn

British Library Cataloguing in Publication Data
A catalogue record for this book is available from the British Library

Library of Congress Cataloguing in Publication Data
A catalogue record for this book has been requested

ISBN 0-415-05206-8 (hbk)
ISBN 0-415-14424-8 (pbk)

Contents

Plates

Acknowledgements

Without the aid of librarians and archivists an enterprise such as this would be, literally, unthinkable. I therefore thank the staffs of Berkshire Record Office, the British Museum, the British Library, the Bodleian Library, Cambridge University Library, Chester Record Office, Northamptonshire Record Office, the National Library of Wales, and, perhaps most of all, those who work in the University Library and Brotherton Collection at my home base in Leeds.

Colleagues in the School of English at Leeds have been unfailingly generous with their time in answering questions and suggesting sources of information. Especial thanks go to Michael Brennan, Martin Butler, Andrew Hadfield, Paul Hammond and Stephanie Wright for their advice and help. The supportive and encouraging environment of the School has played a major part in sustaining my work.

At a time when so much in our culture seems to be driving towards individualism and privatisation, it is refreshing to remark the fact that instincts of mutual support and generous sharing of information are very much alive and well within the community of academics. I am enormously grateful to a number of people, often encountered briefly at academic conferences, who have put me in touch with material of many kinds, and have plugged many a gap in my knowledge. To A.R. Braunmuller, Pauline Croft, David Harley, Lynn Hulse and Lois Potter I express my gratitude. An especial debt is owed to Arthur Marotti, Alastair Bellany, Jeremy Maule and Bruce R. Smith, who each drew my attention to important manuscript sources that I would otherwise have overlooked, and which have proved of great significance in the argument of the book. This study would have been materially the poorer without their generosity. I am grateful also to Matilde Coletta and Stephen Ryle for their translation of Italian and Latin texts.

To Jane Hayward, whose careful reading of the typescript saved me from many stylistic infelicities and aided the clarity of my presentation in innumerable ways, I owe a great deal; though, of course, neither she nor any of those whose help I gratefully acknowledge here bears any responsibility for the final product.

Finally, in these pressured times, when research and writing becomes increasingly difficult, I wholeheartedly express my gratitude to the British Academy for a grant from the Small Grants Fund for Research in the Humanities which enabled me to spend time in London, and to the Leverhulme Trust, whose award to Leeds University gave me that most precious resource of all, a year free from teaching and other responsibilities in which the book was completed.

The author and publishers wish to thank the following for permission to use pictorial material:

Plates 1 and 2 are reproduced by courtesy of the National Portrait Gallery, London.
Plate 3, from MS Dd.3.63, by permission of the Syndics of Cambridge University Library.
Plates 4, 5(a), 6 and 9 are copyright the British Museum, London.
Plate 5(b) is reproduced from *Bazilil logia*, Rawlinson 4°.170, by permission of the Bodleian Library, Oxford.
Plates 7, 11, 12 and 13 are reproduced by permission of the Society of Antiquaries of London.
Plate 8 is reproduced from a copy in the Brotherton Collection, University of Leeds.
Plate 10 is reproduced from the Devonshire Collection, Chatsworth, by permission of the Chatsworth Settlement Trustees.

Note: In quotations from primary sources I have used modernised editions where possible. When citing manuscripts, seventeenth-century editions or modern old-spelling texts I have reproduced the spelling of the originals, but silently regularised i/j and u/v and expanded contractions. I have occasionally modified punctuation where this has seemed necessary to aid clarity. All quotations from Shakespeare are taken from *The Oxford Shakespeare: The Complete Works,* ed. Stanley Wells and Gary Taylor (Oxford: Clarendon Press, 1988); Jonson's masques are quoted from *Ben Jonson: The Complete Masques,* ed. Stephen Orgel (New Haven and London: Yale University Press, 1969).

David Lindley
The University of Leeds, January 1993

Abbreviations

The following abbreviations are used in text and notes:

BL   British Library

Chamberlain   *The Letters of John Chamberlain,* ed. Norman Egbert
              McClure (Philadelphia: The American Philosophical
              Society, 1939)

CSP   Calendar of State Papers

CUL   Cambridge University Library

HMC   Reports of the Historical Manuscripts Commission

SP   State Papers

ST   *Complete Collection of State Trials,* ed. T.B. Howell, vol. II
              (London, 1816)

Introduction

On 24 May 1616, in a crowded Westminster Hall, Frances Howard, Countess of Somerset, pleaded guilty to having planned the murder of Sir Thomas Overbury three years earlier, while he was a prisoner in the Tower. With the conviction on the following day of her husband, Robert Carr, the greatest scandal of the Jacobean age came to its conclusion. In the case of Frances Howard it was the climactic event in an already chequered life. Born in 1592/3, she had been married in 1606 to the third Earl of Essex. The marriage failed, and in 1613 Frances sued for its annulment on the grounds of her husband's impotence. Immediately the annulment was secured she was married again to Robert Carr, the King's favourite. These events had outraged the Jacobean moral majority, but scandal reached its peak in 1615 when it was revealed that she had been implicated in murdering Sir Thomas Overbury, Carr's friend and political adviser, to prevent his opposition to her divorce. In the trials allegations of witchcraft and more than a suspicion of corruption at the highest political level added to the potent brew, and it is little wonder that the story made such a powerful impact upon contemporary society.

It is a story which has often been retold since,[1] and it might legitimately be asked what justification there is for a further book on the subject. The purpose of this study is not, however, merely to provide another consecutive narrative account of Frances Howard's life (though in the course of what follows many of the details of the received story will be questioned). I will be concerned much more with issues that are raised by and through the accounts of these events, and particularly by the characterisation that Frances Howard has received, both in her own time and in the writings of subsequent historians. The sensation that the Overbury murder trials generated at the time was enormous. Like the lurid tabloid headlines about collapsing marriages in the British royal family, or the news of sexual scandals that have afflicted senior politicians in recent years, the public interest in the revelations of 1615–16 betokens a sense of a symbolic importance in these events which extends far beyond the actual details. There is a further significance in the fact that, both at the time and subsequently, all accounts of Frances Howard have concurred in the representation of her as an epitome of female villainy, malicious, irrational and lustful. The main purpose of this book is to investigate why this scandal should have provoked the response that it did, and to attempt both to understand and to query the stereotypical picture of the woman at its centre. In the process questions inevitably arise about the ways in which narratives are constructed and reproduced, and about the nature and use of historical evidence. It is with those questions that I begin.

Firstly, the documentary evidence upon which the standard picture of Frances Howard has been based must be examined. It is immediately striking that almost nothing that is known about her derives from anything she herself wrote or said. The evidence of the annulment hearings and of the Overbury murder trials leaves many gaps, and those gaps in her history have been filled in largely with gossip and scandal derived from later accounts by writers who clearly had an axe to grind. Arthur Wilson, for example, whose *History of Great Britain* was published in 1653, had been the servant of Frances Howard's first husband, the Earl of Essex – but only after he was divorced.[2] Wilson was a Parliamentarian, and keen therefore to depict the luxury, immorality and vanity of the Stuart courts as justification for the uprising of the Civil War. Sir Anthony Weldon, author of the *Court and Character of King James* (1650) was also a strong Parliamentarian, and had earlier been dismissed from the court of James I for lampooning the Scots. Again he seems unlikely to be the most disinterested of reporters. There were accounts by royalists, one by Bishop Godfrey Goodman, which was not published until 1839, and Sir William Sanderson's *Aulicus Coquinariae* of 1650, designed specifically to answer Weldon; but, though they are much more benign in their representation of Carr and the Howards, their accounts, like those of their opponents, are largely undifferentiated compilations of gossip, rumour and so-called eye-witness reports.

It might properly be objected that it is the job of the historian to see through the bias of contemporary scandal-mongers, and to weigh dispassionately the evidence put before the juries at the Overbury trials. But in recent years there has been increasing recognition that no history is ever utterly impartial. Hayden White has gone further than most in claiming that all historical writing is itself a species of narrative, and that:

what the historian brings to his consideration of the historical record is a notion of the types of configurations of events that can be recognised as stories by the audience for which he is writing... How a given historical situation is to be configured depends on the historian's subtlety in matching up a specific plot structure with the set of historical events that he wishes to endow with meaning of a particular kind. This is essentially a literary, that is to say fiction-making operation.[3]

White suggests that any historian's approach to documentary material is inevitably already conditioned by a range of pre-existent story-patterns into which a narrative might be cast. The model, in his view, precedes particular examples. His theories have come under fierce attack from historians who hold fast to the possibility of objectivity, and to the view that the true historian confronts the documentary record with an open mind.[4] Whatever claims might be made for the objectivity of certain kinds of historical writing, however, it will become very obvious indeed that Frances Howard's story is filled out in accordance with paradigms that derive from somewhere other than 'hard evidence' – and that this is as true of modern historians' accounts as it is of the more transparently biased near-contemporary witnesses.

And this raises the second general problem. If one wants to reconstruct the influences and assumptions which dictated the way contemporaries saw and recorded the story of Frances Howard, then the obvious place to look is to the literature of the period. In its literature a culture represents itself to itself, and from it it derives its sense of what constitutes a satisfying story. Historians have traditionally been sceptical of the value of literary evidence, but a major argument of this book is that literary models do not just provide a background for the story of Frances Howard, a fortunate coincidence between her lurid history and the stockpile of motifs that provided the source material for many Renaissance writers. I will be arguing that there is a continuous interplay between real and fictional worlds, and that literary texts do far more than merely reduplicate the concerns that are evident in the history of Frances Howard. In them, I will be suggesting, we can more clearly perceive the matrix of assumptions that conditioned the way her contemporaries saw her, and through them we can understand the ideology that dictated the manner in which they represented her.

In saying this, of course, I am drawing upon many of the ideas that recent critical theories, particularly those of 'cultural materialists' and 'new historicists' have put into circulation. They have argued that the old distinction between literary 'foreground' and historical 'background' is unsustainable. As Jean Howard summarises it:

> Rather than passively reflecting an external reality, literature is an agent in constructing a culture's sense of reality. It is part of a much larger symbolic order through which the world at a particular historical moment is conceptualized and through which a culture imagines its relationship to the actual conditions of its existence.[5]

Historical and literary evidence, then, may be regarded as in important respects complementary one to another, and I will be exploring the relationship between them throughout the book.

There is a further ingredient in the traditional story that needs to be considered. A great deal of the evidence about Frances Howard's career was produced in legal contexts, in the annulment hearings and in the murder trials. It can be argued that these proceedings, like the writing of history or of literature, are also always conditioned by particular cultural assumptions, and that lawyers, like historians or the authors of plays and poems, are intent primarily on producing satisfying narrative structures. Then and now, the court-room is a place where stories are recounted with a particular purpose in view – the production of a verdict of guilt or innocence. Bennett and Feldman have argued that all modern trials are founded upon processes of story-making. As they succinctly put it:

> in order to understand, take part in, and communicate about criminal trials, people transform the evidence introduced in trials into stories about the alleged criminal activities.[6]

As we will see, the way trials in seventeenth-century England were conducted meant that lawyers were even freer to make and to impose their narrative upon the world than are their modern counterparts. But the central point is manifest – the 'history' of Frances Howard which emerged at the trials for murder was constructed with only one end in view. With the recent lengthening series of overturned convictions in British courts, the unreliability of trial evidence, including the confession of the accused, scarcely needs to be stressed.

At this point it might seem that there is nothing left that is fixed and stable – historical narrative, literary texts and lawyers' arguments are all reduced to story-making. It is not my intention to become deeply involved in theoretical debates for their own sake, although it will be obvious that the direction this book takes owes a great deal to these newer approaches to law, as well as to history and literature. I will, instead, be offering a re-examination of Frances Howard's story as a kind of practical case-history, which might test some of the current presuppositions of such theories. In one important respect this study departs significantly from them. The tendency of many of these approaches has been to insist that ultimately there is nothing that is knowable outside language, and, since language is always dictated by the ideology of its period, it is argued that to search for a 'truth' which lies beyond the linguistic traces of the archive becomes a pursuit of the pot of gold at the end of the rainbow. It is an argument that is seductive, but, in the end, I believe, unsustainable.

At the simplest level there is, after all, a profound difference between an historical and a fictional account of a character. In Webster's *The White Devil*, for example, Vittoria, the central female figure, is put on trial for the murder of her husband. She defends herself vigorously, and in her confrontation with her judges earns admiration from most readers. The scene raises many questions about the position of women in the face of male power and the systems of law which embody it, questions which, as we will see, are immediately relevant to the case of Frances Howard. But within the fictional world which is the play, we know what Vittoria has done; notwithstanding the pity we may feel for her oppression in the court-room, she actually did consent to her husband's death. Furthermore, though an actress in interpreting the role might give different emphasis to aspects of her character, there is nothing that we can know about Vittoria that is not contained within Webster's text. But when we consider the case of Frances Howard we know that a person existed beyond the records that survive, however comprehensively they have been researched, and therefore we are always aware that the question of whether or not she did the things for which she was found guilty remains potentially open.

During the early stages of thinking about this book I was called to do jury service. The experience of acting as a juror in a real trial, rather than a literary debate, forced me to contemplate this problem in a very direct and pressing fashion. As an academic I might go into the court supplied with all kinds of theories about the way stories are made, and about the ultimate unknowability of facts outside the language in which they were represented; I might be fully aware that the trial would be at one level a story-telling contest. In the jury room, however, forced to adjudicate between those stories, and then go back to deliver a verdict which meant imprisonment for the accused, I could not avoid the recognition that the decision of the jury had very material consequence for the individual concerned. To this day, of course, I do not know absolutely whether the story we agreed to believe was 'true' or not; I do know that a decision about the character of the accused was necessary in order to choose one story over its competitor, but that, at the same time, to assent to one of the available stories itself determined how that person was perceived.

All this may seem a long way from a book about the career of a long-dead woman. But I want to argue that, just as in real-life jury service, the decisions one makes about a character and the judgement one comes to upon the truth of a particular story are absolutely intertwined. If one believes that Frances Howard was indeed a lustful and appetitive woman who seduced Robert Carr, and if one accepts that she committed multiple adultery and followed it up with murder, then one's response to her will be very different from that which would follow from a belief in her partial or total innocence. As will become apparent, I argue that there is a real possibility that the early part of her life has been misrepresented, and that she was far from the promiscuous figure of legend. But, at the same time, I believe it is most likely that she did intend to murder Thomas Overbury. What then becomes interesting is the consequence of separating the two halves of a story that has for centuries been persuasive precisely because it seemed to be so inevitable a sequence. In focusing upon the real complexity of the sequence of events that makes up Frances Howard's history, the cultural force of the narrative patterns imposed upon it becomes even more striking.

The arguments of this book do not ultimately stand or fall on the question of Frances Howard's actual guilt. Put crudely, if she was indeed the 'wicked woman' of legend, then the analysis of the implications of her representation will function as, for example, a discussion of the character of Lady Macbeth might, in leading to an understanding of the ideology that lies behind the exaggerated horror with which such female villains are regarded. If she were partially or totally innocent of the charges, however, then we might want to protest more strongly at the actual consequences that the power of such stereotypes had, and perhaps still has, for women.

As a prelude, and as a miniature case-study of the problems involved, it is helpful to consider the particular example of the way in which the portrait of Frances Howard attributed to William Larkin (Plate 1) has been read by three recent writers.

In David Riggs's magisterial biography of Ben Jonson the portrait is reproduced with the comment: 'the anonymous painter evokes Lady Somerset's unabashed sexuality and menacing gaze'.[7] G.P.V. Akrigg responds in a very similar way, remarking that: 'the descending curve of her dress takes advantage of contemporary fashion to display her breasts. An amused sensuality lurks about her mouth. A coldly appraising stare marks the eyes'.[8] Aileen Ribiero writes: 'Frances Howard, court beauty and centre of a scandal involving adultery and murder, was no doubt aware of the erotic contrast between her imprisoning lace cartwheel ruff, and what the moralist Brathwaith called "those rising mounts, your displayed breasts".[9]

All three commentators confidently agree in reading the low-cut dress as a sign of sensuality. It is significant that the only woman I quote, aware perhaps of the possibility that the male gaze of other commentators might be held to import their own response into their apparently 'objective' descriptions, attributes the sexuality of the portrait to Frances Howard's own conscious purpose. But decoding the significance of bodily display, in art or in real life, is always fraught with ambiguity. A 'page three' model, a woman on a topless beach in the Mediterranean, or a mother breastfeeding in a public place will today provoke very different reactions in different beholders. At one level the projection of lustful purpose into this image of Frances Howard is uncomfortably close to the way in which in our society it is still possible for a rapist to plead that a girl's short skirt might be taken as a mitigation of his crime.[10] The desire of the beholder is converted into the intent and the fault of the object. There will be many occasions in the course of the recounting of the tale of Frances Howard where precisely such transference of lust, guilt and blame takes place, both in the minds of those who prosecuted her at the time and those who have retold her story subsequently. But more significant for the moment is the question of what reaction this image would have provoked in its own contemporary cultural context. In the seventeenth century the response to such physical display was no less variable than it is to comparable images today, but it was inevitably constituted within and by assumptions that are very different from those of our own time. And this is one of the fundamental issues to which we will be returning time and again in the pages that follow. One of the striking characteristics of modern commentary has been its unquestioning transportation into the present of the scandalised commentary on her conduct at the time. Disentangling the one from the other will be a continual challenge, and one which has considerable general implication for the way we both write and use history in our own culture.

As Akrigg recognises, low-cut dresses were fashionable during the period. Many court ladies of unimpeachable moral life were depicted in exactly the same kind of costume that Frances Howard wears in this portrait.[11] The fashion was encouraged by Queen Anne, who, according to the Venetian ambassador, displayed her bosom 'bare down to the pit of her stomach'.[12] In the previous century the French ambassador had reported on an audience with Queen Elizabeth, who 'kept the front of her dress open, and one could see the whole of her bosom, and passing low, and often she would open the front of this robe with her hands as if she was too hot . . . Her bosom is somewhat wrinkled . . . but lower down her flesh is exceeding white and delicate.'[13] Elizabeth's self-conscious use of her erotic power has been much commented on in recent years, but it is nonetheless possible to claim that in her own portrait Frances Howard had no desire to do anything more than see herself represented as one who dressed fashionably.

Merely because it was fashionable, however, such female display was not universally applauded. Robert Niccols, in his satirical picture of the unchaste court, *The Cuckow* (1607), characterises the wanton woman thus:

> Loosely she was aray'd in wanton weed
> Which wanderers eies did with inticement feed,
> For she was clad in robe of tissue thinne
> Through which so brim appeared her snowie skin
> That it did seem to those, that did it see
> No whit obscured, but farre more white to bee;
> Her Ivorie brests did ever open lie
> To readie spoyle of gazers greedie eie,
> And both her lillie paps were bare to winne
> Her lovers melting heart to wanton sinne.
>
>   (p. 15)

Niccols' Spenserian portrait can be complemented by the writings of many other satirists, for whom Nathanael Richards may stand as representative. In his 'Vicious Courtier' he mounts a vitriolic attack on court women:

> A *Drab of State*, is a consuming flame,
> Oft fiers the Hearts of Princes past reclaime.
> Turns Joy, to deepe and Melancholy sadnesse,
> Poysons the bloud, and fils the braine with madnesse.
> Why should she else, with painting seeme more faire?
> Suffer her naked *Breasts* lie open bare?
>
>   . . .
>
> If not like CIRCE, by enchantments strange
> Men into Beasts and Beast-like nature change.[14]

The collocation of women's sexuality, poison and the myth of Circe was deployed powerfully in commentary on the latter part of Frances Howard's story. But for the moment these quotations are sufficient evidence that the fashion for low-cut dresses amongst court women provoked a hostile response, and one that was not just a matter of generalised moral disapproval, but more specifically an attack upon the dress of upper-class women.

The conflation of moral outrage and class antagonism in this antipathy to court dress becomes clearer if one considers the picture that accompanies 'Mistris Turners Farewell to all Women' (Plate 7). Anne Turner, executed for her part in the murder of Sir Thomas Overbury, made, as we will see, a very repentant end on the scaffold. In this pairing of images the contrast between her past life and present mortification is demonstrated both by the 'cover-up' of her former nakedness, and also by the replacement of court attire with the sober dress of the middle classes. The illustrator was not just representing a contemporary perception, for there is a long iconographic tradition behind this popular broadside. In Sebastian Brant's *Ship of Fools*, for example, the choice made by Hercules between the paths of pleasure and virtue is symbolised by a naked woman on one side, and a soberly dressed matron with distaff on the other (Plate 9). The incorporation in a popular news-sheet of an existing pictorial stereotype exemplifies another main strand in all of the ensuing discussion – the way current events are accommodated to patterns that are already donated by a narrative and moral tradition.

There are, of course, other traditions of interpretation of the naked or near-naked female figure. In Ripa's *Iconologia* 'Veritas' or 'Truth' is represented naked; the nurturing breast figures in representations of Charity (as in Spenser's *The Faerie Queene*, I. x), and in pictures of the Madonna throughout the late Middle Ages and Renaissance.[15] Ellen Chirelstein considers the depiction of Lady Elizabeth Pope with one breast exposed, and concludes that 'her heraldic body restricts the play of erotic meaning to the voluptuous display of wealth and status'.[16] She also, however, contrasts this formal portrait with the more sensuous depiction of the female body in 'private' art forms like the miniature, or in the court masque, where, she points out, the 'corporeal body' is at least theoretically contained within the Neoplatonic theory which saw the beauty of the body as representing the beauty of the soul. The costume design by Inigo Jones (Plate 10) is an example of such a depiction. It must be doubted, however, whether contemporaries were quite so ready to understand these costumes in an abstract manner. Dudley Carleton famously objected to the appearance of Queen Anne and her ladies in *The Masque of Blackness* because their apparel was 'too light and courtesan-like' for such great ladies.[17] (There is a subsidiary, but revealing point to make here. It was during the sixteenth century that the general meaning of 'courtesan' as anyone who attended at court was narrowed and displaced on to the female of dubious virtue. We are left then with a dissymmetry, where there is no single word to act as a female equivalent for the male 'courtier'. The underlying belief that the court and female virtue are incompatible will be further discussed in Chapter 2.)

The point of all this, and its significance for the story of Frances Howard, is to emphasise that the readings of this portrait with which we began are anything but neutral, objective and value-free. The response of contemporary observers would have depended on their attitude to the court in general (and to women in particular), and have been influenced by awareness – conscious or unconscious – of the traditions of representation within which the portrait might be placed. Just as it is important to the reading of this picture to situate it carefully within its own culture, so it will be necessary to consider scrupulously the ways in which seventeenth-century society delimited the boundaries of virtue and vice. What her contemporaries meant by calling Frances Howard a 'whore' or a 'lewd woman' will turn out to be significantly different from what a modern reader might think they implied.

The commentaries on the picture also raise basic questions about the relationship of the representation of Frances Howard to historical 'truth'. Both Riggs and Akrigg comment further on the 'menacing gaze' and 'coldly appraising stare' of the portrait. This seems to me pure fantasy. Or, rather, it is an example of the way in which a knowledge derived from outside the representation is fed back into it. Because both writers have accepted unquestioningly that Frances Howard first committed adultery and then murdered Thomas Overbury, then any painter worth his salt must, in their view, have registered her potential for such dark deeds. There is a circularity in the way the accepted and completed story of Frances Howard's life confirms a reading of the picture, and then that reading itself becomes confirmatory evidence of the supposition that she was an archetypal female villain. It is a circularity exactly like that which affects the juror in the court-room.

The way prior assumptions condition perception is even more dramatically exposed by the fact that it is by no means certain that the portrait is a picture of Frances Howard at all. Another copy of the portrait claims it to be of her sister, the Countess of Salisbury.[18] At one level this may seem to illustrate the fragility of historical evidence, but in a more significant fashion it demonstrates the power that the stereotypical understanding of Frances Howard as a 'wicked women' has to float free of specific referents. This can clearly be seen by considering other contemporary portraits. Plate 4 reproduces an engraving of her with her husband which dresses her in a costume of the early seventeenth century.

It was probably published at the time of the Overbury murder, when the scandal was at its height. A few years later Simon van de Passe produced the 'true picture' of Frances, in two versions (Plate 5). On the bare head of the first version is placed a hat which belongs to the fashion of the 1620s. Somewhat later Martin Droeshout produced the satirical print of Doctor Panurge, curing the ills of his society with purges and alchemical firing (Plate 6). In its centre stands a woman, clearly modelled on the second version of van de Passe's portrait. The correspondence of the two images has led to speculation that the satirical print is intended to comment on Frances Howard, Simon Forman and the Earl of Essex.[19] This seems most unlikely, not least because the 'humour' of which the lady must be purged is her 'manliness', rather than the voracious sexuality or murderous tendency one would have expected to be associated with Frances Howard. What has happened is that the portrait has lost its specificity; the image of Frances Howard has become merely an icon of 'female transgression'. Whereas Riggs and Akrigg give to an image which may or may not be a portrait of the 'real' Frances Howard all the specific resonances of their reading of her life-history, this pictorial sequence demonstrates how the 'true image' may be emptied of particularity as it is converted into unspecific satire. It is this continual sliding from the particular to the stereotype and back again that characterises the representation of Frances Howard throughout history – and it is this slipperiness that I want to expose and to fix in the rest of the book.

Recently the Larkin portrait of Frances Howard has appeared on two very different books. It adorns, first, the cover of a critical book on Shakespeare's *The Merry Wives of Windsor*.[20] The decision to put a portrait of the least merry of Jacobean wives on this cover says a great deal about our post-modern culture, its indifference to history and its facile use of 'signs'. Presumably the editor responded to the display of bosom in the crudest and simplest way – that much cleavage must indicate a 'merry' woman. At the very least, such carelessness prompts one to demand some attention to historical accuracy. But her appearance on the front of another book is much more significant, and much more sinister. Bellerophon Books published in 1989 a book entitled *Infamous Women*, with Frances Howard as its eye-catching icon. The book contains a series of zappy little stories about wicked women from Queen Nitocris to Mata Hari, accompanied by cut-out paper dolls of each of the characters, with appropriate costumes to colour in. For whom, one asks, is this book intended? For girls? Is it intended as a warning – or merely to encourage young people to internalise all the assumptions about the wickedness of women that permeate the history of Frances Howard? The very existence of this book in the 1990s makes clear what is at stake in examining the construction of the received picture of Frances Howard. It is a fundamental principle of everything that follows that the way we read and make our history has profound implications for the way we manufacture our present.

Chapter 1

The first trial: An arranged marriage

On 5 January 1606 Frances Howard was married to Robert Devereux, third Earl of Essex. This wedding is the starting point for the study of Frances Howard in two respects: firstly, at a narrative level, it initiated the series of events that was to lead to her trial and condemnation for the murder of Thomas Overbury a decade later; and secondly, the way it was arranged, and the terms within which it was celebrated, direct attention to many more general issues about the ideology of marriage, the place of women and the nature of court politics in early modern England. These cultural assumptions were significantly to determine the representation of Frances Howard's later career, and analysis of them is therefore also vital preparation for this book's discussion.

To modern eyes this marriage would seem doubly blighted. Not only was it an arranged marriage, engineered for political and dynastic purposes, but also the couple themselves were both very young at the time of the ceremony.[1] In this respect Frances Howard's marriage was typical of her family. Her father, Thomas Howard, Earl of Suffolk, had himself obeyed the injunction of his father, the fourth Duke of Norfolk, who advised the eleven-year-old boy in 1572 to take Mary Dacre as his wife. When she died in 1578 she was still only fifteen.[2] Suffolk reiterated the pattern in arranging the destinies of his own children. At the same time as Frances's marriage to Robert Devereux was planned, her younger sister was affianced to William Cecil, Lord Cranborne, the son of the Earl of Salisbury (the marriage was finally concluded in 1608). In 1606 Suffolk also contracted his eldest son Theophilus to the daughter of the Earl of Dunbar when she was but six years old:

> with the full assent and good-liking of Theophilus Lord Walden, and also with the full assent and good-liking of Lady Elizabeth Hume that a marriage should heareafter in good time be solemnized between

them, if it should please God, within three months after the said Lady Elizabeth should accomplish the age of twelve years.[3]

One might wonder how far a girl of six might be able to assent to a future marriage, but the crucial phrase is the last. Children were assumed competent in law to give their own consent to marriage once the woman reached twelve, the man fourteen. 'If a formal engagement was entered into earlier, it could be broken by either party at the age of consent' as Lawrence Stone points out.[4] The parents obviously wanted to leave as little room as possible for the youngsters to disavow their politically advantageous match. (Ironically, of course, the fact that Frances and Robert were – just – above the age of consent at the time of their wedding had important consequences when its annulment came to trial seven years later.) But it was not just in prosecuting such youthful unions that Suffolk made earnest attempts to secure advantageous alliances. At Christmas 1605 Frances Howard's elder sister Elizabeth had been married to William, Lord Knollys only a few months after his first wife died. The bride was about eighteen, her husband fifty-eight. Suffolk, it seems, was quite prepared to ignore the other standard objection to forced marriages – the comic stereotype of January and May.[5]

In seeking to make 'good' marriages for his family Suffolk was endeavouring to do no more nor less than most parents in the upper levels of his society. Arranged marriages, with varying degrees of complacence on the part of the couples involved, were commonplace. In prosecuting the matches so young, however, Suffolk was flying somewhat against the practices of his age. If it was ever thought that the projected marriage of the fourteen-year-old Juliet in Shakespeare's play was typical of the period, recent researches have established conclusively that the average age at first marriage was surprisingly late. In most of English society couples characteristically married in their mid- to late twenties.[6] Compared with the lower orders, the pressures of dynastic ambition were greater upon the upper classes, while there was less need for them to wait until financial competence on the part of those wishing to be married was assured. But even here the average age crept up between the late sixteenth and early seventeenth centuries. Lawrence Stone suggests that 'by the early seventeenth century very young aristocratic marriages were becoming rare'.[7] Though there were precedents for Suffolk's eagerness to marry his children young, he was behaving somewhat unusually.

In all such marriages children, boys and girls alike, were pawns in parental power-games. It is no coincidence that Suffolk embarked upon a flurry of matrimonial arrangements in the early years of James's reign.

The arrival of the new king had signalled a restoration of the Howard family to positions of power and influence, and the need to consolidate his rising political fortunes would have seemed particularly pressing. In pursuit of such ambition the marriage of Frances Howard to the Earl of Essex must have seemed ideal. Robert Devereux was the son of the second Earl of Essex, also named Robert, the last great favourite of Queen Elizabeth. In February 1601, thwarted, as he saw it, by the influence of the Cecil faction at court, smarting from his failures in Ireland and his repudiation by the Queen, the second Earl had attempted rebellion, riding into London and hoping to raise the citizens against the queen's 'evil advisers'. The rising, described by Lawrence Stone as 'that absurd fiasco of gang-warfare and semi-rebellion',[8] but rather more richly analysed by Mervyn James as the 'last honour revolt', having its roots in an older (and increasingly threatened) concept of aristocratic honour and privilege,[9] had proved a spectacular flop. Despite the admiration in which the people undoubtedly held the Earl of Essex, neither they, nor many of the aristocracy in other respects allied to him, were prepared to put their ties to the Earl above their duty to the Queen. They knew a crack-brained plot when they saw one. The Earl was arrested, tried and executed along with some few of his followers. Frances's father was closely involved in his arrest, but the chief instrument in Essex's destruction was held to be Robert Cecil.

After James's accession in 1603, Robert Cecil and the Howard family seemed decisively to have outmanoeuvred the former associates of the Earl of Essex in the race for court appointments. As Neil Cuddy observes: 'Although James sweetened some survivors of the defeated Essex faction with considerable patronage, he thereafter gave them neither office nor influence.'[10] The old 'Essexians', however, remained an identifiable grouping, and their rivalry with the Howards will be a constant feature of this narrative. The King was keen to try to ameliorate this friction, for he had been in correspondence with the second Earl of Essex before he began dealings with Cecil, and immediately upon his assumption of the throne had met Robert, taken him in his arms and kissed him, 'loudly declaring him the son of the most noble knight that the English had ever begotten'.[11] For Suffolk, therefore, a marriage of his daughter to Essex's son would seem appealing, both gratifying the King and claiming the Earl for his family's interest. Arthur Wilson in his *History* described the political situation thus:

> the Treasurer *Salisbury*, that great Engine of the *State* to whom all wheels moved, held an intimate correspondence with the House of

> Suffolk ... And being mindful of the asperity and sharpness that was betwixt him, and the late Earl of *Essex*, he thought it a good Act of *Policy* and *Piety*, and therefore he was a great *means* in marrying the young Earl of *Essex* to the *Lady Frances Howard* ... that the Fathers *Enmity* might be closed up by the sons *Nuptial Fraternity*. The Earl of *Essex* was fourteen years of Age, and she thirteen, when they married, too young to consider, but old enough to consent.[12]

Wilson was writing well after the event, but the Venetian ambassador suggested at the time a similar political ambition when he wrote:

> the marriage of a daughter of the Chamberlain [Suffolk] to the Earl of Essex is to be celebrated on New Year's Day; and his Majesty intends to be present. Six months later another daughter of the Chamberlain is to marry a son of Lord Salisbury. The object is to reconcile the young Earl of Essex to Lord Salisbury if possible. Essex is but little the friend of Salisbury, who was the sole and governing cause of the late Earl's execution. Nothing is more earnestly desired by Salisbury than not to leave this legacy of hatred to his son, for though Essex is not rich nor in enjoyment of the power Lord Salisbury wields, yet if the latter were to die his son would not succeed to the influence and authority which his father possesses, whereas Essex has an infinite number of friends all devoted to the memory of his father; and there is no doubt but that, when the Earl of Essex is a little older, suggestions and persuasions to revenge will not be wanting. Lord Salisbury hopes by creating ties of relationship to cancel the memory of these ancient enmities; many, however, are of opinion that this is too feeble a medicine for so great an ill.[13]

These accounts imply that the marriage of Frances Howard was not only an attempt to hijack the Earl of Essex before he came of age and could be dangerous, but was part of a larger political and factional design in which the Earl of Suffolk acted as a middleman, offering two of his daughters as the instruments to forge a chain linking the old adversaries. Salisbury himself had been working to influence the young Essex, who had been made a ward of the Crown, and therefore technically came under his guardianship in his role as Master of Wards. He had had some success, since Essex had become 'the closest of friends' with Salisbury's son, Lord Cranborne, and had begun himself to correspond with Cecil.[14] Suffolk's daughters must have seemed convenient counters for the most influential of all early Jacobean politicians to use to cement his control. For Suffolk himself the double marriage of his daughters hitched him ever more firmly to the powerful figure of Salisbury.

What the young Earl himself felt about the match is nowhere recorded. There is a tantalisingly vague letter addressed to him from Edward Reynolds which suggests that Essex's friends themselves may have wanted to see him safely married. He refers to whisperings he has heard about the Earl's conduct:

> that your Lordship hath of late somewhat declined from that path wherein heretofore you have, without straying, directed your steps, and a litle blemished your honor by the company of some persons, that have abused the goodness and facility of your noble nature.[15]

Reynolds might, of course, have been anxious about Essex's friendship with Cranborne, but the letter indicates, if nothing else, a sense of the need for Essex to be settled down.

We know absolutely nothing, either, of Frances Howard's views on the match. She therefore makes her début on the court stage at the age of thirteen entirely as a function and symbol of the ambitions of her parents. As we will see, her subordination to the demands of factional politics is to be a constant and significant feature of her history, as it was for the great majority of upper-class women in her society.

The fact that this was a politically highly charged marriage is signified by the way its celebration was accompanied by two elaborate court masques, and consideration of those entertainments offers instructive insight into the ideology that underpinned the match, at both a political and a personal level. Historians, until very recently, have been dismissive of the court masque. They have tended to concur in the view (held also by many in the early seventeenth century) that the genre was merely an expression of the conspicuous extravagance and superficial vanity of the Jacobean and Caroline courts. But this verdict has been challenged and qualified in recent years. Rehabilitation of the genre began with attention to the literary ambition of the authors of the masque, focusing on the artistic ingenuity that went into the fashioning of the words, music and staging of the entertainments, and unravelling the intricacies of the learned and arcane allegories that sustained the devices. More recently, commentators have concentrated on the precise political context of individual masques to reveal their embodiment of the ideology of the court and to uncover ways in which the performances might figure the designs and political desires of the king, or contrariwise might encode, in however devious and indirect fashion, the political positions of particular noblemen and women who sponsored or took part in them.[16] The court masque, then, while it might merely seem sycophantically to idealise the court, was in fact attempting to steer and control the understanding of the audience. Jonson, Jones and other purveyors of masques, if one may anachronistically borrow a term from current politics, were the 'spin-doctors' of the Jacobean court, and their work a species of political image-making. Their entertainments are therefore a valuable point of access to the ways in which the politics of the Jacobean court in general and this marriage in particular were represented to, and read by contemporaries.

When Jonson published *Hymenaei*, the wedding-night masque for Frances Howard, he prefaced it with one of his most significant statements of the theory that underpinned and justified the whole enterprise of masquing. Jonson argues that the ephemeral spectacle of the masque is but the surface or 'body' of the show, while its real justification is the 'soul' of which this surface is only a shadow. He claims:

> This it is hath made the most royal princes and greatest persons, who are commonly the personators of these actions, not only studious of riches and magnificence in the outward celebration or show, which rightly becomes them, but curious after the most high and hearty inventions to furnish the inward parts, and those grounded upon antiquity and solid learnings; which, though their voice be taught to sound to present occasions, their sense or doth or should always lay hold on more removed mysteries. (p. 75)

The preface as a whole is built on a number of oppositions: between body and soul, voice and sense, occasion and mystery, ignorance and learning. Jonson argues that so long as the arcane 'mystery' directs the merely occasional, the soul informs the body and the learned control the ignorant, then the masque serves its 'proper' function of exceeding the merely appetitive and transitory, and giving access to higher, more general truths.

Behind all this lies a Platonising theory which invites the spectator to attempt to look through the accidents of the 'real' world to the tran-scendent truths of which they are, indeed must be, but a shadow. To the modern reader, however, this claim that the masque subordinates the temporary and occasional to the divine and eternal seems a very clear example of the way ideologies are constructed. Masque can readily be understood as a genre in which the contradictions of royalist ideology are resolved through a ruthless conversion of dialectic into the seamless surface of praise. If the audience can be persuaded that the specific events being celebrated ought to be seen as validated by a divine truth which lies behind and beyond them, then particular political action is removed from the possibility of question. So for recent critics the task of the reader of masques has been not simply to explicate (and therefore concur with) the ways in which Jonson and other writers transform the mundane into the ideal, but to attempt to focus ever more closely on the ideological operation of the masque text. This involves a multi-levelled reading of the texts, unpicking the carefully crafted surface to elucidate the contradictions that are being ironed out by it. Close attention to the exact details of their 'present occasion' is required if the implications of the brief texts that survive are fully to be revealed.

We will have cause to consider masques at each stage of this book – this first marriage, its successor and the Overbury murder trials are all figured in masques performed at court. In studying each of these masques a number of perspectives need to be kept in play. The text itself, of course, needs carefully to be examined. But at the same time an attempt has to be made to judge what the response of the audience of the masque might have been. It is frequently a limitation of even the most sophisticated of masque criticism that it assumes that those who watched were necessarily taken over by, or in simple agreement with, the position a masque took up. It seems to me much more useful to see masques as engaged in a contest for the political and ideological high ground, their texts as always potentially open to qualification and opposition, even at the time of their presentation. It is too easy to assume that only the enlightened twentieth-century critic, reading against the ideological grain of the text, is gifted with the necessary distance and insight to fracture the smooth surface of the royalist performance. Whilst it is vital to investigate the relationship between the text and its circumstances, to lay bare the nature of the manipulation of understanding it was attempting and the way it encoded and enforced the ideology of the Jacobean court, it is hubristic to assume that none of this perception was available to the original witnesses of a masque's first performance.

Jonson was already becoming established as the chief provider of entertainments for the Jacobean court. *Hymenaei*, the masque he provided for this occasion, is long and elaborate. (Its ambition is in part a reflection of Jonson's own determination to claim the role of court poet as unambiguously his.) Its action may briefly be summarised. It begins with a procession of pages dressed to symbolise Roman marriage rites. They are interrupted by eight masquers representing the 'humours and affections', whose disorderliness threatens the concord of marriage. Their disruptive potential is defused as Reason carefully explains the iconology of marriage, and the triumph of order is symbolised by the entry of Juno, goddess of marriage, accompanied by eight female masquers who 'represent her powers'. The reconciliation of order and passion is figured by the dance in which the male and female masquers join. After the 'revels' in which masquers and spectators join together, the masque concludes with an epithalamion. Compared with later masques this one, though elaborate, is not particularly complex. Indeed, its elaboration is not so much of scene or action, as of explication and clarification. The published text is covered in notes wherein Jonson demonstrates the richness of his classical learning, and the speeches of Reason in the performance itself patiently explain the iconology of each stage of the masque and each set of performers to the audience. The amplitude of its annotation and the pedantic explanations built into the performance suggest that Jonson was by no means convinced that he could trust his spectators to read aright the images he set before them. There is a characteristic tetchiness running throughout the commentary, from the opening preface to comments like this, on the significance of the entrance of the humours and affections:

> And for the allegory, though here it be very clear and such as might well escape a candle, yet because there are some must complain of darkness that have but thick eyes, I am contented to hold them this light. (p. 341)

Jonson might well have been right in suspecting that many of the spectators cared rather more for the dancing and the feast which followed than they did for the accuracy and intricacy of his scholarship – but this very nervousness about the capabilities of his audience indicates the essential fragility of the ideological operation the masque attempted.[17]

At the most basic level Jonson translates the actual marriage of Frances Howard and Robert Devereux into classical terms, borrowing the symbolism of Roman marriage rites to afford dignity to the celebration and to honour the match. But he is attempting much more by this strategy. As D.J. Gordon pointed out in a seminal article,[18] the 'removed mystery' which the work attempts to derive from the particular occasion concerns the idea of Union, which is developed on a number of levels. Through the particular union of Frances Howard and the Earl of Essex the audience is invited to reflect upon the proper relationship between reason and the passions, both in the individual and the married couple, and is then led through that meditation to contemplate an image of the harmonious unity of the universe itself. In addition to this moral meaning, the masque's emphasis on Union alluded to, transformed and endorsed James's political ambition to unite the two realms of England and Scotland, his pet project in the early years of his reign, and one already running into severe difficulties. The particular marriage and the political issue of Anglo-

Scottish union are both validated by their absorption into the picture of cosmic harmony.

The thirteen-year-old girl and almost fifteen-year-old boy to whom the masque was ostensibly addressed are left a long way behind. In this representation their marriage is indeed a 'sacrifice' (the word is often repeated) to an idea of political and cosmic union. But the masque does contain material intended to convey a picture of the ideal married life to the couple as well as to the wider audience, a picture that, though steeped in Roman imagery, is close to the standard prescriptions of the marriage manuals and preacherly advice of the period. The advice is, typically, addressed largely to the woman. Reason explains the iconology of the procession of pages, and concentrates on the representation of the bride:

> Her hair,
> That flows so liberal and so fair,
> Is shed with grey, to intimate,
> She ent'reth to a matron's state,
> For which those utensils are borne.
> And that she should not labour scorn,
> Herself a snowy fleece doth wear,
> And these her rock and spindle bear,
> (ll. 163–70)

The domestic destiny of the woman is clearly marked out. So too, Reason praises the conjunction of Juno and Hymen because:

> Without your presence Venus can do nought,
>   Save what with shame is bought;
> No father can himself a parent show,
> Nor any house with prosp'rous issue grow.
> (ll. 300–3)

In this passage the control of potentially 'shameful' sexuality within marriage is essential for the preservation of secure paternity and maintenance of family blood lines.

Throughout the masque there is an emphasis upon the wedding night itself. The published masque concludes with a long 'Epithalamion', closely modelled on classical prescription, which is largely intent on persuading the bride, assumed to be modest and frightened, to admit her husband to her bed and body. Earlier in the masque Reason had explained:

> The blushing veil shows shamefastness
> The ingenuous virgin should profess
> At meeting with the man.
>
> (ll. 161–3)

And in the Epithalamion the bride is told:

> Shrink not, soft virgin, you will love
> Anon what you so fear to prove.
>   This is no killing war
>   To which you pressèd are,
>   But fair and gentle strife
>   Which lovers call their life.
>
> (ll. 410–15)

The depiction of a shamefast and passive bride awaiting the amorous advances of the husband that will convert her from maid to wife represents a standard view of female sexuality, supposed to remain dormant until aroused by the male. Frances Howard was to confront the prevalence and cultural force of these assumptions in her later suit for divorce, as we will see. But there is a more immediate problem with the reading of this Epithalamion, for, as Jonson tells us, only the first stanza of this poem was sung at the masque itself. As he crossly observes:

> After them, the musicians with this song, of which then only one staff was sung; but because I made it both in form and matter to emulate that kind of poem which was called epithalamium, and by the ancients used to be sung when the bride was led into her chamber, I have here set it down whole, and do heartily forgive their ignorance whom it chanceth not to please. (ll. 392–7)

Jonson's epithalamion, however, may have been curtailed at the performance not so much because of the objections of the unlearned to its scholarly amplitude as from an uncomfortableness in so explicitly bidding this particular couple off to bed, when everyone knew that this was not their destination that night.

It was customary in early marriages such as this, even though the partners were legally old enough to give consent and to begin sexual relations, for the couple to be separated for some time, and the marriage to be consummated later. Alan MacFarlane indicates the reasons for postponing intercourse:

> An early sixteenth century text argued: 'Many great sicknesses do spring thereof; young mothers also have no just strength, neither to

nourish nor to bring forth the fruit... Likewise the children which were born of children, became sick and feeble.' Here were a number of separate arguments rolled into one, each of which was repeated elsewhere. Over-young marriages could have several harmful effects. They would weaken the man: he was still growing up and would be drained by sexual activity; part of his vital fluid, his sperm, would flow out of him... The effects on a growing woman were even worse, for she was subjected to the strains of childbearing at too young an age... Thirdly, the effects on the offspring of such children were harmful: they would be stunted and sickly because their parents had been immature.[19]

But whatever the reasoning, everyone in the audience for *Hymenaei* must have been fully aware that the couple were not to be bedded together immediately. The separation of the political and moral ideology of the masque from the reality of the young couple could not be sharper. We may admire Jonson's aesthetic art and industry in translating the marriage into an image of larger political considerations, or applaud his scholarship in the classically accurate epithalamion, while at the same time recognising the degree to which the couple themselves are totally misrepresented in the text of the masque as an ordinary married pair urgently awaiting their wedding night and the consummation of their marriage. As events transpired, of course, it was precisely the gap between this ideal and the reality of non-consummation that made the annulment of this marriage possible.

Commentators have pointed to the further irony that the masque dismisses those 'humours and affections' which were in later fact to separate the couple. But equally symptomatic of the ironic distance between the masque's adulatory purpose and the political realities it sought to translate is its representation of the King and Queen. Early in the masque Jonson had presented James and Anne as patrons of the marriage and extolled their exemplary function:

> O you, whose better blisses
> Have proved the strict embrace
> Of Union with chaste kisses,
> And seen it flow so in your happy race;
>
> That know how well it binds
> The fighting seeds of things,
> Wins natures, sexes, minds,
> And every discord in true music brings:

> Sit now propitious aids
> To rites so duly prized . . .
>   (ll. 84–94)

Apart from the question as to whether the assembled courtiers would, even at this date, have been provoked to a wry smile at the idealisation of a couple who lived largely apart, the Queen's enmity to the Howards and her links to the old Essexians were to prove of considerable political significance to the future of Frances Howard. The point here is not to criticise Jonson for a failure of prophetic gifts, but rather to mark out the degree to which the gap between idealised surface and actuality was, even at the time, open for any to see.

On the following night a further entertainment was staged for the couple. This took the form of a tournament or 'barriers'. Jousts had provided aristocratic entertainment throughout the Tudor period, and though their popularity began to wane in the reign of James, Jonson was to provide elaborate texts for three such occasions, two of them for the marriages of Frances Howard.[20] In each case a debate is set up to provide a literary pretext for combat between groups of men fighting across a barrier on horseback, or, as here, on foot with pikes and swords. On this Twelfth Night occasion, the device presented two female figures identically attired, one representing Truth, the other Opinion. The subject of their debate is marriage, Truth upholding the dignity of the married state, Opinion defending virginity.

Not surprisingly, the contest ends with Truth victorious. But in the course of the debate Opinion's defence of (female) celibacy articulates an opposition to marriage which raises a number of interesting questions.

> Untouched virginity, laugh out to see
> Freedom in fetters placed, and urged 'gainst thee.
> What griefs lie groaning on the nuptial bed?
> What dull satiety? In what sheets of lead
> Tumble and toss the restless married pair,
> Each oft offended with the others' air?
>
>   . . .
>
> And then, what rules husbands prescribe their wives!
> In their eyes' circle they must bound their lives.
> The moon when farthest from the sun she shines
> Is most refulgent; nearest, most declines:
> But your poor wives far off must never roam,
> But waste their beauties near their lords at home;

And when their lords range out, at home must hide
(Like to begged monopolies) all their pride.
When their lords list to feed a serious fit,
They must be serious; when to show their wit
In jests and laughter, they must laugh and jest;
When they wake, wake; and when they rest, must rest.
And to their wives men give such narrow scopes,
As if they meant to make them walk on ropes:
No tumblers bide more peril of their necks
In all their tricks than wives in husbands' checks.

(ll. 685–90, 701–16)

This speech begins by addressing both man and woman, the 'married pair', but moves swiftly to considering the position of the woman in marriage. It therefore operates within the same language as the masque of the previous night, which also aims itself at the married couple, but asserts, without really needing to argue it, that the transformation of the wedding night is primarily in the state of the bride, not the bridegroom. The central position of female virginity in these marriage masques is symptomatic in a fairly obvious way of something that will have considerable significance in the reading of the divorce hearings in Chapter 3. For the moment, it is enough to draw attention to the way in which the transition from virginity to matrimony is marked out upon the female partner, even in the speech of an opponent of marriage.

It is, of course, ironic indeed that this speech, so accurate in its prophecy of the actual future of Frances and Robert, should have been offered on this occasion. But much more significant is the way that words which might seem to a modern reader only too accurate in their description of the power relations in traditional marriage clearly expect the audience to respond negatively to them. Opinion's speech is transgressive precisely because its resentful account of the life of the married woman is barely a parody or exaggeration of the customary advice that the dutiful and obedient wife was expected to follow. Opinion presents a catalogue of wifely inconveniences that many men in the audience would see as a list of entirely proper controls over the conduct of women. Robert Greene's *Penelope's Web* (1587), a collection of stories explicitly offered to women to reinforce the ideals of chastity, silence and obedience, asserts:

a woman, though rich and beautiful, deserveth smal prayse of favour, if the course of her life be not directed after her husbands compasse. And as the Mathematicall lines which Geometricians doe figure in their carrecters, have no motion of themselves, but in the bodyes wherein they are placed, so ought a wife to have no proper nor peculiar passion or affection, unless framed after the speciall disposition of her husband.[21]

On the next page Greene uses the same image that Jonson's Opinion deploys in the passage quoted above, but to quite opposite effect:

> But sayth Antisthenes, some wives resemble the nature of the Moone, which the further she is removed from the spheare of the sunne, is the more radiant, and the neerer she approacheth to his beames, the more eclipsed and obscured: so the longer the distance is betweene them and ther husbands, the better chere; when in place they are ever sorrowfull and pensive.

Jonson's text allows the expression of objections to conventional marriage theory, but makes sure that potential rebellion is contained by giving the words to a figure who can be dismissed as representing typical womanly wilfulness. It is a frequent strategy in many of the literary texts we will be encountering in the course of this study. Objections to the unequal power of marriage partners were being voiced during the period, but in the *Barriers* there is no such departure from tradition; its speeches make clear the ways in which wifely subordination was both celebrated and inculcated.

It is not only through the speeches of the characters that this work reinforces a conventional view of marriage. For, though it presents a contest between two *female* speakers, representing Truth and Opinion, their battle is fought out by *male* protagonists. This aptly images the way in which women in general, and Frances Howard in particular, were objects of exchange and contest between men. When one considers the line-up of combatants in the *Barriers* this becomes even clearer. The contest was supervised by Frances's uncle, the Earl of Nottingham, Lord High Admiral, between whom and the second Earl of Essex there had been a continual struggle for credit and favour in the conduct of sundry expeditions in the previous reign, and by the Earl of Worcester, who had been one of the lords sent to apprehend Essex in 1601. Combatants on the side of Truth included supporters, clients and members of the Howard family. Five Howard males took the lists, and among those accompanying them were Sir Thomas Monson and Sir Roger Dalison, both long-time clients of the Suffolk family. Amongst those contesting for Opinion, on the other hand, were no less than three – the Earl of Sussex, Sir Oliver Cromwell and Sir William Constable – who had been imprisoned for their real or suspected part in Essex's uprising. The last two, indeed, had been in fear of execution. Sir Carey Reynolds had come under suspicion of involvement, and at least three others had been knighted by the Earl of Essex on his various military expeditions.[22]

In a very real and obvious sense, then, the *Barriers* staged before the eyes of the court the factional rivalry that it was the business of the marriage to patch up. One can only conjecture what degree of personal animosity some of the combatants might have brought to the ritual, and cannot know with what relish the courtly audience, fully cognisant of the various ties of clientage and loyalty of the contestants, read the spectacle being enacted before them. But what is certain is that no one could have mistaken, if it crossed their minds to think about it, the way in which the married couple, and the female partner in particular, though the ostensible subjects of the debate, were simply tokens and occasions of this political exchange.

The combat is thus described:

> Here the champions on both sides addressed themselves for fight, first single, after three to three; and performed it with that alacrity and vigor as if Mars himself had been to triumph before Venus and invented a new music. (ll. 788–91)

No sense is given here of either side having the better of the tournament itself. But after the battle an Angel descends and declares the victory of Truth. Truth herself consoles the losers with the words:

> Nor, though my brightness do undo her [Opinion's] charms,
> Let these her knights think that their equal arms
> Are wronged therein: for valour wins applause
> That dares but to maintain the weaker cause.
>
> (ll. 831–4)

One wonders how satisfied the Essexians would have been by this attempt at consolation. If they, or the court audience in general, saw any political realism in the charade of the contest, then they might have been less than happy at the victory of the Howard clan that this tournament could be deemed to represent. Their triumph is depicted in this entertainment not as a victory achieved through superior skill, but merely as a consequence of the chance of enlisting on the 'right' side. This might well have seemed an all too accurate representation of the political scene, and a convincing reason for the bitter and resentful attitude that characterises the 'Essexians' throughout the early Jacobean period.

I have spent some time in discussing these two entertainments because they demonstrate the kind of representation and manner of reading that the marriage of Frances Howard and Robert Devereux received in the culture of the court. In them we recognise the degree to which the actuality of the youthful couple is buried beneath a weight of political and moral symbolism, and perceive too the outlines of the view of marriage which Frances Howard was so desperately to contest in seeking to free herself from this match.

In order fully to lay the ground for later discussion of the annulment hearings, it is necessary to consider further the contemporary attitudes to marriage, particularly to young, arranged marriages such as this. In the wedding masque, *Hymenaei*, there is a great deal of emphasis on the orderliness of marriage and its correspondence to the well-ordered kingdom. In the *Barriers* Truth offers a similar proposition:

> Love (whose strong virtue wrapped heav'n's soul in earth,
> And made a woman glory in his birth)
> In marriage opens his inflamèd breast;
> And lest in him nature should stifled rest,
> His genial fire about the world he darts,
> Which lips with lips combines, and hearts with hearts.
> Marriage Love's object is, at whose bright eyes
> He lights his torches, and calls them his skies.
>
> (ll. 659–66)

This high valuation placed on love seems rather misplaced in the celebration of so young, and so arranged a marriage. It signals, however, the way in which mutual affection was coming to be perceived as a more central element in the ideal marriage, and therefore as a more significant factor in parental negotiations.

Many commentators at the time were aware of the potential contradiction between the wishes of parents and the desires of their children. William Gataker, for example, in his *Marriage Duties* wrote:

> Where commeth to bee taxed the foolish and preposterous course that is taken by divers parents, who match their sonnes young to wives, and then send them a travailing: so that they part as sone as they meete, ere their affections be wel fastened; and so oft either returne with them estranged on their part, or at returne finde them estranged on the other part; while their absence hath made way for some strangers enticement.[23]

Writing in 1620, Gataker might even have had the subsequent history of Frances Howard's career in mind, though his sentiments can be paralleled in any number of sermons and treatises. Even Swetnam, in his *The Araignment of Lewd, Idle, Froward and Unconstant Women*, a misogynist tract

which provoked a number of counterblasts from women writers, could
still observe:

> when matches are made by the Parents, and the dowry tolde and paid
> before the young couple have any knowledge of it, and so many times
> are forced against their minds, fearing the rigour and displeasure of
> their parents, they often promise with their mouthes that which they
> refuse with their hearts.[24]

Since the force of parental compulsion tended to fall more often on
daughters than sons it is tempting to see arranged marriage simply as a
product of a patriarchal society, and a blatant symptom of the oppression
of women. This, however, would be to oversimplify. For mothers were
frequently to be found negotiating in the marriage market on behalf of
both male and female children. In Middleton's *A Chaste Maid in Cheapside*,
for example, it is Maudline Yellowhammer who drags her daughter by the
hair away from her lover, and back to the marriage designed for her, to
the surprise of the Waterman who comments 'You are a cruel mother'.[25] So
too, many commentators recognised that the evils of compelled affection
affected male and female alike. George Wilkins' play, *The Miseries of
Enforced Marriage* (1607), for example, focuses on the damage done to the
male hero by his arranged marriage. In Middleton's *Women Beware Women*
(c. 1621) we pity the case of Isabella, paraded before the foolish Ward to
whom she must be married but, as David Atkinson points out in his useful
article on this topic, the language of enforcement used to the Ward himself
is very similar to that earlier used against Isabella.[26] At the present moment
there is a cultural pressure to make questions of gender the prime focus of
attention, and a master-story for historical investigation. But, important
though such issues are, it is vital not to let this tendency skew explanation
of the multiple foundations of social practice. Arranged marriage is a
symptom of cultural patterns that include the inferior place accorded to
women, but go beyond to encompass the more general authority of parents
over children, and the claims of family and class interest over the individual
will. Sir Walter Raleigh indicated the link between husbandly and parental
authority in these terms:

> The rule of the husband over the wife, and of parents over their children
> is natural, and appointed by God himself: so that it is always, and simply,
> allowable and good. The former of these, is, as the dominion of Reason
> over Appetite; the latter is the whole authority, which one free man
> can have over another.[27]

The hierarchical principle, sustained by analogies, operates to justify both kinds of authority, but they are distinguished one from the other.

Nonetheless, since the constraints of the married state fell more heavily upon women, who surrendered almost all power and all possessions to their husbands, and since the existence of the moral double standard permitted men to console themselves with extra-marital affairs but treated such indiscretion in the wife with much harsher judgement, it is young women who had most to complain of, and whose protests are most often articulated in the literature of the period. Atkinson cites the character of Ursula in Sampson's *The Vow Breaker*, who fulminates:

> by my virginity, a young wench were better be heir to a swineherd's chines than a rich man's bags! We must be coupled in wedlock like your Barbary horse and Spanish gennet, for breed's sake, house to house, and land to land, the devil a jot of love! Poor simple virginity, that used to be our best dowry, is now grown as bare as a serving-man's cloak that has not had a good nap this seven years. (I.i.137–44)[28]

In *The Atheist's Tragedy* when Castabella is compelled by her father to marry Rousard, the sickly elder son of D'Amville, his younger brother Sebastian cries out 'A rape, a rape, a rape!' and defends his intervention by asserting 'why what is't but a rape to force a wench to marry, since it forces her to lie with him she would not'.[29] These sentiments, in fact and in fiction, were commonplace. In Webster's *The Devil's Law Case*, when Jolenta is forcibly affianced to Ercole, rather than to Contarino whom she loves, Winifred the waiting woman comments:

> plague of these
> Unsanctified matches! They make us loath
> The most natural desire our grandame Eve ever left us.
> Force one to marry against their will! why, 'tis
> A more ungodly work than enclosing the commons.

But her mistress answers wearily:

> Prithee peace!
> This is indeed an argument so common,
> I cannot think of matter new enough
> To express it bad enough. [30]

Arranged marriages were frequent, in real life and in fiction. While Frances Howard and many others may have gone willingly enough to their youthful marriages, Frances Coke, for example, daughter of Sir Edward (the Lord Chief Justice who was to play such a major part in Frances Howard's later history), rebelled against her father's determination to marry her off to

John Villiers, the mentally unstable brother of the Duke of Buckingham. Even if the story that she 'was tyed to a bed-poste and severely whipped' to obtain her consent is untrue in detail, she was certainly forced to submit to fatherly authority.[31] Of course, many children must have been content to accept their parents' choice of partner; but the tensions that frequently arose in real life are reflected in the anxieties of preachers and moralists, and in fictional treatments of marriage and love, which suggest the degree to which the ideological contradictions inherent in the early seventeenth-century view and practice of matrimony were becoming visible and problematic.

The theory of marriage was forced to negotiate potential contradiction between the claims of parental authority and of individual self-deter-mination. This contradiction operated simultaneously on a number of levels. Parental authority, especially that of the father, was validated by the way it echoed fundamental notions of hierarchy and reduplicated at the level of the family the patterns that operated in society at large. Ben Jonson's *Hymenaei*, as we have seen, rests upon precisely that possibility of viewing marriage as an example of ordered passions on the personal level which both validate and are validated by analogy with the desirability of order on the political and cosmic level. This tidy reinforcement of the ideology of marriage by situating it within an all-embracing system of analogy and correspondence was, however, always potentially at odds with the fact that the marriage ceremony is a regulation of the individual appetite, a remedy against fornication and the means by which individuals avoid sin.

Since it is the love and affection which individuals demonstrate towards one another that increasingly was felt to be central to the bond of marriage, inevitably it followed that deeply divided perceptions of love itself should be focused in the controversies over the institution. From one perspective love is dangerous, since it privileges passion over reason and elevates evanescent feeling into a permanent principle. Erotic appetite therefore threatens the hierarchy of the sexes, since in courtship the male is imagined as losing rational control in surrendering authority and power to the woman he loves. Once the lover's suit is granted, then, of course, this inversion is righted – as Sidney's Astrophil exults at the moment of Stella's apparent surrender:

> For Stella hath, with words where faith doth shine,
> Of her high heart giv'n me the monarchy;
> I, I, O I may say, that she is mine.[32]

The danger of founding marriage upon so unruly a passion was often stressed. Montaigne, translated by Florio, put it forcefully:

> I see no mariages faile sooner, or more troubled, then such as are
> concluded for beauties sake, and hudled up for amorous desires. There
> are required more solide foundations and more constant grounds, and
> a more warie marching to it: this earnest youthly heate serveth to no
> purpose.[33]

On the other side, of course, are the claims made for love as a feeling not
sub- but supra-rational, and for sexual desire as a sign of human involvement with the creative principle of God himself, claims endorsed, as we
have seen, in *Hymenaei*.

If uncertainty about the status of sexual desire and love helped to fuel
the debate about marriage, the collision between parental authority and
individual liberty was actually rooted in the law of marriage itself. For
though the law insisted that parents' consent *ought* to be given to a match,
yet, as MacFarlane says:

> We have a situation where marriages needed no consent or witnesses
> in order to be valid. Parents, employer, lord, friends, could all advise,
> could put enormous physical, moral and economic pressure on the
> individuals, but ultimately the simple words of the pair – if the man
> was over the age of 14 and the woman 12 – would constitute an
> unbreakable marriage from the twelfth to the twentieth century in
> England (with a lapse between 1754 and 1823). It is difficult to envisage
> a more subversively individualistic and contractual foundation for a
> marriage system.[34]

In historical terms it is difficult to assert any coherent, or coherently
developing pattern of negotiation between these conflicting demands. It
used to be argued that Protestantism, with its emphasis upon the individual
spiritual life and its privileging of the married state over celibacy, played a
significant part in tipping the balance. Lawrence Stone, for example,
suggests that 'the doctrine of the absolute right of parents over the disposal
of their children was slowly weakening in the late sixteenth and early
seventeenth centuries', and argues that 'When one looks for the causes of
this change of attitude, it seems likely that a preponderant part was played
by the puritan ethic.'[35] But this view has been challenged by Kathleen M.
Davies[36] amongst others, insisting on the continuity of advice about
marriage and the essential similarity of writings in both Catholic and
Protestant traditions. So too, the attribution of the growth of a 'liberal' view
of marriage to an emergent bourgeois individualism in the Renaissance is
questioned by writers such as MacFarlane, who claims that 'the revolution

to conjugality and companionate marriage, which is both unusual and so influential, had occurred at least by the time of Chaucer in England, if not long before'.[37] It is not my purpose to adjudicate between these opposing views of the origins or of the novelty of the debate. But it is important to recognise that the conflict assumed a particular force in the late sixteenth and early seventeenth centuries. The frequent expression of opposition to arranged marriage in treatises and fictional works suggests a pressing concern with the problem in this period, and at the same time created a climate of feeling in which those like Frances Howard, married, but not for love, might have felt their predicament with especial sharpness.

Among many factors that might help to account for the apparently increased preoccupation with the evils of arranged marriage two in particular seem relevant here. The first concerns marriage and social class. The treatises frequently demand that marriages should be made between those of equivalent social status. One of the reasons for the rights of parents to control their children's choice of partner is that mere affection might lead the young to neglect proper regard for their class position. In practical terms this concern meant that control over marriage was much more exercised at the upper end of the social ladder. This leads to a common complaint – hinted at in Ursula's comments already quoted – that high-born ladies are subject to a pressure their lowly sisters do not suffer. In Marston's *Sophonisba* the heroine, married to Massanissa but pursued by Syphax, complains:

> O happiness
> Of those that know not pride or lust of city!
> *There's no man blessed but those that most men pity.*
> O fortunate poor maids, that are not forced
> To wed for state, nor are for state divorced;
> But pure affection makes to love or vary;
> You feel no love which you dare not to show,
> Nor show a love which doth not truly grow.
> O, you are surely blessèd of the sky![38]

She borrows a standard literary topos – the same lament at the predicament of the high and mighty as is uttered by Henry VI on his molehill or Henry IV in his sickness – but uses it to bemoan her lack of freedom in the specific area of marriage.

If preservation of class identity was a reason for parents to claim control over the errant passions of their offspring, the increasing social mobility of the period and the shifts in economic power which forced merchant and aristocrat to find mutual convenience in intermarriage threatened to make arranged marriages serve rather different ends. Ursula's complaint, it should be noted, is about the subordination of marriage to economic, rather than to class or kinship interest. Equally threatening is the sense that arranged marriages were being used to breach rather than to preserve the fixities of a hierarchical society. It is the social ambition of the Yellowhammer family in Middleton's *A Chaste Maid in Cheapside* which leads them to forbid the marriage their daughter desires to Touchwood Junior in favour of an alliance with Sir Walter Whorehound, and drives them to prosecute a union between their son and the Welsh whore, whom they are led to believe is a rich heiress. The ridicule of their social aspirations is what, by contrast, validates the love match their daughter desires. To the long-standing condemnation of arranged marriages for their bringing together of old and young was added a criticism of their link with improper social aspiration. The motivation of parents therefore became more open to question, and their claim to know better than their children what is good for them was consequently weakened.

But not the least important influence on the way people thought about marriage must have been the ever-widening accessibility of literary treatments of love and of marriage. Literature, as has already been suggested, does much more than reflect social practice; it also has a significant part in constituting that practice. It is, I think, right to claim that attitudes in general must have been influenced by the literary texts circulating in the period and important to recognise that such texts were becoming ever more easily accessible to young women of some education. Women are indeed singled out as the target audience of an increasing number of literary works, especially of prose romances.[39] If romantic love is finally instated as an ideal basis for marriage in the period, then the widespread dissemination in published sonnet sequences, romances and dramas of notions that derive originally from medieval codes of *fine amour* must have played some part in celebrating and fixing such an attitude. In a paradoxical fashion, the idealisations of women which seem to modern eyes intrinsic to their imprisonment, may, as Shelley suggested, have had a more positive effect. He wrote:

> The true relation borne to each other by the sexes into which human kind is distributed, has become less misunderstood; and if the error which confounded diversity with inequality of the powers of the two sexes has been partially recognised in the opinions and institutions of modern Europe, we owe this great benefit to the worship of which chivalry was the law and poets the prophets.[40]

Many strands of twentieth-century criticism, while insisting on the implication of literature in its contemporary culture, have at the same time disempowered literary texts as agents of change. In this they are quite at variance with seventeenth-century commentators. Puritan critics of the theatre berated the stage for the way it corrupted the attitudes of its audience. Robert Anton, for example, lamented:

> Why doe our *lustfull Theaters* entice,
> And personate in lively actions *vice*:
> Drawe to the Cities shame, with guilded clothes,
> Such swarmes of wives, to break their nuptiall othes;
> Or why are women rather growne so mad
> That their immodest feete like planets gad
> With such irregular motion to base Playes,
> Where all the deadly sinnes keepe hollidaies.

And he adjures good wives to avoid:

> this hellish confluence of the stage,
> That breeds more grosse infections to the age
> Of separations and religious bonds
> Then e're religion with her hallowed hands
> Can reunite: rather renew the web
> With chast Penelope, then staine thy bed
> With such base incantations. [41]

Such tirades might seem faintly comic to the modern reader – but at least Anton and writers like him thought that literature might make a difference to the way people acted in their daily lives. Literary texts presented powerful ideas of romantic love in marriage, and staged the conflict between the competing ideologies of individual affection and parental control in a way which allowed space for oppositional views to find expression, and readers or audiences to entertain ideas that questioned the machineries of power within which they lived.

How far Frances Howard's receptiveness towards the love-letters Robert Carr may have sent her (whether or not they were penned for him by Thomas Overbury) derived from their intrinsic forcefulness, how far from a sense generated by reading love-poetry or the protestations of the heroes of romances like the *Arcadia* that desire ought in some way to be prosecuted by such ambassades cannot be established. But there can be little doubt that when comedies revisited the old Plautine and Terentian stories of the defeat of fathers' attempts to block the love-matches of their children they confirmed and encouraged a set of attitudes that were ripe for such reinforcement in the period. Literature staged the tensions implicit in contemporary matrimonial practice.

Shakespeare's *A Midsummer Night's Dream* opens with one of the clearest of depictions of the contested view of marriage. Egeus enters, and complains:

> Full of vexation come I, with complaint
> Against my child, my daughter Hermia. –
> Stand forth Demetrius. – My noble lord,
> This man hath my consent to marry her. –
> Stand forth Lysander. – And, my gracious Duke,
> This hath bewitched the bosom of my child.
> Thou, thou, Lysander, thou hast given her rhymes,
> And interchanged love tokens with my child.
> Thou hast by moonlight at her window sung
> With feigning voice verses of feigning love,
> And stol'n the impression of her fantasy
> With bracelets of thy hair, rings, gauds, conceits,
> Knacks, trifles, nosegays, sweetmeats – messengers
> Of strong prevailment in unhardened youth.
> With cunning hast thou filched my daughter's heart,
> Turned her obedience which is due to me
> To stubborn harshness. And, my gracious Duke,
> Be it so she will not here before your grace
> Consent to marry with Demetrius,
> I beg the ancient privilege of Athens:
> As she is mine, I may dispose of her,
> Which shall be either to this gentleman
> Or to her death, according to our law
> Immediately provided in that case.
>
> (I.i.22–45)

All the ingredients of the patriarchal view of marriage are here: Egeus has provided a good potential partner, and claims of his daughter her due obedience. At the same time he characterises the threat to his authority as deriving from the seductive power of love. At this point in the play Theseus endorses the authority of Egeus, but Hermia's wish that 'my father looked but with my eyes' is ultimately to be borne out by the action of the play. (Though even at the end Egeus is overruled by Theseus, rather than converted to a genuinely different perception of his relationship with his daughter.) But this witty and slippery play does not simply sustain the position that the child's view should be privileged and that love should dictate the choice of marriage partner. The happenstance of love, the very frailty that renders it so suspect to the fatherly eye, is embodied in the fluctuating attachments of the four lovers under the influence of Oberon and Puck. Their pairings are sorted out by the end and the potentially tragic outcome of thwarted love is comically diverted into the mechanicals' play of Pyramus and Thisbe, but the audience is left in no doubt of the fragility of the eye's perceptions. In this respect, *A Midsummer Night's Dream*, like so many of Shakespeare's comedies, curbs its transgressive potential, and sits on the ideological fence.

George Wilkins' *The Miseries of Enforced Marriage* seems, by contrast, very much more obviously to question the rights of parents to overrule their children's affections. In this play the central figure, William Scarborow, first contracts himself to Clare Harcop, only for his guardian Lord Falconbridge to compel him to marry his niece Katherine. William cannot avoid the match, and when it is completed Clare Harcop kills herself and Scarborow reacts by abandoning his wife and giving himself up to prodigality, before Lord Falconbridge's acknowledgement of his injustice enables a reconciliation between Scarborow and Katherine. But whilst this is the most sustained condemnation of arranged marriage to be put upon the stage in the period, its ideological underpinning is by no means without ambiguity. Where romantic comedy can use the tricks and turns of the genre to evade full confrontation of the contest between parental authority and youthful love, this play buys its final reconciliation at the price of killing off the girl to whom Scarborow first pledged his love. Its solution to the problem of arranged marriage is to require both hero and audience to accept that, even though the guardian acted badly, virtue is to be found in obedience to the inalienable demands of the marriage contract, rather than in repudiation of them. By presenting a male figure as the victim of an arranged marriage this play usefully reminds us that the pressures were not only felt by women, even if they were more often the passive objects of exchange. But at the same time, the play marginalises the sufferings both of Clare Harcop, the deserted woman, and of the wife Katherine who simply demonstrates an 'ideal' womanly dutifulness and obedience in putting up with Scarborow's monstrous behaviour.

Many plays dramatise the problems inherent in the demands for parental control over marriage, but none can finally escape the doubleness of contemporary ideology. In social practice an accommodation was sought between the extremes of parental domination and children's rights of self-determination. So, for example, William Heale writes:

Marriage of al humane actions is the one and only weightiest. It is the present disposall of the whole life of man: it is a *Gordian* knot that may not be loosed but by the sworde of death: it is the ring of union whose poesie is *Pure* and *endlesse*. In a word it is that state which either imparadizeth a man in the Eden of felicitie, or els exposeth him unto a world of miserie. Hence it is that so mature deliberation is required, before such an eternal bond be united. The mutual affection of each partie, the consent of parents, the approbation of friends, the trial of acquaintance: besides the special observance of disposition, of kindred, of education, of behaviour.[42]

It is revealing that, even in a treatise ostensibly written for women, he should still present marriage as a potential paradise for *men*, but his effort is to assert that while the ideal marriage is founded first upon mutual affection, there is still a requirement for the approval of friends and acquaintances.[43] The potential collision of the two sides is avoided by a benign hope for reconciliation between competing interests, blandly ignoring the frequent fact of conflict between them.

Shakespeare's *The Tempest* is a wonderful demonstration of the art of papering over ideological fissures. The wise Prospero, in fatherly care of his daughter Miranda, claiming to do 'nothing but in care of thee', takes the opportunity presented by Fate, which brings his enemies into his power, to prosecute the return of his dukedom. The treaty of friendship between himself and Alonso, King of Naples, is guaranteed by the marriage of his daughter to the King's son. From the perspective of the two youngsters, theirs appears to be a love-match, a spontaneous effusion of affection, which Prospero opposes. Acting the traditional blocking father he makes Ferdinand win his wife by servile toil. Throughout the play, however, the true nature of his control and political manipulation is never made apparent to the young lovers. Even the audience (or at least the modern audience) might be inclined to forget the very specifically political function their marriage serves, so preoccupied is Prospero with instructing the young lovers on the need for their individual self-control and sexual abstinence. At the play's end, as Prospero presents his erstwhile enemy with his restored, and now married son, it is carefully dramatised as a personal, rather than a political restoration.

The Tempest was performed as part of the marriage celebrations for King James's daughter Elizabeth to the Elector Palatine in 1613. It might seem a particularly appropriate play to have chosen, for the royal couple were also young – both sixteen years of age – and, though their marriage was of great political importance, James apparently followed the increasingly approved custom of allowing his daughter the power of final decision over the mate he had chosen for her. According to the Venetian ambassador the conclusion of the match was 'subject to the Princess's pleasure, who wishes first to see the Palatine and be wooed a while'.[44] Fortunately Frederick proved an ardent suitor. John Chamberlain reported that:

> he is everyday at court, and plies his mistresse hard and takes no delight in running at ring, nor tennis, nor riding with the Prince . . . but only in her [Elizabeth's] conversation.[45]

The Princess was presumably satisfied, and so there was no problem in matching her liking to her father's wishes. It is almost unimaginable that Elizabeth should have rejected Frederick – just as it is impossible to imagine what Prospero might have said to his daughter if she had found Ferdinand unattractive. But on many occasions, in fact and fiction, resolution was not so easily won.

The strain in keeping together the requirements of filial duty and romantic love is dramatised in *Romeo and Juliet*. Early in the play Capulet tells Paris to woo his daughter, since:

> My will to her consent is but a part,
> And, she agreed, within her scope of choice
> Lies my consent and fair-according voice.
> (I.ii.15–17)

Juliet herself, encouraged by her mother to consider whether she can love Paris, replies:

> I'll look to like, if looking liking move;
> But no more deep will I endart mine eye
> Than your consent gives strength to make it fly.
> (I.iv.99–101)

Thus far the Capulets behave as concerned parents should, and Juliet responds as the dutiful daughter ought; but, of course, once the romantic attachment to Romeo supervenes, Juliet stops being an obedient Princess Elizabeth or Miranda, and refuses to follow her parents' wishes. Then the vocabulary changes, and Capulet fulminates:

> God's bread, it makes me mad. Day, night; work, play;
> Alone, in company, still my care hath been
> To have her matched; and having now provided
> A gentleman of noble parentage,

Of fair demesnes, youthful, and nobly lined,
Stuffed, as they say, with honourable parts,
Proportioned as one's thought would wish a man –
And then to have a wretched puling fool,
A whining maumet, in her fortune's tender,
To answer 'I'll not wed, I cannot love;
I am too young, I pray you pardon me'!
But an you will not wed, I'll pardon you!
Graze where you will, you shall not house with me.
Look to't, think on't. I do not use to jest.
Thursday is near. Lay hand on heart. Advise.
An you be mine, I'll give you to my friend.
An you be not, hang, beg, starve, die in the streets,
For, by my soul, I'll ne'er acknowledge thee,
Nor what is mine shall never do thee good.

(III.v.176–95)

It is too modern a reaction to condemn Capulet out of hand. Whilst his vocabulary and conduct are excessively violent, there can be little doubt that many a father in the Globe Theatre would have identified with Capulet's feelings. Nor is it clear that the play as a whole endorses the position of Romeo and Juliet themselves – the tragic outcome of the play is, in part, a vindication of the attitude which sees young, romantic love as excessive and dangerous in its self-preoccupation.

There is, however, a further important dimension to this outburst. As the audience knows, but Capulet does not, Juliet is resisting the marriage not merely out of the promptings of her feelings, but because she is already married, and has already slept with her husband. As we have seen, in canon and civil law, whether parental consent has been given or not, a marriage contracted between young people over the age of consent was legally binding. At one level, then, Capulet's outburst articulates precisely the fear that parental control is ultimately unenforceable. So it was in the marriage of Maria Audley to Thomas Thynne. These children of feuding families married secretly in 1594 when both were sixteen, and despite the protracted efforts of the Thynne family to have the match declared invalid, in 1601 Daniel Dunne (later to be involved in Frances Howard's divorce hearings) finally gave judgement in favour of the young couple in the Court of Arches.[46]

In William Painter's popular collection of stories, *The Palace of Pleasure*, the 34th Novell of the First Book concerns the King of England's daughter, who, disguised as an abbot on a journey to the Pope, precipitately falls in love with Alexandro, invites him to bed, and, after formal espousals and exchange of rings, consummates the union. Arriving at the Papal court, she explains that, while she was running away from a match designed for her by her father with the decrepit Scottish King, God had placed Alexandro before her eyes, and she declares to the Pope: 'him will I have and none other'. Though secret, private and without parental approval, because due ceremony was observed, and, above all, because the couple had had sexual intercourse, the Pope recognises that nothing can be done but to accept the match.[47]

In English society in the late sixteenth and early seventeenth centuries such clandestine contracts were frowned upon, and those who contracted such unions might be punished by the ecclesiastical courts, but, as Martin Ingram observes: 'The law prescribed that clandestine marriages, though irregular, were valid and binding'.[48] The importance of this for the future story of Frances Howard is, of course, that her marriage, though legally conducted, and not arranged, as far as one knows, against her will, was alleged not to have been consummated. In the end, for all the controls and wider cultural influences upon the ideology of marriage, its very existence turns upon the most private of acts.

Painter's collection is not uniform in the position it adopts, however. The 15th Novell in Book Two declares its moral directly:

> Euphimia fondly maried against hir father's will, and therefore deserv-edly afterwards bare the penaunce of hir fault: and albeit she declare hir selfe to be constant, yet duty to lovinge father ought to have withdrawen hir rash and heady love ... Yet the tender Damosell or lovinge childe, be they never so noble or rich, ought to attend the father's tyme and choyse, and naturally encline to parent's will and likinge, otherwise great harme and detriment ensue.[49]

The coexistence in a single volume of stories of models which seem both to condemn and to validate youthful self-determination is a clear enough mark of the deeply embedded contradictions in the period.

The importance of all of this for Frances Howard's story is threefold. In the first place, though at the beginning of the chapter I suggested that her youthful, arranged marriage was a problem from a modern perspective, it should by now be clear that it was problematic also in the seventeenth century – it is for this reason that I have called this chapter the 'first trial'. When Frances Howard came to sue for the annulment of her marriage one detects signs of guilt amongst those who surrounded her for having married her off so young. Even the King himself 'fell to inveighing against the marriage of young couples, before they be acquainted one with another' (*ST*, 814). Secondly, the existence of a model of marriage based upon love cannot but have influenced her own thinking about her married state, for good or ill. Thirdly, and perhaps most powerfully of all, her subsequent suit for the annulment of her marriage to the Earl of Essex dramatically exposed many of the uncertainties and ambiguities within the ideology of the period. As we will see, the depth of her challenge is reflected in the animosity which is returned upon Frances Howard, a hostility which frantically seeks to shore up the dominant ideology by demonising the woman who confronted it.

Chapter 2

Interlude: Filling in the blanks

After their marriage in 1606 Frances Howard and Robert Devereux were separated. She returned to her family, he continued his education, which was completed by the increasingly obligatory tour abroad between 1607 and early 1609. The marriage quickly deteriorated after Essex's return to claim his bride, and early in 1613 moves were set on foot for its annulment. There are very few documented facts concerning Frances's conduct during these intervening years. They can briefly be summarised.

On 2 February 1609 she danced in Jonson's *The Masque of Queens*.

On 5 June 1610 she performed in Daniel's masque *Tethys Festival*, the Queen's celebration of Prince Henry's installation as Prince of Wales, in the role of 'the nymph of Lea'.

Sometime before September 1611 she wrote two letters, one to her confidante Mrs Anne Turner, the other to the conjuror Simon Forman pleading with them to help her in her attempts to win a lord (assumed to be Robert Carr) to her love, and inhibit the desires of her husband. (These letters became public in 1615 during the trials for the Overbury murder.)

In 1612 John Chamberlain reported that, at the Twelfth Night masque, *Love Restored*, Frances and her younger sister discomfited the gentlemen masquers by refusing to dance with them in the revels.[1]

The divorce hearings charted the various places at which Frances Howard and Essex stayed during their life together.

During the Overbury trials Weston and Franklin alleged that there had been a number of meetings between Frances Howard and Robert Carr at various places during the year or so before the divorce hearings.

Three items of less direct testimony survive. On 25 July 1610 Samuel Calvert wrote to William Trumbull, suggesting that the Earl of Essex had cause to look to his lady 'for they say plots have been laid by [her] to poison him'.[2] In 1612 Philip, Earl of Montgomery wrote to the lords of the Privy Council to deny that he had sought to obtain some unspecified favour from the Countess of Essex which might impugn her virtue.[3] In 1613 the divorce case was halted for a while as Mary Woods accused Frances Howard of having approached her for a powder to poison her husband.

These are the only direct and contemporaneous testimonies to her actions between her marriage and the beginning of the annulment proceedings. But she has been charged with much more. It has been suggested:

(a)   that she had an affair with Prince Henry;
(b)   that she was generally promiscuous;
(c)   that her relationship with Robert Carr was consummated before the divorce was secured.

All historians who have attempted to narrate the course of events leading up to the divorce and the Overbury murder have relied heavily upon the accounts published later in the seventeenth century by Arthur Wilson, Anthony Weldon, Godfrey Goodman, William Sanderson, Francis Osborne and others. It is almost entirely from them that the mud is added to the few pieces of straw that constitute documented fact. Beatrice White appositely comments on these 'histories':

> So much of the intimate history of James's reign has been distorted by the scandalmongering of partisan writers of the Commonwealth and Restoration that it is difficult to separate truth from fiction. An originally hazardous remark is repeated so often and with such a ring of conviction that it gains at last the credit of authority.[4]

But all the caution in the world cannot inhibit narrators of Frances Howard's history from relishing the scandalous details that these writers offer, so that no account is above slipping in comments from them as if they were attested fact.

Any life-writing is, moreover, bound to proceed by a kind of narrative back-formation – attempting to derive from later, more fully documented events a psychology of character which can provide the narrative impulse for the story as a whole. But both the choice of which incidents are held to be significant and the psychology of character derived from those incidents will inevitably be constructed within a range of possibilities largely determined by cultural norms as to what constitutes an acceptable match of story and character. The very attempt to locate the causes of future action in the nature of early experience and in the psychology of the individual is itself a kind of understanding of 'character' which belongs to our novelistic age. It is by no means clear that seventeenth-century writers thought of causation, or of personality, in these terms. Modern historians, however, do, and we may see the pressure of such assumptions very clearly in William McElwee's account of the blank years from 1606 to 1612:

> One old friend of the family considered that she had always been 'of the best nature and the sweetest disposition of all her father's children, exceeding them also in the delicacy and comeliness of her person'. But like so many enchanting children she was already thoroughly spoilt. She had a kittenish charm which grown-ups found irresistible and there was nobody who thought it worth while to try to give her any solid education or any sense of responsibility. Even if she had been sent back to Audley End by her mother in 1606 to wait until her husband was ready to claim her, the marriage could hardly have been a success. Self-interest and a love of pleasure were the most marked characteristics of her family and the Countess of Suffolk was the greediest and most selfish of them all. Frances was already ungovernably self-willed and completely feather-headed and unlikely to grow up into a suitable companion for the rather solid and solemn young man to whom she had been married. Kept up in London with her mother and allowed almost immediately to take part in all the gaiety that was going at Court, she never really had a chance. Almost every influence to which she was exposed was likely to bring out the worst in her. She saw far too much of her wicked old uncle, Northampton ... One of her mother's intimates, of whom she saw a great deal, was a Mrs. Thornborough, wife of the Bishop of Bristol, who encouraged in her an interest in palmistry and fortune-telling and a great deal of silly superstition. Mrs Thornborough's other hobby was equally unfortunate: she was something of an amateur chemist and 'given to making extracts and powders'. But far the worst influence of all was, of course, the Court itself. The atmosphere of cut-throat competition, of open and unscrupulous self-interest and almost continuous self-indulgence, would have undermined the character of most girls of her age. As it was, she grew up with the mind of a self-willed child interested only in clothes and success at parties, artful and rather silly, quite ungoverned in her passions, and obstinately unable to see any point of view but her own or understand any opposition to her desires.[5]

I have quoted this character-construction at length, since it is one of the most fully elaborated versions of the commonplace description of Frances

Howard (even if rather kinder in tone than some). It might seem persuasive in its presentation of a rather flighty character, one who could slip into irresponsible and criminal action out of a blind self-will and ignorance. But this persuasiveness floats upon a whole raft of unsubstantiated assertions and implicit assumptions. It will serve admirably as a specimen text on which to base an examination of the ideological underpinning of the standard representation of Frances Howard. There are three elements of it that I want to single out.

In the first place McElwee attributes Frances's failure of character to her being unduly under the influence of her mother. There are two aspects to this. The Countess of Suffolk is regarded herself as a bad character, 'greedy and selfish'; and at the same time it is suggested that her female friends, especially Mrs Thornborough, were suspect. Later in the narrative Anne Turner, Frances's confidante, is similarly to be presented as a malign influence upon her. The historian constructs a picture of a gaggle of women, silly and superstitious, but also avaricious and egotistical – and therefore threatening.

The second major factor in the corruption of Frances Howard is held to be her presence in the court itself, characterised as a place of moral laxity and vain self-indulgence. Apart from anything else, there is a straightforward historical misrepresentation here. Frances Howard's first performance at court was in *The Masque of Queens* in 1609. This might seem to an impartial observer to suggest that her full participation in courtly activity was delayed until she was sixteen years of age and her husband was shortly to return to her. But taking part in court entertainments is enough to signal to McElwee her weakness for 'success at parties' and to suggest her predisposition to moral degradation.

Thirdly, running throughout McElwee's characterisation is an assumption that Frances Howard was neither educated nor encouraged in proper female virtues. These virtues include a passive readiness to sit and wait for her husband's return; but above all it is the virtues of self-control and self-abnegation that McElwee most wants from his subject. Self-will, he implies, is dangerous, lack of government of the passions heinous, and Frances Howard's reluctance to bow to those who oppose her becomes a mark of her hopelessly transgressive (and characteristically female) nature.

It is saddening (if not entirely surprising) that McElwee, writing almost four hundred years after the events he describes, should so relentlessly reduplicate many of the assumptions – especially the assumptions about proper womanly behaviour – that were current in the early seventeenth century. As I have suggested in the Introduction, the power of this story to bring its ideological baggage with it into modern times, surreptitiously hidden under the very coherence that accounts like McElwee's appear to give it, is one of the most striking – and significant – features of it. I want, therefore, to take these three aspects of McElwee's characterisation of Frances Howard in turn and situate them in terms of early seventeenth-century culture.

First, then, to consider the significance McElwee bestows on the 'mothering' Frances Howard received. Catherine Knyvett, the second wife of the Earl of Suffolk, was indeed a powerful figure, close to Queen Anne, and deeply involved in the competition for status and prestige which characterised the upper levels of the Jacobean court. To sustain her ambitions she took large pensions from Spain, and was involved in many shady financial dealings.[6] Whether these dubious transactions were taken on her own initiative, or whether, as Stone suggests, the highest officers of state 'tried to save their faces by keeping in the background, often adopting the time-honoured device, mentioned by Tacitus, of using their wives as agents'[7] scarcely matters. She and her husband were prosecuted for corruption in 1618 and found guilty. Evidence produced at that trial indicates that the Suffolks, both husband and wife, used their social and political positions to extort bribes and kickbacks on a massive scale. Stone suggests that their corruption and extortion, which still failed to make the finances balance, was dictated in no small measure by the ludicrous ambition of the building of the huge house at Audley End, and by the costs of having so many children who survived into adulthood. But it is essential to recognise that the Suffolks were but more visible in their 'corruption' than the great majority of Jacobean courtiers because they were brought to trial, and that the Countess was neither more nor less implicated than her husband.

It is nonetheless revealing that McElwee's narrative should single out the Countess. There is an implication that her career not only transgresses the boundary between honesty and corruption, but also contravenes the expectation that dealings in financial matters and court influence should be the preserve of men. Women like Bess of Hardwick or Anne Clifford can be regarded by modern writers as heroines because of their deter-mination to control their own fortunes and to take on the male estab-lishment which opposed them, but the general attitude to the influence of women at court in the seventeenth century was one of suspicion and sometimes of derision. So, for example, as Barbara Lewalski points out: 'In 1618, one of Sir Dudley Carleton's well-wishers advised him to press his request for a secretaryship through "mylady of Bedford (who is above measure powerfull with both the Marquesses and mylord Chamberlaine)".'[8] George Trevelyan complained, in 1614, that he lost a promised command because 'the femall sex bares to great a swaye in altering his [Sir Arthur Chichester's] mynd which he intended otherwise.'[9] When Drayton revised his satirical poem 'The Owle' in 1619 he included a passage about Frances Howard, represented as a wren, in which her desire for power is explicitly suggested as the motivation for her actions:

> Quoth the Wren, gossip, be you rul'd by me,
> And though men say, the weaker sex we be,
> Whate'r they thinke, yet gossip, they shall know,
> That we were made for something else then show.
> Few things shall passe that now in working are,
> But you and I therein will have a share.[10]

It is a double-pronged attack, where the Countess of Suffolk and her daughter are simultaneously chided for superficial female vanity, and yet cast as dangerously ambitious women. (One consequence of the persistence of such attitudes has been seriously to minimise the nature and kinds of influence that women might have had on the politics of the period – a lack that is only now beginning to be repaired.)[11]

The attack on the Countess's maternal failure is supplemented in this account by allusion to her association with Mrs Thornborough. Whence, one might ask, came this lady in? The wife of the Bishop of Bristol actually became visible in the story only in the latter stages of Coke's attempt to gather evidence for the trial of Frances Howard for the murder of Thomas Overbury in 1616. He was alerted to her possible involvement by an anonymous letter which Sir Thomas Fanshawe sent to the Lord Chief Justice, saying that he had found it on the stairs leading to his room. The letter claimed:

> It is the part of every good subject to set forward the discoverie of such foule facts. And for that reason I have attempted to acquaint your Lordship with the name of one very fitt for such imployment. If your Honour wilbe pleased to examine the Bishop of Bristol's wife, I meane she that nowe lives with him it may be your wisdome will discover some thinges worthie your Lordship's knowledge. The rather for that she hath bene famelier and extraordinarily nere in kindnesse and privatie to the Countesse of Somerset, and her mother. She is knowne to practise chimistrie much, and to make extractions oyntments powders and waters in great varietie: for what purpose god knowes.[12]

Coke pursued the matter further, conducting examinations of Frances Brittan, who called Mrs Thornborough 'a fatt comlye woman' and testified that she 'did much converse both with the countesse of Suffolk and with the countesse of Essex', and of Anne Horne and Stephen Clapham.[13] Coke prepared notes for an interrogation of Mrs Thornborough, but no record of an examination survives, and the matter seems to have gone no further. None of these witnesses was able to claim with any certainty that they knew of Mrs Thornborough 'dabbling' in chemistry or any other activity, and even Coke, who could make any vestigial connection serve his ends, seems to have given up on this one.

McElwee's evidence for the malign influence of the bishop's wife is based entirely upon hearsay, and imports material which only came to light under the special circumstances of a murder trial back into the narrative of earlier years. Including this 'information' allows him to claim that Frances Howard from her early years was associated with dubious dealings in poisons, a claim made plausible by her later conduct. More powerfully and insidiously, it permits a hint of the Suffolk household as a witches' coven. (The very different attitude that an historian takes to Mrs Thornborough's husband, the Bishop of Bristol, who actually published a book on alchemy, is revealing. Where the wife scandalises McElwee, the husband's 'dabblings' merely amuse A.L. Rowse.)[14] The point here is not to deny that Frances Howard seems to have consulted a number of wise men and cunning women, nor to deny that Mrs Thornborough and the Countess of Suffolk may have been interested in that area lying between 'chemistry', medicine, witchcraft and superstition. (Jonson, in his 'Conversations' with William Drummond, told him of a play – now lost – called *The May Lord*, in which, amongst various contemporary figures shadowed under false names was 'the old Countess of Suffolk, an enchantress', which might suggest that this propensity was well known.)[15] What is vital is to recognise the way in which Frances Howard's character is indelibly, if tangentially, associated with the ultimate female sin of witchcraft.

There are, however, significant differences between modern and seventeenth-century attitudes to these matters. The characteristic modern reading of such interest in the vaguely occult as 'dabbling' and weak-minded superstition represents a much simpler reaction to the consultation of conjurors than many contemporaries would have had. The wise man or cunning woman offered a wide variety of services, from healing to the recovery of lost property, astrological prediction and fortune telling, as well as powders and potions to procure love or alienation of affection. Though they were prosecuted by the church courts under suspicion of witchcraft or trafficking with the Devil, and were attacked and ridiculed by the medical establishment, yet they were nonetheless widespread, and widely consulted.[16] Nor was it just in rural villages that such practitioners functioned, attracting the poorly educated. The London-based Simon Forman and others like him attracted their extensive and socially varied clientele by appealing to the same nexus of attitudes as did the village cunning folk. As Keith Thomas observes, 'The astrologers' enemies liked to dismiss their customers as "the silly sort of ignorant and profane people" . . . But men and women were almost equally represented, and many customers were members of the nobility or persons of social distinction.'[17] Jonson's *The Alchemist*, after all, derives its satiric comprehensiveness from the possibility that Sir Epicure Mammon, as well as the humble Abel Drugger, might consult the con men. It would be foolish to assume that Jonson's ultimately condemnatory presentation of the rogues Subtle, Face and Doll is symptomatic of the dominance of a sceptical attitude towards alchemical and other marginal practices in his society at large. Indeed, the play would not be as animated as it is (and the interest in the production of Forman's magical charms at the trial of Anne Turner would not have been so titillating to the crowd as it was) if the belief that such practices were possible, even if often abused by confidence tricksters, had not been strong. The boundaries between 'science', alchemy and astrology, between the theories that underpinned official medical practice and the charms of the village wise woman were difficult to draw. What made John Dee respected by many, but Simon Forman universally to be reviled, had as much to do with social status, with the possession of official qualifications, and with the company each kept, as it had to do with profound differences in fundamental outlook.

It is in these contexts that we can consider the case of Mary Woods, which threatened the opening of Frances Howard's divorce hearings. On 6 May 1613 Chamberlain reported:

> There was speach of a divorce to be prosecuted this terme twixt the earle of Essex and his Lady, and to that end he was content to confesse (whether true or fained) insufficiencie in himself; but there happened an accident that hath altered the case, for she having sought out a certain wise woman had much conference with her, and she after the nature of such creatures drawing much monie from her, at last cousened her of a jewell of great value, for the which beeing apprehended and clapt up, she accuses the Lady of divers straunge questions and projects, and in conclusion that she dealt with her for the making away of her Lord (as ayming at another marke) upon which scandall and slaunder the Lord Chamberlain and his frends thincke yt not fit to proceed with the divorce.[18]

Even if rather belated, Chamberlain's account tallies with the examination

of Mary Woods herself on 26 February 1613. She asserted that she had
been given a diamond ring and gold chain to 'procure a kynde of poyson
that would lye in a mans bodye three or four dayes without swelling'.[19] At
first Frances Howard, through a servant Richard Grimstone, deposed that
she had given the objects to Mary Woods, characterised as a laundress at
Salisbury House, as a temporary measure, because she had been hurrying
to a masque at court and feared that the ring might come off if she were
taken out to dance, and the chain would be vulnerable to pickpockets.
Later Mrs Isabel Peel provided a completely different version, in which
Mary Woods had cozened a number of women with her promises to
procure husbands, or pregnancy. She testified that Mary Woods had 'told
her she had a diamond ring of my La. of Essex to buy a powder which
was verie costly to hange about her necke that wold make her to be with
child',[20] suggesting that Frances wanted to emulate her younger sister who
was then pregnant.

   None of these stories inspires much confidence in their veracity. Given
the state of Frances Howard's marriage it is difficult to believe that she
was anxious to recover the ring because it had been 'sent to her by the
Earle of Essex her husband when he was in Fraunce'. It would seem also
highly improbable that she was searching for some aid to fertility, as Mrs
Peel suggested (unless she were already anticipating her second marriage
to Robert Carr). But Mary Woods' suggestion that she had been hired to
procure a poison for Essex is also dubious. Why should Frances Howard
have recourse to poison precisely at the point when the annulment of her
marriage was about to proceed? Could she have been daft enough to
pursue the woman for the return of her jewels if she had indeed been
treating with her for poison? Did she assume that her own social status
was powerful enough to override anything the cunning woman said? It is
not impossible, but other explanations are equally plausible. It is (just)
possible that her own story might be true. It is also conceivable that she
might have consulted Mary Woods about some other matter, but wanted
to disown any dealings with a wise woman, given that all such figures
operated on the borders of respectability. After all Charles Richardson not
only exhorted magistrates to punish severely all cunning men and women,
but declared 'all that seeke unto these instruments of the divell, are every
whit as abominable to God as themselves are'.[21] Another motive for
keeping things hidden might well have been shame at being made to
appear a fool. Mary Woods was transparently fraudulent. Mrs Peel also
claimed to have received a pregnancy powder wrapped in a little bag, but
when she opened it she found it was 'a littell dust swept out of the flower
[floor]'. But the strongest suggestion that Frances Howard was being

maligned came from the testimony of a weaver of Norwich (Mary Woods' home city) that the charlatan's standard response when threatened with exposure was to claim that she had been hired to procure poison to murder a husband. (It was a potent blackmail threat, since, as we will see, the fear of husband-murder was particularly virulent at the time.)

The truth is irrecoverable. But the ready assumption of Frances Howard's guilt rests on the congruity of this episode with her known traffic with Forman and Turner, supplemented by the belief that she might have 'turned in her perplexity to another of those despicable beings who prey on the desperation of unhappy people', as Beatrice White puts it.[22] Though her formulation implies a rather more sympathetic understanding of Frances's plight than many are prepared to afford, it still assumes that nobody in their right mind would deal with such conjurors, whereas there is ample evidence that many people of all social ranks regularly consulted cunning folk for astrological predictions about their everyday affairs, and for medicines, as well as for rather more exotic powders and potions. Resisting too simple a notion of the place of the wise men and cunning women in seventeenth-century society is important in permitting a balanced verdict upon Frances Howard's conduct. If such figures were reviled or ridiculed by many writers, part of the reason was a fear that they could do real damage (as we will see in looking at the claims of *maleficium* in the divorce hearings). One characteristic inflection of this fear was to tie it in with the danger of insubordinate wives.

In Jonson's *Epicoene*, Truewit tries to persuade Morose not to marry by listing all the horrors of having a wife. His grisly catalogue of her potential misdemeanours concludes with this:

> And then her going in disguise to that conjuror and this cunning woman, where the first question is, how soon you shall die? next, if her present servant love her? next that, if she shall have a new servant? and how many? which of her family would make the best bawd, male or female? what precedence she shall have by her next match? And sets down the answers, and believes 'em above the scriptures. Nay, perhaps she'll study the art.[23]

In this narrative, designed to make Morose fearful, Truewit stresses the idea that his future wife will use conjurors as sources for information about his own death.

Perhaps Truewit had in mind an earlier play, *A Warning for Fair Women* (1590). This drama was based on a real-life murder committed by Anne Saunders upon her husband in 1573. Early in the play Anne speaks to Mistress Drurie, who has been insinuated into her company by her would-be-lover George Brown to further his suit. Drurie looks at her palm, and says:

> I see disciphered,
> Within this palme of yours, to quite that evil,
> Faire signes of better fortune to ensue,
> Cheere up youre heart, you shortly shalbe free
> From al your troubles. See you this character
> Directly fixed to the line of life?
> It signifies a dissolution,
> You must be (mistris *Anne*) a widdow shortly.

Anne questions her:

> Have you such knowledge then in palmestrie?

to which Mistress Drurie replies:

> More then in surgerie, though I do make
> That my profession, this is my best living,
> And where I cure one sicknesse or disease,
> I tell a hundred fortunes in a yeere.
> What makes my house so haunted as it is,
> With merchants wives, bachlers and yong maides,
> But for my matchlesse skil in palmestrie?[24]

She later goes on to 'prophesy' that Anne will make a better marriage, and suggests to her that she reads in her palm the identity of her future husband. Drurie is clearly a fraud, and, unlike the erring wife of Truewit's imagining, Anne does not search her out for consultation – but she is shown as entirely ready to swallow her message.

In both these scenes, the 'faction' and the imaginary projection, a connection is established between the restive wife and consultation of cunning folk. Wife and conjuror confirm each other in their subversion of authority, husbandly or religious. It is a fear that might have some roots in actuality, for Thomas notes 'the frequent inquiry about the life expectation of close relatives' in the surviving records of the astrologers' practices.[25] These dramatic representations raise that fear in order that it might be demonised and exorcised. In McElwee's account the question of Mrs Thornborough's dabblings in dubious practices is a significant element in building up the picture of, and case against, Frances Howard. But it is only one part of his suggestion that the inadequacy of her education is attributable to her being left to the company of women.

In plays and satires the representation of groups of women in conversation is frequently encountered. The picture entitled 'Tittle-tattle' (Plate 9) is crowded with women depicted in a variety of environments where they are thought to waste their time in gossip. (Interestingly, there is only one male figure in the whole print. The point is not to represent the danger of women to men, but instead to attack them in themselves.) Linda Woodbridge has charted various functions that the spectacle of women talking or acting together without the company of men might be called upon to serve.[26] Two have particular resonance here. Male writers assume that women left alone discuss sex. In William Goddard's misogynist *Satyricall Dialogue*, for example, Diogenes disabuses Alexander of his notion that maidens' tongues 'will not trip immodestly', with the claim:

> till theire by themselves
> Maydes in talke are modest bashfull elves.
> But beinge from the companie of men
> The lawe of modestie is broken then.
> Twas not long since I stood to maydens neere
> But Lord! thou't ne're beleeve what I did heare
> For onelie that same wench esteem'd was well
> Which could the ribauldst dreame, relate and tell.[27]

Diogenes goes on to give examples of maidens dreaming about their sexual initiation. Goddard's assumption that behind the modest exterior women are really only interested in lust is part of the staple of the period's misogyny. But even in scenes between virtuous women, sex is suddenly a permitted subject – as in the exchange of Hero and her maid Margaret in *Much Ado About Nothing*, III.iv, for example.

This shifting of male sexual guilt on to women is, of course, a standard and omnipresent characteristic of male discourse. It articulates, among many other things, men's fear of their own sexuality, and at the same time their sexual vulnerability. In the early Tudor poem 'A Talk of Ten Wives on their Husbands' Ware'[28] the ten women take a stanza or so each to belittle (in every sense) their husbands' penises. This extended dramatisation of every male's secret fear is related to the fear that witches could cause impotence – a matter that is going to be of considerable significance in the next chapter. Manipulative women in the drama can be comic and fearful – as in *Epicoene* – or far more deeply threatening, as is Livia in Middleton's *Women Beware Women*. But the general sense of a company of women as potentially menacing to male security is pervasive in Renaissance drama. It is by no means an insignificant ingredient in the creation of a ground for the depiction of Frances Howard as irrational and sexually voracious.

The second element in McElwee's account, I suggested, was the claim that being brought up in the court was necessarily bad for a young girl. It would be unnecessarily pedantic to exemplify the fact that the court was seen throughout this period in a double light, as both the fount of courtesy and sophistication, and the source of corruption and depravity. Whether in the whole literary career of Ben Jonson, who acted as the court's idealising mouthpiece in his masques but yet wrote poems urging the likes of Sir Robert Wroth to stay away from its dangerous seductions, or in a drama such as Webster's *Duchess of Malfi*, which opens with an idealised picture of the French court as a contrast to the multiple corruptions of the court that is to be the play's scene, the tension is a permanent feature of Jacobean writing, whether sermon, satire or drama. In the context of the representation of Frances Howard's early years, however, it is especially relevant to consider ways in which anti-court feeling focused upon sexual transgression, and particularly upon what might happen to young women in a courtly environment. It is not only modern writers who have blamed the influence of the court for Frances Howard's transgressions. McElwee's claim is an echo of Wilson's assertion that when Essex returned from his travels he 'found that *Beauty*, which he had left *innocent*, so *farded* and *sophisticated* with some Court *Drug* which had wrought upon her, that he became the greatest Stranger at home'.[29]

Whether or not it was factually true that sexual morality at the court of James was laxer than that of his predecessor (or, for that matter, whether the much trumpeted marital fidelity of his son actually produced a moral reformation) there is no doubt that it was perceived so to be. Anne Clifford wrote in her diary in 1603 that 'all the ladies about the Court had gotten such ill names that it was grown a scandalous place.'[30] In 1607 the satirist Robert Niccols suggested that:

Heere need not Jove come take a sleeplesse nap
With golden showers in Danaes lovely lap,
For heere our lustie Danaes, if he want
Will shower down gold on him, if he but graunt.[31]

Writers of all kinds concurred in presenting a picture of a court where sexual licence ruled. In particular it was a commonplace to suggest that young girls at court were unlikely to remain virgins long. In *The Maid's Tragedy* Evadne has just been married to Amintor, and we are offered a dialogue between her and her maid Dula as she prepares for her bedding:

Evadne   I am soon undone.

Dula   And as soon done
         Good store of clothes will trouble you at both.

Evadne   Art thou drunk, Dula?

Dula   Why, here's none but we.

Evadne   Thou thinkst belike there is no modesty
         When we're alone.

Dula   Ay, by my troth, you hit my thoughts aright.

Evadne   You prick me, lady.

1 Lady   'Tis against my will.

Dula   Anon you must endure more and lie still;
         You're best to practise.

Evadne   Sure, this wench is mad.

Dula   No, 'faith, this is a trick that I have had
         Since I was fourteen.[32]

Dula's knowingness confirms the already mentioned belief that women when alone talk dirty, but in her case it is shown to proceed from her own sexual experience, beginning at the early age of fourteen. Evadne's modesty in this preparation for her wedding night is soon revealed as fraudulent. As Amintor approaches her she refuses his embraces. He cannot understand her actions, but assumes that she must have sworn to preserve her maidenhead for a night. Evadne responds with the show-stopping line: 'A maidenhead, Amintor, At my years?'(II.i. 194–5). She reveals that she is the King's mistress, and that the marriage has been arranged to cover up the affair. The line is a dramatic shock, since, as Kathleen McLuskie says, it

> brings to a halt all Amintor's coyly expressed assumptions about the behaviour of brides, throwing into question both the narrative and the social conventions which assume that marriage will achieve the happy and automatic conjunction of social form and sexual pleasure.[33]

Its ridicule of Amintor's naiveté invites the knowing audience to concur in the view that a court virgin is an impossibility.

The same assumption is represented in Massinger's *The Renegado*, where Donusa, having seduced Vitelli and surrendered her virginity to him, asks her maid, Manto, whether she is a virgin, to which she replies:

>   A Virgine Madame?
> At my yeeres being a wayting-woman, and in Court to?
> That were miraculous. I so long since lost
> That barren burthen, I almost forget
> That ever I was one.[34]

To Chamberlain the assumption becomes a casual joke when he writes that the Queen would bear the charges of a celebration of the marriage of Lord Roxborough 'which must be a maske of maides, yf they may be found'.[35] Francis Osborne, in his 'factional' play on the Overbury affair, *The True Tragicomedy*, has Frances, at her first entrance (ostensibly the morning after her marriage to Essex) declare to her sister 'you know I am no virgin'[36] as a prelude to a bawdy conversation about Essex's impotence. In this representation Frances is subsumed into the general convention that no court lady was likely to be a virgin. The literary origins of Osborne's characterisation are obvious; we need to ask how far the historians' confident condemnation of Frances Howard's sexual conduct is similarly constructed, similarly dependent upon cultural assumptions.

Moralists, then as now, saw the collapse of sexual continence everywhere in their contemporary society, but yet the court was represented as a particularly virulent source of moral corruption. In part this was a necessary consequence of the complementarity believed to subsist between the court and society as a whole. If the court is corrupt, the argument runs, then society will be contaminated – and conversely, therefore, if society is corrupt the source must be the moral degradation of the court itself. In part, no doubt, it is also the product of that fascinated envy with which those with little access to the centres of wealth and power regard the doings of their 'betters'. (One only has to think of the current treatment of the marital problems of the British royal family, or the gossip about film stars and other gilded folk to recognise, for all the differences, some common link.) But there are more culturally specific reasons that might be advanced.

In a sermon preached to the King and court in 1621 Francis Mason chose as his subject David's adultery. In the Epistle to the Reader he explained why he took that text:

> First of all I considered what sins are likely to be found in Princes Courts. And among sundry other, two especially did offer themselves to my cogitation; carnall concupiscence and politick Practices. For, where there is pomp in apparell, delicacie in diet, and beautifull objects, all concurring many times with idlenesse and ease, there a man walketh in the midst of snares, and is in danger to be set in combustion with the fiery darts of the Divell.[37]

(Needless to say, Mason was careful to insist that he didn't mean his treatment of King David to suggest that King James himself was in any way open to criticism for these sins.) His suggestion that idleness provides opportunity, and the incitement of the eye and feasting of the body the preparatives to lust is absolutely standard. Dod and Cleaver write:

> For idleness is the mother of foule lusts. As a standing poole (not having any course of running) groweth filthy of it selfe, and full of todes and noysome vermine: so the heart that is not taken up in some good and honest calling is a fit place for the devill, wherein to breed and ingender all monstrous and filthy lusts.[38]

William Whately pointed out more pithily that 'the belly and the groyne, you know, are neare neighboures; he that stuffes the one provokes the other.'[39]

The court, with its extravagant consumption, is therefore precisely the place which provides all the stimuli for the heating of the blood which leads to lustful action. One might add to this catalogue the intrinsic danger, in many moralists' eyes, of that other courtly pastime – dancing. Thomas Beard's comment is typical: 'Concerning Dancing... there is none of sound judgement that know not, that they are baites and allurements to uncleannesse, and as it were, instruments of bawdrie.' He suggests that mummeries and masques 'are derived from the same fountaine ... and oftentimes are so pernitious, that divers honourable women have beene ravished and conveyed away by their meanes.'[40] This view of masques is, essentially, that which supports McElwee's characterisation of the vanity of Frances Howard. There might have been some contemporary reason for such an attitude – after all, Carleton reported of *The Masque of Blackness* in 1605:

> It were infinit to tell you what losses there were of chaynes, Jewels, purces, and such like loose ware, and one woeman amongst the rest lost her honesty, for which she was caried to the porters lodge being surprised at her busines on the top of the Taras.[41]

(Though, incidentally, this account might also give some credibility to the reason Frances Howard gave for entrusting her jewels to Mary Woods.) Harington's famous description of the drunken dissolution that attended the masque presented to Christian IV of Denmark at Theobalds would be further testimony. Certainly to those writing the 'histories' of the Stuarts in the period of the Commonwealth, masques typified the debauchery of the court. Sir Edward Peyton, for example, fulminated:

> the masks and plays at Whitehal were used onely for incentives of lust: therefore the courtiers invited the citizens wives to those shews, on purpose to defile them in such sort. There is not a lobby nor chamber (if it could speak) but would verify this.[42]

It was a well-enough established topos for Middleton/Tourneur to use in *The Revenger's Tragedy*. There Antonio describes the seduction of his wife:

> Last revelling night,
> when torchlight made an artificial noon
> About the court, some courtiers in the masque,
> Putting on better faces than their own,
> Being full of fraud and flattery – amongst whom,
> The duchess' youngest son (that moth to honour)
> Fill'd up a room; and with long lust to eat
> Into my wearing, amongst all the ladies,
> Singled out that dear form, who ever liv'd
> As cold in lust as she is now in death
> (Which that step-duchess' monster knew too well);
> And therefore, in the height of all the revels,
> When music was heard loudest, courtiers busiest,
> And ladies great with laughter – O, vicious minute,
> Unfit but for relation to be spoke of! –
> Then, with a face more impudent than his vizard,
> He harried her amidst a throng of panders
> That live upon damnation of both kinds,
> And fed the ravenous vulture of his lust.[43]

In this play, of course, masques not only typify the court's immorality, but become, as elsewhere in Jacobean drama, the means by which that court implodes in an orgy of violence at the end of the play.

But, as in reading the Puritan attacks on the theatres as places of lascivious meeting (as well as provocative subject matter), we need to take into account the perspective of those who wrote in these terms. Precisely because masques were symbols of the court their reporting and reception has at least as much to do with the attitude of the onlooker or historian as with the 'truth' of the individual occasion. The fact that masques are built upon disguise makes them a ready symbol of political and moral duplicity at court in the work of a number of dramatists writing for the popular stage. It is easy to slip into an endorsement of such opinions, but we must not lose sight of the way in which writers and performers genuinely believed that participators and spectators alike could be transformed and educated by the activity of masquing. Many masques are indeed alert to the potential criticism of their preoccupation with love and their foundation upon the dangerous skill of dancing. In *Pleasure Reconciled to Virtue*, for example, a masque which makes the potential dangers of revelling its subject, the masquers are invited to take out the ladies but are sternly reminded:

> Go choose among – but with a mind
>   As gentle as the stroking wind
>   Runs o'er the gentler flowers.
> And so let all your actions smile
>   As if they meant not to beguile
> The ladies, but the hours.
> Grace, laughter and discourse may meet,
>   And yet the beauty not go less:
> For what is noble should be sweet,
>   But not dissolved in wantonness.
>   (ll.274–83)

Frances Howard took part in a number of court masques. In *The Masque of Queens* she represented one of a troop of heroically virtuous women; in Daniel's *Tethys Festival* she was 'the beauteous nymph of crystal-streaming Lea', one of the Queen's attendants doing honour to Prince Henry. It is possible to view her participation with more neutrality than McElwee managed. But perhaps her most interesting intervention is that recorded in one of Chamberlain's letters. Much of the letter is illegible, but the relevant part is this:

> When they came to take out Ladies, beginning... of Essex and Cran-bourn, they were refused... example of the rest, so that they were fain... alone and make court one to another.[44]

All trace of this refusal is excluded from Jonson's printed text of the masque. Its device had been the restoration of Love in place of worldly desire of money; the masquers, figuring 'the ten ornaments/That do each courtly presence grace' had performed a dance whose motion 'was of love begot'. As they turned to take out the ladies Jonson provided this song:

> Have men beheld the Graces dance,
>   Or seen the upper orbs to move?
> So did these turn, return, advance,
>   Drawn back by doubt, put on by love.
> And now, like earth, themselves they fix,
> Till greater powers vouchsafe to mix
>   Their motions with them. Do not fear,
>   You brighter planets of this sphere:
>   Not one male heart you see

> But rather to his female eyes
> Would die a destined sacrifice
> Than live at home and free.
> (ll. 265–76)

Why Frances Howard and her sister refused to respond to this invitation can only be a matter of speculation. It may have been nothing more than that they were not attracted by the masquers, who were generally second-rank courtiers. One should probably resist the temptation to suggest that they were imitating the Princess and her ladies in *Love's Labour's Lost* who disconcert their suitors by refusing to play their courtly game. Nonetheless, in a context where Frances Howard's participation in masques is immediately made a symptom of her feminine vanity, it is tempting to see her resistance to the transparently coercive compliment of Jonson's verses as something of an heroic gesture.

Be that as it may, the claim that the court is a dangerous place for women is a common topos. Sylvester's warning to women at court is typical. It begins:

> Beware fayre mayd of Musky courtiers oathes
> Take heed what guiftes and favors you receive
> Lett not the fading glosse of silken clothes
> Dazell your vertue, or your fame bereave
> > For loose but once the hold you have of grace
> > Who will regard your fortune or your face.[45]

But the court is also often represented not so much as a place where women are in danger, as a place itself characterised by a dangerous femininity. The frequent suggestion is that, as a place of ease, of music and feasting, the court is intrinsically effeminate, subject to passions and pastimes rather than the nurse of heroic and manly virtues. Beard, again, lamenting the signs that the world is drawing to its evil end, says that:

> to [wickedness] also many great men give elbow-room and permission to sinne, whilest justice slumbereth... A mischiefe to be lamented above the rest, drawing after it a horrible overflow of all evils, and like a violent stream spoiling everywhere it goeth: when as they ought to governe the sterne of the Commonwealth let all go at randome, suffering themselves to bee rocked asleep with the false and deceitfull lullabie of effeminate pleasures and delights of the flesh.[46]

Music, dancing and pleasures were inevitably likely to be perceived as 'effeminate', for they, like women in conventional Renaissance terms, are not rational but appetitive in their delights, and therefore, like women, are siren songs, weakening the heroic male virtues of reason, self-government and control.

Women's vain desires were often suggested as the reason for the growth of a London 'season'. James himself, in a speech to Star Chamber, argued that 'one of the greatest causes of all gentlemen's desire, that have no calling or errand to dwel in London, is apparently the pride of women ... because the new fashion is to be had no where but in London'.[47] Alexander Niccholes warns husbands:

> bring her to the city, enter her into that schoole of vanity, set but example before her eies, she shall in time become a new creature ... She shall not blush to do that unlawfully which before shee was bashful to thinke on lawfully.[48]

The city, like the court at its centre, was, as Lawrence Manley points out, itself frequently characterised as a woman. In the topographical writing which is his subject, this female characterisation is ideologically conservative. London was represented 'as heroic matron, symbolically submissive intermediary between nature and the higher claims of political culture', thereby, Manley argues, effectively masking the troubling diversity of the city. But, as he points out, in satiric or critical writing this female persona could take on the conventionally double nature of women. He cites Dekker's observation that London 'hast all things in thee to make thee fairest, and all things in thee to make thee foulest: for thou art attir'd like a Bride ... but there is much harlot in thine eyes.'[49]

A little example of the way these contrary perceptions of the court might issue in practice is given in John Holles's advice to his son, apparently dissuading him from pursuing some particular woman:

> Concerning the new grown heyre, by the late death of her brother, shee is a great courtier for bals and masks and great meetings; always one, of no birth, no kinred, her father a scholler only; besyds shee hath been in love, and so will shee agayn, by Diogenes his rule: rather I wishe yow a gentlewoman of good bloud, good kinred, un-blowne, and un-acquaynted with court conversation, dexterities, and intertainments.[50]

The desire for a woman uncorrupted by the court is obvious. But the same son had been told, when he set out on foreign travel a decade earlier, that he would find 'in France an assured, free, and civill conversation, running at the ring, dauncing vyz, qualities in these times most respected in our Court', and had been instructed to acquire the skills of riding, weapons and dancing 'as so necessarie to a young gentleman, as who cannot expresse himself in them as he ought, shall be disesteemed and neglected of his felloes.'[51] Who, one might ask, is he going to dance with? Clearly, in Holles's mind, not with his future bride.

Behind all these warnings and fears lies a strong sense that in the city, and in the court in particular, women were able, and therefore only too likely, to run free. When Ben Jonson presents a picture of renunciation of the vanities of the world his female speaker concludes:

> Nor for my peace will I go far,
>   As wanderers do that still do roam,
> But make my strengths such as they are
>   Here in my bosom and at home.[52]

Though the stoic self-reliance of this ending is a commonplace in poems of retreat for male as well as female speakers, that sense of the proper domestic space for women as their salvation is particularly loaded.

And this brings us to the third element in McElwee's account, the underlying suggestion that what Frances Howard needed was education in submissiveness, in the subjugation of self-will and obedience to authority. That the Renaissance viewed the position of women as essentially one of inferiority to men, and required of them obedience first to their parents, and then to their husbands is such a commonplace that it does not need exemplification here. Greene's comments already cited can stand adequately in the place of countless books of advice and sermons which enforced these attitudes upon the women of the period. But, as Linda Pollock has argued in a notably balanced article on the education of upper-class women, parents did not have an easy time in plotting the course of appropriate upbringing for their children, and especially for their daughters. As she points out, women were often expected to run estates in the absence of their husbands and to show themselves competent in a range of activities which overlapped the male sphere. In the course of their education 'Both sexes were conditioned in the necessity of obedience to parents. But daughters had to be even more meticulously schooled in deference because, as married women, they would be under the governance of their husbands.'[53] Pollock insists that this did not mean that parents wished their daughters to grow up without abilities or independence of mind. As she says:

> The upbringing of girls was intended to ensure adult women were deferential to men, but not to preclude the possibility of independent thought or action. Thus, women as adults switched between roles,

choosing according to the circumstances to utilize what were conventionally held to be masculine skills or feminine qualities. This versatility of the female sex, although a desired consequence of their rearing regime, caused problems for the smooth operation of a patriarchal society.[54]

One might add that it caused problems also for the women caught in this trap, problems which might be seen as continuing down to the present day in various transmuted forms. One of the ways of looking at Frances Howard's career is precisely to see her as oscillating between the independence of mind that her social status and, presumably, her education gave her, and the demands of obedience operative in her culture.

Of the detail of Frances Howard's education we know nothing. But the absence of any mention of her between 1606 and 1609 does suggest that, whether or not she spent time at court with her mother, she would probably, like her husband, be completing her education, an education that taught her to write a neat italic hand [Plate 3] (even if she had difficulty, as Franklin was to claim in his trial, in reading the secretary hand of Gervase Elwes), and social skills, including training in dance, and some instruction in domestic management appropriate to one who might in future be expected to cope with the running of her husband's estates. The ideal conduct from a woman in Frances's position is indicated in a letter the Earl of Salisbury wrote to his son shortly after he had married Frances's sister, and, like Essex, gone abroad to complete his education:

> I saw your wife, who is a goodly young lady, kind to you and modest in her carriage, refusing to come to Court or London as places she will take no pleasure in during the time of her virginal widowhood.[55]

If only, McElwee's argument goes, Frances Howard had been content to follow the wishes of her parents, to accommodate herself to her marriage and preserve that idealised chastity, then she might have led a life of reassuring obscurity. There is no actual evidence that she did not pursue this course at least until 1609.

But that has not been the customary story. It is time to return to the charges set out at the beginning of the chapter, to test their validity and question the sources which give these accusations their plausibility. If we begin with the suggestion that Frances Howard was the mistress of Prince Henry, then we find that there is no contemporaneous evidence for such an attachment. Two comments in the Venetian archive have been advanced, but neither can be taken seriously. On 19 August 1612, shortly before the Prince's death, Foscarini was writing that 'Both the King and Queen think it desirable to marry the Prince as soon as possible, as his Highness has begun to show a leaning to a certain lady of Court.'[56] But whatever else is unknown, it is certain that by this date Frances was set on the course that was to lead to her marriage with Robert Carr; whoever the threatening lady was, she was unlikely to have been Frances Howard. Even less to be credited is the letter of 13 November 1615 when Foscarini claimed 'The countess, his wife, confesses to having had recourse to witchcraft in order to obtain the love of the deceased prince, and the bronze statue made for this purpose has been found'.[57] This letter just postdates the trial of Anne Turner, on 7 November, and it was then that Frances Howard's letters to Turner and Forman were first read, and that the models purported to have been used to prosecute her love for Carr were exhibited. The Venetian ambassador seems to have conflated these revelations with the rumours going round that the poisoning of Overbury was but the tip of a huge poison plot which had already claimed Henry and others, and was set to kill off half the court. These rumours were to be given further momentum at the trial of Franklin by the Lord Chief Justice himself – and will be discussed later in the book.

The real 'evidence' that historians have drawn upon emanates chiefly from Wilson's *History*. He suggests that Frances tried to seduce Henry, and reports that after she had given up on him and turned to Carr, the Prince reacted angrily, spurning a courtier who proffered him Frances's glove, dropped during a dance, with the words: 'He would not have it, it is strecht by another'. Wilson's testimony is amplified by Sir Simonds D'Ewes, who wrote:

> She was so delicate in her youth as, notwithstanding the inestimable Prince Henry's martial desires, and initiation into the ways of godliness, she, being set on by the Earl of Northampton, her father's uncle, first taught his eye and heart, and afterwards prostituted herself to him, who reaped the first fruits. But those sparks of grace which even then began to show their lustre in him, with those more heroic innate qualities derived from virtue, which gave the law to his more advised actions, soon raised him out of the slumber of that distemper, and taught him to reject her following temptations with indignation and super-ciliousness.[58]

D'Ewes cannot have been speaking from first-hand knowledge, since he was born only in 1602. Whatever access he or Wilson might have had to 'sources close to the palace', the fact is that all suggestion of an affair between Henry and Frances postdates the event, and, more importantly, postdates the Overbury murder trial. For if D'Ewes's account is considered more closely, then the pattern of the story he relates has an obvious correspondence with the commonplace narrative of her affair with Carr. She is set on by her wicked uncle; she is the active seducer, and blame attaches not to the man who took her virginity, but to her for offering herself to him.

Indeed, for D'Ewes the character of Frances Howard herself is significant only insofar as she contributes to the eulogy of Prince Henry, making him human enough to have felt some spark of sexual attraction, but heroic and manly enough to resist female blandishments. In this Henry is set up as an anti-type to Carr, who showed no such moral restraint. As we will see, the characterisation of the affair of Robert Carr and Frances Howard as one of a virtuous man led astray by Circean female charms is a frequent and powerful one. What is important at present is to recognise the way in which the suggested affair with the Prince conforms to this stereotype – which might lead one to think that the stereotype is what produces the story, rather than the other way around.

In a recent treatment of this same affair, we find J.W. Williamson also dismissing the rumour, since it 'began only after Henry's death and was precipitated by anti-Stuart writers who had never known the prince or the extent to which his personal myth made him distinctly different from the stereotypical rakes who crowded into the Court of James I'.[59] But, far from redeeming Frances Howard, Williamson, intent on purifying his hero from any taint, suggests that she was anathema to him precisely because of her sexuality. He observes of her: 'By the time she was seventeen, when her husband had returned from Europe not much improved, she had become a common property among both gallants and wits.' In this more general accusation Williamson is echoed by many historians. Stone, for example, writes that she secured the annulment of her marriage to Essex 'on the grounds that she was *virgo intacta* – a hypothesis to the falsity of which a number of men about town could testify'.[60] Again, there is no contemporaneous evidence that Frances Howard conducted liaisons with anyone but Robert Carr. The source for Stone, Williamson and others is the remark by Weldon of the trial of Frances Howard's virginity during the annulment hearings, that the midwives 'gave verdict, she was *intacta virgo*, which was thought very strange; for the world took notice, that her way was very near beaten so plain, as if *regia via*, and in truth, was a common way before Somerset did ever travell that way'.[61] The dependence of the modern historians upon Weldon's words is obvious. One has to ask whether the picture of a promiscuous Frances Howard which Weldon and others presented is not a retrospective construction fabricated within the assumptions about court women that we have earlier examined.

Coppélia Kahn makes an interesting observation in this context:

> Though prostitutes and promiscuous women appear in Renaissance drama, the term 'whore' is most often applied not to women who sleep with many men, but to women who don't – to wives, for the most part, who sleep or are thought to sleep with one other man. If a woman does not belong exclusively to one man, like a whore she is thought common to many men. Through the category of the whore, the male imagination seeks to justify its control over women. These words, spoken by De Flores in Middleton's *Changeling*, epitomize the fantasy of women's sexual appetite on which the term of whore is founded:

> > if a woman
> > Fly from one point, from him she makes a husband,
> > She spreads and mounts like arithmetic,
> > One, ten, a hundred, a thousand, ten thousand,
> > Proves in time sutler to an army royal.
> >   (II.ii.60–4)[62]

Frances Howard, having offended once with Robert Carr must, therefore, have offended many times. The assumption made by the fictional character, De Flores, is identical to that which sustains Weldon's account, and underprops many more recent historians' representations.

If hypotheses about Frances Howard's affair with the Prince and her more general promiscuity are demonstrably built upon shaky factual ground, the same is not true of her affair with Robert Carr. It would seem clear that when Essex returned from his foreign travels his marriage ran into immediate difficulties. He himself may well have been seriously ill with smallpox. Wilson's testimony that Frances Howard tried to avoid living with her husband and loathed leaving London for his house at Chartley in Staffordshire is borne out by the letters that we will examine shortly. Whether the Earl was impotent or not (a subject to which we will return in the next chapter), his wife made every effort to discourage his attentions. She writes to this effect to Turner and Forman sometime before Forman's death in September 1611, and the evidence of Anne Turner at her trial was that after Forman's demise she and Frances had recourse to another conjuror, one Dr Savery, in efforts to incapacitate Essex. In the course of the investigations of the murder of Overbury, testimony was given of meetings between Frances Howard and Robert Carr. Richard Weston, in his examination of 6 October 1615, testified to meetings at 'a

house betwene hammersmyth and Branford over against a common' where
they stayed for at least an hour and a half, and at Turner's house in
Paternoster Row. At the trial Lawrence Hyde elaborated on Weston's role
as a pander to the affair, arranging meetings 'where they committed
lewedenes togeather', and reminding the jurors that 'all this while shee
was the countess of Essex'.[63] In the later trial of James Franklin – a man
who, as we will see, could be relied on to say what he thought the
prosecution wanted to hear – a rather juicier account was given of his
own meetings with Frances Howard at Turner's house. He claimed that
'he knewe alwaies when my Lo: of Rochester lay there, for then when he
came in the morninge hee was not admitted into the La: bedchamber, but
Mrs Turner was sent to talke with him; and once she complayned that the
Countesse had not made her privy to the Earles lyinge there'.[64] The
trustworthiness of this specific testimony must be doubted, but yet it
appears certain that Frances Howard and Robert Carr did meet on a
number of occasions before the annulment of her marriage to Essex.

The Earl of Northampton testified both to the meetings, and to the
potential danger of them, when he wrote to Carr during the divorce
hearings:

> Touching the remove of the swet lady to Cawsom we are all of one
> mind, as I gather upon your Lo. last letter; that is, your Lo., my Lord
> and Lady, the prety lady and I; for since she findes that yor Lo. can not
> come thither she for her part desires not to remaine there especiallye
> considering that the same conveniency of sendinge to hir in that hows
> cannot be so ordinarily currant as it is nowe by me to the satisfaction
> of all partyes.
>
> Upon the remove therfor we are all agreed and differ only in the
> place. Your Lo. likes of London which can not be so fitte in my ladies
> [Countess of Suffolk's] absence whom my Lo. affaires drawe downe for
> a while; for the Q., my Lo. of Southampton who is nowe arrived,
> Pembruch etc. would take occasion upon hir aboad in this place without
> company to runne upon the matter. Awdley ende they take to be the
> better and fitter place and free from occasiones of discourse in the
> meane while till the knotte be tied.[65]

Meetings there have clearly been, but Northampton is concerned that any
breath of scandal must be avoided during the divorce hearings. It is possible,
indeed probable, that if Frances Howard had been engaging in private
meetings where she and Carr shared a bed, she might not have made this
known even to Northampton, in other respects her confidant. But, as so
often, there is a significant clash of testimony. The centrality of Weston's

role in the whole affair was confirmed at his trial by the claim that only he was the bearer of letters between Frances and Robert. Anne Turner, however, even in her final confession before her execution, still maintained that 'all the letters that came from the Earl of Somerset to the Lady came in the packet of the earle of northampton and from him she had them'.[66] Northampton's surviving letters corroborate her version, as does Henry Savile's communication with Sir Henry Neville on 24 August 1613: 'Packetts passe night and day from Court to Greenewich from whence footemen be sent away at Midnight with letters to the La: Frances'.[67] But whether or not Weston and Franklin had been leaned on to provide or invent the evidence of adultery that was necessary to the prosecution case, we may take it that some meetings, chaperoned or not, had taken place at some time before the annulment was finalised.

There is, however, a further dimension to the problem. It is by no means clear when the relationship had begun, or, indeed, who initiated it. The letters to Forman and Turner belong at the latest to September 1611, yet Weston claimed in his examination that the meetings between the couple only took place in the twelve months before he was appointed Overbury's keeper, on 7 May 1613. Overbury suggested that he had assisted Carr in the early stages of the affair by writing love letters for him, though others maintained that it was Frances who seduced Carr. A frustratingly undated fragment of a letter by John Holles gives another, and very different account of the beginning of their relationship:

> My Lord in answear to your Lordships letter I will sett down what I remember that passed betwixt your Lordship and my Lady, before my Lady of Suffolk and my self at Clarkenwell house: and omitting sum by speeches, that which was most insisted on, was of your Lordships and my Ladies first cumming together. Yow there protested, that notwithstanding severall sollicitations from her, it was not your seeking, and that after my Lord of Essex had delivered her up to my Lord of Suffolk her father, my Lady writt to yow to cum to Chesterford park, where then my Lord of Lennox was; as I remember; then your Lordship sayd, that shee tould yow, shee was a free woman, your Lordship replyed that yow had as yet made no fortune, that yow were at the Kinges bestowing: and that he was hard to deale with all in any suche matter: nevertheless shee pressing yow still, and my Lord of Lennox in her behalf, your Lordship sayd yow would try the King, how yow could frame him therunto.[68]

Without any context for this letter it is difficult to evaluate it. Why should Carr have been asking Holles to remind him of what one would have thought he knew full well? Why was Holles writing on the subject apparently some years after the event? It is, however, a signally interesting document. Somerset may, of course, have been hiding the truth in presenting himself as the innocent object of Frances Howard's attentions. If, however, these recollections are accurate, then it casts the whole relationship in a very different light. In this version Frances Howard in her own mind was free from her marriage to Essex even before the divorce hearings were over. (It is perhaps relevant that she signed herself with her maiden name at the end of the letter reproduced in Plate 3.) Once Somerset had secured the consent of the King, the match might have been confirmed with a formal (if secret) betrothal, at which point both of them could have considered themselves married in all but outward ceremony (the position of Claudio and Julia in *Measure for Measure*, for example). If this were the case, then to meet, or even to share a bed, would not have seemed to them as flagrantly immoral as it was represented as the murder trials. Betrothed couples were permitted considerable licence in early seventeenth-century society – albeit that the circumstances of this affair were scarcely normal.

Whoever made the first move, however, the depth of Frances's feeling for Robert Carr once their relationship was established is touchingly suggested in Northampton's letters. He speaks, for example, of 'the prety Nimphe that loves you more then hir owne life' and 'the prety lady who lives by the life of your letters as a chameleon doth by aire'.[69] But more than this, Northampton, who perhaps had more opportunity than any other of knowing how the relationship proceeded, suggests by implication in his letters that, whether they met or not, Frances Howard preserved her virginity until after she was married to Carr. His letters are not all dated, so their sequence is difficult to reconstruct, but in a number of them he makes jokes which turn upon Frances's virginity, and the promise that marriage brings. He writes in one:

> God will blesse the nexte bargain and here in this ladyes chamber from whence I write nowe I shall hope one day to find better pen and Inke then I have at this present as you may perceave by my letter.

In another letter, seeming to answer some apologetic noises in a letter from Carr about the difficulty of reading his handwriting, he observes:

> your Lo. shall assure your self that notwithstanding any blotte whereof you speake yet your character [handwriting] is not redde by me with any paine that am nowe as well acquainted with your hand as with my owne, and though it wear it wear but that which a man takes in

crackinge a swete nutte to tast the kirnell or but lyke the payne which my La. Fraunces shall feele when the swete streame followes.

And in yet another letter asks:

My sute in the meane time is that she be rewarded with a kisse from your owne lippes which shall pass for the broade seale till you come to the privye seale wherin if I make anie staie let the K. take my office.[70]

Versions of some of these letters were quoted at Carr's trial. The *State Trials* reports that the Lord Chief Justice left off reading 'for the bawdiness of it' (*ST*, 935); one manuscript account speaks of the 'beastly and bawdy letters';[71] and they provoked John Castle to exclaim 'It would turn chaste blood into water to hear the unchaste and unclean phrases that were contained in them';[72] but however indecorous they might be, their tenor is self-evident. In Northampton's eyes their relationship remains unconsummated. He may have been deliberately misled, of course, but his testimony must be taken into account.

Still to be considered, however, are the two letters which provide the compelling evidence of her resort to powders and potions to inhibit her husband and provoke her lover. They are so central to a reading of her, and to the later representation of her conduct, that they need to be quoted in full. No holograph survives of these letters, which seem to have been kept back by Forman's widow from the searches Turner instituted at Forman's house in an attempt to destroy potentially damaging evidence. They exist now only in the versions that have come down from accounts of the trials, which may or may not be accurate. The first which was quoted at Turner's trial was addressed to her, with the injunction to 'burn this letter':

Sweet Turner; I am out of all hope of any good in this world, for my father, my mother, and my brother said, I should lie with him; and my brother Howard was here, and said, he [Essex] would not come from this place [Chartley] all winter; so that all comfort is gone; and which is worst of all, my lord hath complained, that he hath not lain with me, and I would not suffer him to use me. My father and mother are angry, but I had rather die a thousand times over; for besides the sufferings, I shall lose his [Carr's] love if I lie with him [Essex]. I will never desire to see his [Carr's] face, if my lord do that unto me. My lord is very well as ever he was, so as you may see in what a miserable case I am. You may send the party [Forman?] word of all; he sent me word all should be well, but I shall not be so happy as the lord to love me. As you have taken pains all this while for me, so now do all you can, for never so unhappy as now; for I am not able to endure the miseries that are coming on me, but I cannot be happy so long as this man [Essex] liveth: therefore pray for me, for I have need, but I should be better if I had your company to ease my mind. Let him [Forman?] know this ill news: if I can get this done, you shall have as much money as you can demand, this is fair play. – Your sister, Frances Essex.

The second letter was to Forman:

Sweet Father; I must still crave your love, although I hope I have it, and shall deserve it better hereafter: remember the galls, for I fear though I have yet no cause but to lie confident, in you, yet I desire to have it as it is yet remaining well; so continue it still, if it be possible, and if you can you must send me some good fortune, alas! I have need of it. Keep the lord [Carr] still to me, for that I desire; and be careful you name me not to any body, for we have so many spies, that you must use all your wits, and all little enough, for the world is against me, and the heavens favour me not, only happy in your love; I hope you will do me good, and if I be ingrateful, let all mischief come unto me. My lord is lusty and merry, and drinketh with his men; and all the content he gives me, is to abuse me, and use me as doggedly as before: I think I shall never be happy in this world, because he hinders my good, and will ever, I think so; remember, I beg for God's sake, and get me from this vile place. – Your affectionate, loving daughter, Frances Essex. – Give Turner warning of all things, but not the lord: I would not have any thing come out for fear of the Lord Treasurer [Cecil], for so they may tell my father and mother, and fill their ears full of toys. (ST, 931–2)

At the murder trials these letters were both shocking and fascinating to the large audience. They seemed to confirm the villainy of Frances, suggesting a desire to make away her husband, and as John Castle said, when sending copies of the letters to James Miller 'You will see by them how abusively her lust wronged those great judgements that spake for her separation from that noble Essex, upon whom she practised *magiam maleficiam*'.[73] They provided the hard evidence from which Wilson and others elaborated upon the conspiracy to 'imbecillitate' Essex. But whilst these letters undoubtedly show that she was consulting Forman and Turner in the hope of procuring means both of inhibiting Essex's desires and promoting the love of Carr – or of some other 'lord' – a more sensitive and careful reading of them suggests very strongly that the conventional picture of Frances Howard is mistaken. The letters do not even confirm that she was plotting to murder her husband. They do, to be sure, register a despairing recognition that, tied to an apparently indissoluble marriage, she was consigned to a life-long prison. Only the phrase 'if I can get this done, you shall have as much money as you can demand' can be taken as hinting at a design to murder. 'This' could mean 'murder', but it is by no means the only possible reading. Even the supporting evidence of Calvert's letter, saying that 'plots have been laid to poison' Essex does not prove the case beyond doubt. As we will see, fear that discontented wives would try to poison their husbands was such a standard projection of male anxiety that it might indicate no more than that he had heard that Frances had been seen consulting Forman, and was known to be hostile to her husband. We will return to this matter when discussing the murder trials.

More significantly for the moment, the letter to Turner suggests that she was far from the sexually experienced whore of common fantasy. She fears the 'suffering' of lying with her husband, and this I take to indicate not an aesthetic distaste, but apprehension at sexual initiation itself. Frances Howard here is not the lusty maid of gynophobic convention, but rather the Amoret of Spenser's *Faerie Queene*, inhibited from accepting her sexuality by the literary myths of the painful surrender of her maidenhead, or else a woman who has been convinced by the standard propaganda of the epithalamic convention which guarantees the virginity of the bride by requiring her to experience pain. If Frances had been already the 'common property' of the gallants she could not have written this sentence. Moreover, her fear that she will lose Carr's love if she accepts her husband's embraces demonstrates how completely she is subject in her own mind to the cultural demands upon female chastity.

Part of the commonplace characterisation of the lustfulness of the court was that women there were not only unlikely to be virgins, but made a habit of using marriage to cover their love affairs. Massinger frequently expounds this notion. In *The Fatal Dowry*, for example, there is this exchange between Beaumelle and her maid Bellapert:

> *Beaumelle*   I would meete love and marriage both at once.
> *Bellapert*   Why then you are out of the fashion and wilbe contemn'd:
> For (I'll assure you) there are few women i' the world, but either
> they have married first, and love after, or love first, and marryed
> after... A husband these dayes is but a cloake to bee oftner layde
> upon your bed, then in your bed. (II.ii.43–57)[74]

And in *The Renegado* Donusa, a Turkish woman, asks Carazie about the condition of women in England. Of the court lady Carazie observes:

Carazie   as I have heard
    They are growne of late so learn'd that they maintaine
    A strange position, which their Lords with all
    Their witt cannot confute.
Donusa   What's that I prethee?
Carazie   Marry that it is not onely fit but lawfull,
    Your Madame there, her much rest, and high feeding
    Duely considered, should to ease her husband
    Bee allow'd a private friend. They have drawne a Bill
    To this good purpose, and the next assembly
    Doubt not to passe it.

(I.ii.39–48)[75]

Commonplace such conduct may have been, but on the evidence of these letters Frances Howard did not even countenance the option that she might continue in her marriage but take a lover on the side. She believed, furthermore, that Carr would only love her if she remained a virgin, and no other possibility was entertained.

The letters also speak movingly of the pressure put upon her by her family, and her panic lest her parents should be alerted to her state. Her fear again reflects the degree to which she has internalised the patriarchal norms of her society, as does the way she writes of Essex's desire to 'use' her sexually. To the modern reader, whatever attitude one might take to the course of action on which Frances Howard embarked, the picture she draws of Essex carousing with male friends, intent only on 'using' and 'abusing' his wife, is a distasteful one. The evidence of these two letters, I would suggest, far from demonstrating a determined and transgressive woman, gives us a picture of one who has internalised the expectations of her society only too completely, and sees herself utterly trapped by them. Her situation mirrors the terrifying picture of the married state given by Alexander Niccholes:

> This knot can neither bee cut nor loosed but by death, therefore as wise prisoners inclosed in narrow roomes suite their mindes to their limites, and not, impatient they can go no further, augment their paine by knocking their heades against the walles, so should the wisdom both of Husbands and Wives . . . make it unto them to beare it with patience and content the asswages of all maladies, and misfortunes, and not storme against that which will but the deeper plunge them into their own misery.[76]

In the eyes of her contemporaries, Frances Howard should have borne the absence of her husband, her 'virginal widowhood', like a Penelope waiting for Ulysses. On his return she should simply have accommodated herself to her prison. It is not surprising that commentators of the seventeenth century should have taken her refusal to do so as a sign of a total moral depravity and therefore represented her in their stereotypes of female disobedience. It is, however, discouraging, to say the least, that modern commentators should so uniformly and unthinkingly have drawn their representations of Frances Howard according to the same prescription. It is not just a matter of sympathy for her distress, though even Walter Devereux, in other respects extremely hostile to her, could still write:

> Notwithstanding the great crimes into which the passions of Lady Essex hurried her, and the horror one must feel at the deliberate planning of the death of her husband which is shown in the latter part of this letter, one cannot but feel some sympathy for her situation. Married, when a child, to one who, being sent abroad, remained a stranger to her, she became attached, during his absence, to another, and now resisted courageously all the efforts and authority of her parents, brother, and husband, to make her unfaithful to the man she adored. Had she rested here, her unhappy situation would have called for our compassion.[77]

Devereux' sympathy is severely qualified by the fact that he can neither offer nor imagine any way she can escape the situation in which she found herself. There is an absolute paralysis. McElwee's account with which we began this chapter wriggles out of the problem by loading blame entirely onto Frances herself through the representation of her as a silly, but self-willed girl.

In the course of this chapter we have seen how assumptions about the court, about masquing, and about women in general all play their part in manufacturing the mould from which the character of Frances Howard is cast. My argument is in some respects a very simple one. Once the revelations of the Overbury murder allowed contemporaries to 'fix' her character as 'wicked woman', then everything else was simply drawn down upon her. The stereotypes of moralists and of literary texts existed as powerful mental and narrative 'sets' which could then take over and determine the nature of her representation. With a dreadful circularity Frances Howard grows into the standard image of the infamous female and the blanks of her life are filled in from the model. It is true that in more recent narratives the vile sorceress of seventeenth-century commentators is transformed into the feather-brained bimbo of McElwee or Le Comte,[78] but, as we have seen, there is a continuity between them.

This is not, emphatically not, an attempt to restore Frances Howard to a moral blamelessness – that would simply be to stay within the binary model which characterises women as virgin or whore, dutiful wife or lecherous transgressive. But it is possible to argue that Frances Howard did not seduce Prince Henry; it is possible to claim that she did not put herself about to all and sundry. It is possible to suggest that she fell in love with one man when she reached the age where she might know her own mind, only to run into the impossibility, in English society in the early seventeenth century, of doing anything about it. I would suggest that this might modify our response to her transgressions. For though one might reasonably deplore the fact that she tried out the resources of conjurors and wise women to solve her problems, her recourse to them was not necessarily simply idiotic, as may now appear. That she should resort to the murder of Thomas Overbury, and possibly have attempted to murder the Earl of Essex, needs to be understood, though not justified, in the light of the situation in which she found herself. But before attending to these criminal acts we will consider her attempt to secure a legal way out of her hated marriage. For here, too, she was to run full-face into the very net of assumptions about proper female conduct which would give further power to the construction of the villainous sorceress which has, by and large, remained the unquestioned representation of her down to the present day.

Plates

1 The most famous portrait of Frances Howard, attributed to William Larkin.

2 Robert Carr, in a miniature after the manner of Hilliard.

3 Frances Howard's note appended to one of the Earl of Northampton's letters to Robert Carr at the time of the

The portraiture of Robert Car Earle of Somerset Vicount Rochester, Knight of the most noble order of the Garter &c. And of the Ladie Francis his wife

4 An engraving of Carr and Howard by Renold Elstrack, probably issued
at the time of the Overbury murder trials.

VERA EFFIGIES FRANCISCÆ COMITISSÆ SOMERSETIÆ / VICECOM · ROFFEN · ETc ·

The lively portraict of the Lady Francis Countesse of Somerset.

S. Pa: sculp: Lon:.

Comp: Holl: excud.

5 (a & b) Two versions of 'the true portrait' of Frances Howard by Simon van de Passe, dating from 1618–20.

VERA EFFIGIES FRANCISCÆ COMITISSÆ SOMERSETIÆ VICECOM: ROFFEN: ETc.

The liuely portraict of the Lady Francis Countesse of Somerset.

S. Pa: sculp: Lon:.   Comp: Holl: excud.

(b)

6 It has been claimed that the figures of the doctor, the woman [and the man are] Forman, Frances Howard and the Earl of Essex.

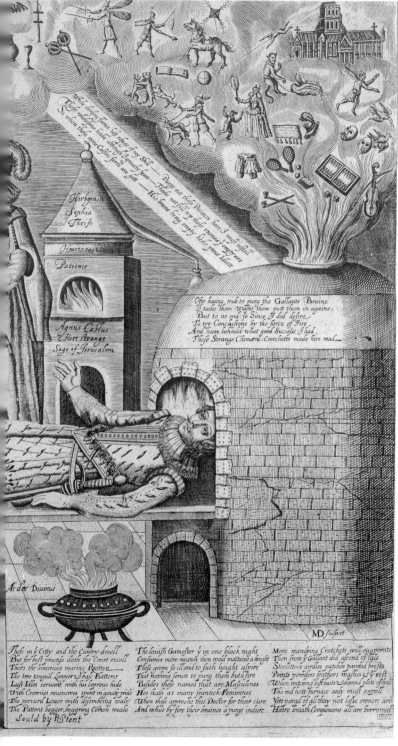

and the man lying on the right in this satirical print represent

7 A moralising broadside produced after the execution of Anne Turner.

8 The choice of Hercules between the paths of Pleasure and Virtue, from Samuel Brant's *Ship of Fools*.

AT THE CHILDBED

AT THE HOTTEHOUSE

AT THE CONDI

AT THE BAKEHOUSE

AT Child-bed when the Goffips meet,
   Fine Stories we are told ;
And if they get a Cup too much,
   Their Tongues they cannot hold.

At Market when good Housewives meet,
   Their Market being done,

Together they will crack a Pot,
   Before they can get Home.

The Bake-house is a Place you know,
   Where Maids a Story hold,
And if their Miftreffes will prate,
   They muft not be control'd.

At Alehouse you fee how jovial
   With every one her Noggin
For till the Skull and Belly be
   None of them will be joggi

To Church fine Ladies do refor
   New Fafhions for to fpy ;

9 A satirical print (c.1603) representing the 'evils' of gossiping women.

Branches of Gossipping.

AT THE MARKET

WASHERS AT THE RIVER

AT THE ALLE HOVS

...o to Church sometimes
...heir Bravery.

...se makes a rough Skin smooth
...t beautify;

...use it every Week,
...s to purify.

At the Conduit striving for their Turn,
  The Quarrel it grows great,
That up in Arms they are at last,
  And one another beat.

Washing at the River's Side
  Good Housewives take Delight;

But scolding Sluts care not to work,
  Like wrangling Queens they fight.

Then Gossips all a Warning take,
  Pray cease your Tongue to rattle;
Go knit, and Sew, and Brew, and Bake,
  And leave off TITTLE-TATTLE.

10 A costume design for a female masquer, by Inigo Jones (c.1610–12).

11 Renold Elstrack's portrait of Thomas Overbury.

12 Samuel Rowlands' broadside representing the discovery of the murder of Thomas Overbury as a Triumph of Time.

The picture of the vnfortunate gentleman, Sir Geruis Eluies Knight. late leiftenant of his Maiesties Tower of London.

Behold him aright whose office & estate,
Vnwisely manag'd, made him vnfortunate:
And whose starring hopes of popular grace,
Rob'd him of life, fanoures dignity, and place.
Yet let the worst o' him thus much conceale,
A foe to him selfe, in ftriuing to be great:
Worshipfull by birth, deborate and kind,
Perfect in all, but the purpose o' min'e.
Thorough which, heauenly ayming ouer hye,
Deceiued him selfe and won blame thereby:
For in ftriking to better his degree,
Fortune betray'd him with falfe hopes we fee.
The golden meanes was not his harts content,
Nor courtesy life, with quiet flumbers spent:
But watchful cares, and charges of estate,

The onely aymes his hart made leuel at.
So aiming vp to dignity & fame,
Forgot what dangers dwell about the fame:
Butfeated on the top of Fortunes mount,
He little thought fo foone to giue account,
Ofhis amiffe: and deeds o' fecret fin,
Ofwhich by law he was found guilty in.
And being caft, as Iuftice had ordain'd,
His foule for heauenly mercy ftill complain'd:
And fo with true repentance leauing earth,
Tooke patiently his iuft deferued death.
Reft then in peace on Sions holy hill,
Perfwafions trayn'd thee vnto this curfed ill:
Which if fo it thou neuer had'ft giuen confent,
Thy dayes had better in gracious maner spent.

Printed at London in the Black-Friers, by
Paul Boulenger. 1615.

13 Broadside depicting Sir Gervase Elwes on the way to execution.

Chapter 3

The second trial: Seeking an annulment

Whenever the annulment of the marriage of Frances Howard and Robert Devereux is mentioned by historians or literary critics it is described as 'squalid', 'sordid', 'disgusting' or, most frequently, 'scandalous'.[1] It was certainly a notorious event in 1613, but, as with so much else in the story of Frances Howard, the responses of subsequent commentators seem to reduplicate with disconcerting complacency the attitudes of the seventeenth century. Heather Dubrow, for example, associates herself directly with the moral distaste of a nineteenth-century chronicler when she writes:

> In reviewing the background to this marriage [of Frances Howard and Robert Carr] one is tempted to sympathize with the fastidious descendant of the bride who is said to have declared, "Nor shall I dwell on the disgusting particulars", for an account of those particulars makes the *National Enquirer* seem restrained and elliptical.[2]

It is curious that a writer in the late twentieth century should find abhorrent the discussion of erection and impotence and of the inspection of a woman to establish her virginity that are the 'particulars' of the case, but Dubrow's comment, in averting its eyes from the examination of those details, typifies the way in which so many scholars have refused to confront what was actually at stake in the divorce hearings. One strand of the argument of this chapter is that the assumptions which prompted the disapproval of Frances Howard's contemporaries need to be interrogated, rather than merely parroted.

As a first step in this enquiry it is essential to separate the evidence of 1613, when the annulment hearings were in process, from the evidence produced three years later at the trials for Thomas Overbury's murder. Conflation of the two episodes is fatally easy, and began early. In accounts of the Overbury trials the divorce was invoked as the motivation for the murder, thus prompting contemporaries to see the one as narrative preparation for the other. The manuscript record compiled for Overbury's father, for example, heads its table of contents with 'The proceedings of the Divorce between the Lady Frances Howard, & Robert Earle of Essex: which divorce was the occasion of all the mischeefes following'.[3] For the modern reader the sense of a necessary connection between divorce and murder is reinforced by historians' effort to produce a chronological narrative of the events of 1613. We are made aware of the recourse to Forman and other conjurors and of the plots with Weston, Turner, Franklin and Elwes to murder Overbury simultaneously with the proceedings in the annulment. It then becomes easy to follow seventeenth-century commentators in assuming a kind of moral domino effect by which the lesser crime of adultery leads to the greater sin of murder in neat and necessary narrative succession. The final temptation is to reinforce the potency of this narrative sequence by deriving from its completed shape a construction of Frances Howard's character which will endorse that moral scenario. Accordingly she becomes a quasi-tragic figure who demonstrates a deepening slide into moral depravity.

Middleton's *The Changeling*, a play influenced by the history of Frances Howard, articulates just such a moral sequence. The heroine, Beatrice-Joanna, escapes from the marriage her father has arranged for her by persuading De Flores to murder the intended husband and thus enable her to marry Alsemero, the object of her love. As the play proceeds Beatrice-Joanna finds herself ever more firmly enchained to the assassin, who is in turn bound to her by his own lust. As she attempts to repudiate him, De Flores ripostes:

> settle you
> In what the act has made you, y'are no more now;
> You must forget your parentage to me:
> Y'are the deed's creature; by that name
> You lost your first condition, and I challenge you,
> As peace and innocency has turn'd you out,
> And made you one with me.[4]

De Flores's words are an accurate summary of Frances Howard's fate in subsequent narratives. She has been represented ever since 1616 as 'the deed's creature', and the deed that defines her is the murder of Overbury. The later-known crime is imported back into the reading of the divorce, which then becomes a sign of Frances Howard's essential moral turpitude. De Flores's lines hint also at another powerful cultural motif which plays a significant part in determining the response to Frances Howard. The 'first condition' of which he speaks is also the original female 'deed' of Eve's betrayal in the Garden of Eden. Female innocence is always already lost, and woman's prior guilt therefore always assumed.

Revealingly, the critical verdict on the character of Beatrice-Joanna in Middleton's play strikingly parallels the personality historians have constructed for Frances Howard. Eliot's formulation is typical, and has been very influential:

> The tragedy of *The Changeling* is an eternal tragedy, as permanent as *Oedipus* or *Antony and Cleopatra*; it is the tragedy of the not naturally bad but irresponsible and undeveloped nature, caught in the consequences of its own action. In every age and in every civilization there are instances of the same things: the unmoral nature, suddenly trapped in the inexorable toil of morality.[5]

It is perhaps not surprising, if Middleton intended his dramatic character to recall Frances Howard to the minds of his audience, that there should be this overlap. But the similarity between Eliot's formulation and, for example, the 'character study' of Frances quoted in the last chapter might also indicate how pre-existing and culturally determined matrices of story and character determine our perceptions of fictional and historical figures alike.

Middleton was writing in 1622, but to those involved in and commenting upon the divorce hearings in 1613 the complete story was unavailable. Those most closely involved in the case, as well as the most assiduous of news-letter writers, seem to have made no connection between the death of Overbury and the annulment; furthermore, they seem to have become aware of Robert Carr's existence as the future husband for Frances Howard only some way through the proceedings. (This itself raises the possibility that Somerset's account of the progress of their relationship quoted in the previous chapter is more truthful than might be thought.) It is, of course, possible that more was known at the time than it was politic to record. Perhaps contemporaries did have strong suspicions that Overbury was murdered because of his opposition to the remarriage of Frances Howard, but in the absence of any solid material evidence it is essential to keep the two issues separate. Otherwise, analysis of the controversy the divorce hearings themselves generated is only too likely to attribute their notoriety to the wrong reasons, and to obscure the real foundations of the antipathy that the annulment provoked. The double pressure to construct a tidy, causal narrative sequence and a psychologically coherent depiction of an essentially flawed female subject must be resisted, at least for a time.

The state of the Essexes' marriage, it would seem, was the subject of as much spicy gossip as the marriages of the royal family in England in the 1990s. Calvert's letter of 1610 quoted earlier indicates as much, and Archbishop Abbot in his narrative of the divorce proceedings says he had 'heard before of some discontentments between that noble couple' (*ST*, 806). Bishop Goodman later claimed that:

> About a year or two before the marriage was questioned, I did hear from a gentleman belonging to the Earl of Huntingdon, but very well known and a great servant to the Earl of Essex, that the Earl of Essex was fully resolved to question the marriage and to prove a nullity; and I am confident that if the Countess had not then at that instant done it, the Earl of Essex himself would have been the plaintiff; so then hereby I conclude that both parties were agreed and were alike interested in the business.[6]

To many observers marital breakdown in upper-class marriages must have seemed far from unusual. Robert Abbot (the Archbishop's brother) in a wedding sermon of 1608 lamented:

> Nature, religion, fidelity, civilitie, equitie, all cry it out that the husband and the wife should walke together; and yet the cry of all these availeth not, but that lamentable ruptures and divisions betwixt husband and wife are everywhere to be seene amongst us, specially amongst men of higher place, yea so common in many places as it were a thing out of fashion for great men and their wives to live and walk together.[7]

The preacher's pessimism is supported by Lawrence Stone's observation that between 1595 and 1620 'something like one-third of the older peers were estranged from or actually separated from their wives'.[8] But none attempted to regularise matters in the manner of Frances Howard and her family. One of the most striking paradoxes of the story is precisely that if Frances Howard had been content to behave as it was alleged many others did, and conduct an illicit affair, she would have remained a forgotten figure, whereas by having the courage and determination (or petulant wilfulness, depending on one's point of view) to seek a way out of her marriage she ensured her notoriety.

Proceedings for the annulment were begun in May 1613, when a preliminary meeting between the earls of Suffolk and Northampton representing Frances Howard, and the Earl of Southampton and Lord Knollys for Robert Devereux agreed the terms of the petition, or 'libel', that

would be submitted. Northampton informed Robert Carr of the negotiations, and concluded optimistically:

> The councell one both sides is agreed upon the Libell; we shall proced
> without impediment. No strife is betwen eyther party in any pointes.[9]

A commission was appointed, headed by George Abbot, Archbishop of
Canterbury, assisted by three other bishops (John King of London, Lancelot
Andrewes of Ely and Richard Neile of Lichfield) and six civilian lawyers
and judges (Julius Caesar, Master of the Rolls; Thomas Parry, Chancellor
of the Duchy of Lancaster; Sir Daniel Dunne, Dean of Arches; Dr Thomas
Edwards; Dr John Bennet; and Dr Frances James). On 17 May the commissioners received the libel setting out the Countess's case. After recording
that the couple were legally married at the ages of thirteen and fourteen, and
that they had lived together as man and wife for three years once the Earl
had reached eighteen, the libel averred that Frances Howard, 'desirous to be
made a mother, from time to time, again and again yielded herself to his
power, and as much as lay in her offered herself and her body to be known;
and earnestly desired conjunction and copulation'. But the Earl, her plea
declared, could not 'have that copulation in any sort which the married bed
alloweth'. The libel went on to testify that the Earl 'hath had, and hath power
and ability of body to deal with other women, and to know them carnally',
and that the lady Frances 'is fit and able to have copulation with a man'.
Frances deposed that she was a virgin, and had not known of Essex's impediment before her marriage to him. The Earl had confessed 'in good earnest,
before Witnesses of good credit, and his friends and kinsfolks, that although
he did his best endeavour, yet he never could; nor at this time can, have
copulation with the said lady Frances, no not once.' A final clause attempts
to allay the gossip about the marriage, suggesting that 'in regard of womanish
modesty, the lady Frances hath concealed all the former matters, and had a
purpose ever to conceal them, if she had not been forced, through false
rumours of disobedience to the said Earl to reveal them' (ST, 785–7). At the
beginning of the hearings it was alleged that Essex's impotence towards
Frances was due to witchcraft (maleficium). This was dropped from the later
stages of the case, but had a powerful effect on public opinion, as we will
see.

A series of witnesses was called to testify that the Earl and Countess had
lain together 'in naked bed' on numerous occasions. In his answer to the
charges, however, Essex reneged on what seems to have been the original
concordat, by suggesting that the impediment to consummation lay in his
wife rather than himself. To answer this new accusation the court asked
for a physical examination of the Countess. Ten matrons and six midwives

were summoned, of whom five matrons and two midwives actually examined Frances and found her *virgo intacta*, but 'fitted with abilities to have carnal copulation, and apt to have children' (*ST,* 805). Frances herself swore an oath to her husband's impotence.

After this the case stalled. Instead of proceeding with the agreement of both parties, as Northampton had hoped, and as Sir Henry Neville had believed on 18 June when he wrote to Winwood of 'the separation intended between my Lord of Essex and his Lady, a Matter no less desyred by my Lord and his friends, then by her and hers',[10] the commissioners were unable to agree, and on 5 July the case was postponed to the next law term. At this point King James intervened by adding two more commissioners to the Court of Delegates, the bishops of Winchester and Rochester, and after a series of stormy meetings the nullity was finally granted on 25 September by a majority of seven to five.

I have made this account as neutral as possible, as a necessary prelude to the discussion of issues that it raises, since from the outset the narrative of the divorce hearings was always contested. Archbishop Abbot produced 'some memorialls touching the nullity ... and the difficulties endured in the same' and to them were added 'some observable things since Sept 25 1613'. In these last it was reported as 'confidently given out, That because the sentence had been opposed there should a book be written in the defence of it' (*ST,* 832). Various possible authors are suggested, among them Sir Daniel Dunne, and an account written by him survives in a number of manuscript copies.[11] In the *State Trials* it is reported that Suffolk vetoed publication, 'for so it might go on to the world's end: for one book might breed another: and so, they whom it concerned should never be in rest'. His views seem to have had some effect at the time, since neither treatise was published, but the decision by the editors of the *State Trials* to enshrine Abbot's account in print has ensured that Dunne's, written 'to prevent that evill which may ensue in a busines of this nature by malevolent or ignorant reporters', lies largely unconsulted. As a result, virtually all subsequent accounts of the divorce proceedings down to the present day have been powerfully skewed by the dominant presence of Archbishop Abbot's view of the matter.

In the opinion of many historians, the Archbishop emerges from the episode with considerable credit. He is frequently depicted as a man, whatever his other limitations, of stern moral integrity in refusing to be bowed by the pressure brought to bear upon him by the King and the Earl of Suffolk. S.R. Gardiner, for example, after describing the presence of Abbot at the wedding of Frances Howard and Robert Carr, rises to a moralising peroration:

To us, who know what the future history of England was, there is something ominous in this scene. It was, as it were, the spirit of Calvinism which had taken up its abode in that silent monitor; the one power in England which could resist the seductions of the Court, and which was capable of rebuking, at any cost, the immorality of the great. Abbot was not a large-minded man, but on that day he stood in a position which placed him far above all the genius and the grandeur about him.[12]

Whether the Archbishop's opposition was so purely motivated as Gardiner suggests is open to question. Like all the participants in the case he was affected by the highly-charged political implications of the marriage.

Frances Howard's attraction to (or for) Robert Carr offered a tremendous opportunity to her family. Since 1607 Carr had steadily been rising in the King's favour, and therefore in political influence; for, as Neil Cuddy observes, James's policy was very consciously to shift power 'away, increasingly, from the Privy Council and a bureaucrat-minister towards the Bedchamber and the royal favourite'.[13] This meant that courtiers vied to ensure that they had the ear of Robert Carr.[14] Under the influence of Thomas Overbury, he had hitherto tended to fall in with the faction led by Pembroke and Southampton, the old Essexians to whom Abbot also owed allegiance. In many areas of domestic and foreign policy they lined up against the Howards, who were pro-Spanish where the Essexians were militant against them, tolerant towards Catholics where they were ardently Protestant. Reading the factional power-games of the early modern period always runs the risk of seeing them as analogous to modern adversarial party-politics, whereas, instead, alliances on grounds of kinship, religious and political allegiance were continually shifting, issue by issue. Nonetheless Northampton, the leader of the Howard clan, perceived factional interest as central to the divorce hearings, and in his letters repeatedly stressed the need to thwart the opposition of Pembroke, Southampton and the Queen. Thomas, Viscount Fenton also described Abbot's actions as politically motivated. On 30 June he writes: 'the nulletye of this mariage is not yet done. The Romage [Romish] metropolitaine makes mutche conscience to doe that quhitche in law he must doe, quherin he shewes his splein but not his judgement', and two weeks later he announces the appointment of more commissioners 'for Cantiburrye hes showin himselfe exceeding partiall against the Chamberlaine, and as it is saide for feare of sume new allaye betuyxt Essex and Rotchester, quherof there is a great lyklyehode.' For Fenton it is the political repercussions of the new marriage that account for Abbot's opposition.[15] Abbot's antipathy to Northampton and Suffolk evidently fuelled his moral indignation at the proposed divorce, and the news that Frances was likely to marry Carr further increased anxiety as he saw the favourite being captured by his opponents. To suggest that his scruples were a consequence of his political affiliation and a more or less conscious attempt to give moral legitimacy to factional interests might be an overstatement, but one should at least be wary of his characterisation as a man of simple, principled moral integrity.

Queen Anne's position in all of this is of some significance and complexity. She was a Catholic sympathiser, and though for a time Catherine Howard and her daughters seem to have been close to her, she yet patronised Pembroke and Southampton and was conspicuously to stand by Essex.[16] In writing to Sir John Digby about the celebrations of the marriage of Lord Roxborough and Mrs Jane Drummond in February 1614, Holles reports that the Queen held a great feast 'to which so many either came or were invited that a table stretching the whole length of the gallery was filled. She herself sat at the boards' end and by her stood the whole time my Lord of Essex'.[17] Northampton reported to Carr his fear that 'the Q. enflamed with passion and rage should out of her hatred to me disorder the maine state of the procedinges'.[18] But the Queen's hostility seems also to have been directed against Carr, chiefly perhaps on account of his friendship with Overbury, whom she loathed.[19] She may be imagined, therefore, to have had a double animosity to the divorce and the proposed remarriage. Her opposition to it was to have significant consequence, as we will see in the next chapter.

The political importance of the divorce and remarriage has other effects upon the way events have subsequently been narrated. Just as Frances Howard in her first marriage had been the coin of factional exchange, so to Weldon in this second match she was little more than the tool of the unscrupulous Northampton. The Earl, he says, 'followed Balaams councel, by sending a Moabitish woman unto him [Carr], in which he made use of Copinger, a gentleman who had spent a fair fortune . . . This Moabitish woman was a daughter of the Earle of Suffolk.'[20] In Ford's *The Fancies Chaste and Noble* of 1638 the same reading of events still seems to have been potent enough to be recalled as a type of courtly corruption. There Troylo-Savelli ironically observes

> He merited well to wear a robe of chamlet
> Who train'd his brother's daughter, scarce a girl
> Into the arms of Mont-Argenterato
> Whiles the young lord of Telamon, her husband,
> Was packeted to France to study courtship . . . [21]

At the end of the previous chapter attention was drawn to competing and contradictory representations of the beginning of the Carr/Howard relationship. The suggestion that Frances Howard was used as bait by her family to seduce Robert Carr adds yet another. Northampton's own comments, however, cast considerable doubt on Weldon's testimony. He wrote to Carr:

> I have receaved great satisfaction by the report which my Lo Chamberlain [Suffolk] hath made of all the procedinges in court, but most of all by that fastenes which I find already to be growne in your affectiones one to another; for though I could not when my soule first thirsted for this inviolable union betwen you two rather then any two within this kingdome thinke of that deynty pot of glewe that will make the bonde more sure . . . [22]

From this letter it would seem that Carr and Suffolk were only becoming reconciled during the course of the annulment hearings,[23] and Northampton clearly suggests that the attraction between Frances and Robert came as a welcome surprise to him. This would seem to contradict the notion that their whole relationship was an elaborately contrived plot. But it is nonetheless significant that, for all Northampton's undoubted affection for Frances and sympathy towards her feelings for Carr, in the end she is, as she had been in her first marriage, the female 'glue' to cement together two politically important males. Her family were doubtless reconciled to her parting from Essex the more easily once they saw an even better prize in prospect, and it is indubitable that Carr's position as favourite persuaded the King to do some heavy leaning on the divorce commission. But, contrary to almost all received narratives, the possibility must be allowed that the annulment proceedings were initiated at a time when Carr and Suffolk were still opponents, and when the family was not fully aware of the seriousness of any relationship between their daughter and the King's favourite. If this account were to be accepted then it places Frances Howard in a very different light. On this reading it must have been her own determined action and persuasion which led her father to contemplate the dissolution of her marriage. She becomes, therefore, a figure braver and more heroic (or more schemingly manipulative) than in the traditional story.

Hitherto I have used the terms 'annulment' and 'divorce' interchangeably – as they were employed at the time. But the particular direction these hearings took, and the premise upon which they were brought – that of the husband's impotence – were dictated by the fact that in the England of the early seventeenth century divorce in the modern meaning of the word was simply not possible. When attempting to assess the attitudes of those who commented on the case at the time it is vital to register the force of this most basic of points. Judicial separations 'from bed and board' were not infrequent in the ecclesiastical courts, but such 'divorces' did not allow either party to remarry. The *Constitutions and Canons Ecclesiasticall* of 1604 made this crystal clear:

> In all sentences pronounced onely for Divorce and Separation *a thoro et mensa* there shall bee a caution and restraint inserted in the Act of the said Sentence, That the parties so separated, shall live chastly and continently: neither shall they, during each others life, contract Matrimony with any other person.

As Roderick Phillips observes 'England was unique in the sixteenth century as the only country where an established or dominant reformed church did not break with the Roman Catholic doctrine of marital indissolubility.'[24]

Protestantism had removed matrimony from the list of sacraments, and substituted a view of it as a secular contract blessed by God and the church (though such a contractual view of marriage had been part of medieval practice too). Faced with the New Testament formulations about marriage, which in many respects tended to tighten up the relative freedoms (for men) of Mosaic law, the general view of reformers was that divorce could be permitted, but only on grounds of adultery (and by extension, of desertion). Both Luther and Calvin allowed the possibility of remarriage, at least for the innocent partner.[25] It must, however, be recognised that these reformers, and many of those who followed them, were still very far from a modern opinion on the question of what constituted good reason for terminating a marriage. Only Martin Bucer adopted a position which 'permitted the dissolution of marriage under a broad range of circumstances, including matrimonial offenses and mutual consent'.[26]

In England during the earlier sixteenth century moves had been made towards a reformist position. Indeed, in the *Reformatio Legum*, proposed in 1552 but never enacted, the tenth chapter extended the grounds beyond Luther or Calvin:

> If deadly hostility should arise between husband and wife, and become inflamed to such an intensity that one attack the other, either by treacherous means or by poison, and should wish to take his life in some way, either by open violence or by hidden malice, we ordain that, as soon as so horrible a crime can be proved, such persons should be by law separated by divorce in the courts: for the person does greater

injury to his marriage partner who attacks health and life than the one who separates himself from the other's society or commits adultery with another. For there cannot be any sort of fellowship between those who have begun the one to plot and the other to dread mortal harm.[27]

The gestures in this statement towards the possibility of breakdown of 'fellowship', albeit of a very extreme kind, as grounds for terminating a marriage were altogether too radical. This reformation of the law never got beyond the drawing-board, though there is some evidence during the later part of the sixteenth century that couples divorced on grounds of adultery did in fact marry again (Bishop Thornborough's wife, whom we encountered earlier, was taken by him after divorce from his first spouse). But the indissolubilist tendency in the church won out, and its triumph was confirmed by the canons of 1604.

The debate continued in the early years of the seventeenth century nonetheless. Writers like Perkins, Rainolds and Whately pressed for the right to divorce and remarry in cases of adultery and desertion, but they were outnumbered, and their campaign had no success. Whately's defence actually provoked his summons before a Court of High Commission to explain himself, an experience which led him to recant his support for divorce in the second edition of his popular conduct-book, *A Bride-Bush*.[28] Bucer's arguments in favour of divorce on grounds something close to temperamental incompatibility found no supporters in England between the *Reformatio Legum* and Milton's passionately argued divorce treatises of the 1640s – with the single exception of Charles Blount, Earl of Devonshire. His response is of particular interest since he had been involved in a scandal analogous to that of Frances Howard's annulment just a few years earlier.

For many years Blount had been the acknowledged lover of Penelope Devereux, sister of the second Earl of Essex, who was unhappily married to Robert, Lord Rich. After she secured a judicial separation from her husband, Blount persuaded his chaplain, William Laud, to marry them in a secret ceremony in 1605. This provoked considerable disquiet; when Blount died shortly afterwards one letter-writer commented:

My Lord of Devonshire is dead, and most say he is happy, for the world began to change the titles of honour into notes of infamy, for his last most dishonourable and both unlawful and ungodly match.[29]

Laud was to remember the day of the marriage as a day of shame to the end of his life. Devonshire, however, wrote a treatise defending his action, and prefaced it with a letter to the King in which he described Penelope Rich's plight:

> A Lady of great birth and vertue, being in the power of her friends, was by them married against her will unto one, against whome she did protest at the very solemnity and ever after: between whom from the first day there insued continual discord; although the same fear that forced her to marry, constrayned her to live with him. Instead of a comforter he did studie in all things to torment her, and by feare, and frawd did practize to deceive her of her Dowry.[30]

In the treatise itself he argues that though indissoluble marriage is an ideal, exception can and should be made:

> if Two that are Married; shall contrarie to th'end and causes of Mariage, instead of comfortable helpes become continuall tormentes unto each other, instead of mutuall consent, doe live in continuall and unconsionable dissention; and instead of beeing one flesh, by abandoning themselves unto others doe beecome one flesh with a nother.[31]

Devonshire's treatise is, of course, special pleading; but its general humanity and readiness to argue with some sophistication for the need to consider marriage law in the light of practical reality rather than idealised principles make it a signal achievement and one which deserves more attention. It is significant that while Devonshire and Penelope Rich had been content to live together unmarried their conduct seems to have been considered only mildly scandalous. What precipitated universal outrage was their attempt to legitimate their union, with all the consequences this brought for inheritance and property. The College of Arms refused to allow Penelope to impale her arms with those of her husband during his funeral pageantry,[32] and in 1607 she was charged with forging Devonshire's will. She could not inherit his estates, it was asserted, because she was not the 'Earl's lawful wife but an Harlot, Adultress, Concubine and Whore'.[33] It is a revealing case to set beside that of Frances Howard. For she, like Penelope Devereux, was a woman tangling with the institution of marriage itself.

She might well have recognised herself in the above passages from Devonshire's writing, as indeed she might have responded sympathetically to Milton's later cry:

> To couple hatred therefore though wedlock try all her golden links, and borrow to her all the iron manacles and fetters of the law, it does but seek to twist a rope of sand, which was a task, they say, that pos'd the divell.[34]

Notoriously, however, Milton's divorce tracts consider only the right of a husband to put away a wife who is an inadequate companion, with little concern for reciprocal rights for women.[35] Though some reformers accepted that male and female adultery were equal crimes, Biblical law and the whole weight of patriarchal assumption militated against the woman who sought to separate herself from her husband.

Thus, it was not the least part of Frances Howard's vulnerability that she was the instigator of the divorce case. The author of *Truth Brought to Light* commented 'it was a question whether a *wife* might sue a divorce, or not, for that the *bill of divorcement* was given to the *husband*, and not to the wife'.[36] In France, where trials for annulment on grounds of impotence were much more common than in England, authorities argued (paradoxically enough) that such actions should only be instigated by the husband. As one legalist put it, only husbands had the right to divorce because 'the ancients were very cognisant of the effrontery and impudence of women, and did accordingly essay to hold in check and as it were bridle this untameable creature'.[37] The very real force of this gendered objection to the annulment hearings can perhaps be more fully understood by reference to other texts. In Robert Snawsel's dialogue, *A Looking Glass for Married Folks*, the virtuous Eulalia reproves the scold Xantippe for offering to beat her husband when he threatened her:

> You are married now unto your husband, what manner of man soever he be, you have no liberty to change him for another, or cast him off. In old time indeed, when couples could not agree, divorcement was permitted and appointed as an extreme remedy, but now that is abolished . . .

To which Xantippe retorts:

> A vengeance on them, whosoever they be, that have taken away that law and liberty from us.[38]

Xantippe is a scold, and quite clearly her comments (like those of Opinion in Jonson's *Barriers* cited in Chapter 1) are meant to provoke disapproval. But Elizabeth Carey approaches the same question in a rather more complex way in her *Tragedy of Mariam*. The fact that this is the first known English play by a woman renders her work of particular interest in the present context. In it two women, Mariam and Salome, each attempt to confront the problem of coping with marriages in which they are not happy. The central figure, Mariam, is married to Herod. He dotes upon her with an excess of passion so great that, when summoned to Rome, he leaves instruction that if he should die Mariam herself should be put to death. If this were not sufficient cause for hatred, Herod has in addition brought about the deaths of both her father and her brother. The play follows the course of a single day, in which an announcement of Herod's death is subsequently overturned by his return. The reader (and it is surely a play designed for reading rather than acting) contemplates the twists and turns of Mariam's reactions as she tries to find a way of dealing with the contradictory feelings she has for her husband. She has taken a vow not to share Herod's bed, but recognises only too clearly that she could yet win him over by pretending love and dutifulness, re-entering, as she puts it, her 'prison once again'. In the event she attempts to maintain her integrity, but Herod, incensed by an apparent plot to poison him, as well as by her unwillingness to play the obedient wife, orders her to be put to death.

Mariam's struggle to find an acceptable way of dealing with her tyrannical husband is framed by the presence of two other women, Herod's sister Salome, and Doris his former wife. Salome has already got rid of one husband, Josephus, but is now tired of Constabarus, his successor, and wishes to marry Silleus. Admitting her wickedness she yet meditates on the reasons why she cannot become Silleus's wife:

> It is the principles of Moses' laws,
> For Constabarus still remains in life.
> If he to me did bear as earnest hate
> As I to him, for him there were an ease:
> A separating bill might free his fate
> From such a yoke that did so much displease.
> Why should such privilege to men be given?
> Or given to them, why barr'd from women then?
> Are men than we in greater grace with Heaven?
> Or cannot women hate as well as men?
> I'll be the custom-breaker and begin
> To show my sex the way to freedom's door.
>
> (1.iv.309–20)[39]

Her husband, Constabarus, reacts violently when she tells him of her intention to secure 'a divorcing bill':

> Are Hebrew women now transformed to men?
> Why do you not as well our battles fight
> And wear our armour? Suffer this, and then
> Let all the world be topsie-turved quite;
> Let fishes graze, beasts swim, and birds descend;

Let fire burn downwards whilst the earth aspires,
Let winter's heat and summer's cold offend...
                              (I.vi.435–41)

(The imputation that Salome is behaving 'mannishly' is one which, as we
will see, Frances Howard also had to confront.) Salome is an unambiguously 'wicked' character, and the play might seem to invite us to share
Constabarus's reaction to her resolve to secure for herself the same liberty
as men. Nonetheless, the cogency of Salome's argument compared with
the hysteria of Constabarus's response at least permits us to recognise the
structural unfairness of the Mosaic law. One might suggest, furthermore,
that the Old Testament setting of the play allows Carey the freedom of
cultural distance to address more directly the possibility of female rebellion.

The issue was taken up by William Terracae in his forty-page poem
defending the nullity. The poem is organised as a series of responses to
the objections that contemporaries had raised. He roundly dismisses the
complaint that the woman's bringing of the suit was improper:

> As if the One, and other, had not right
> And mutuall power alike? as exquisite
> And peremtorie Hers, the wifes, as His,
> Over her bodie in marriadg offices.
> That graunted, what then lettes but both are bound
> And ought complaine alike? Hers to be found
> And heard is just as his.[40]

It is a position strikingly similar to that adopted by Salome in the play.

But Carey's play is further complicated by the figure of Herod's first wife,
Doris. She had been put away by him under the very law that Salome now
challenges. Mariam in her final scene is confronted by her, and accused of
having lived nine years in adultery with Herod. Their dialogue continues:

> *Doris*   I am that Doris that was once beloved,
>   Beloved by Herod, Herod's lawful wife.
>   'Twas you that Doris from his side removed,
>   And robbed from me the glory of my life.
> *Mariam*   Was that adultery? Did not Moses say
>   That he that being matched did deadly hate,
>   Might by permission put his wife away
>   And take a more beloved to be his mate?
> *Doris*   What did he hate me for? for simple truth?
>   For bringing beauteous babes for love to him?

> For riches, noble birth, or tender youth,
> Or for no stain did Doris' honour dim?
> (IV.viii.1857–68)

For all that the chorus later condemn Doris's passion for revenge, the claim of her right to Herod is unanswered. This suggests that Carey has some sympathy for Doris's case, and blames Mariam's plight in part at least on the very existence of the unjust and unequal law. It does not follow, however, that the play is advocating an equal freedom of divorce. In view of her religious conservatism (she was later to convert to Catholicism) Carey might rather have echoed John Dove, who in opposing divorce argued:

> The Libertines of our age, now living, give a prerogative in this case to the man above the woman, because of the Sexe, because the one is a man, the other but a woman . . . they take libertie to themselves out of the scriptures, to maintaine theyr uncleane and licentious life, as that the man may put away the woman and not commit adultery in marrying an other, but the woman may not doo the like, because, say they, the man may have many wives, but the woman may not have many husbands.[41]

For Carey, perhaps, as for Dove, to recognise the justice of Salome's objection to the double standard leads, not to a like liberty for husband and wife, but to a demand for identical restraint.

The play's attitudes are, however, elusive. Catherine Belsey, though celebrating what she sees as a woman writer's ability to present a female character who speaks from a consistent subject-position in the central figure of Mariam, argues that the glimpses of a 'militant feminism' that we get from Salome generate no sympathy.[42] I would argue, however, that the play's inconclusiveness, even confusion about the limits of female opposition to male tyranny (Mariam at her execution is described by a messenger as smiling 'a dutiful, though scornful smile') provokes contradictory and unresolved reactions in the reader. At the very least the play dramatises and recognises the markedly unequal power of women and men in the matrimonial contract. As Betty Travitsky suggests, there is 'an ambivalence in the playwright's mind over woman's stark subordination in marriage in seventeenth-century England'.[43] *The Tragedy of Mariam* registers the forces which constrained women in marriage, and the difficulty they might find in articulating a response or finding an acceptable course of action. It provides an immediately relevant co-text for the consideration of Frances Howard's situation. Like Mariam, Frances chose

to deny her body to her husband; but in determining to seek release from
her marriage rather than settling for the patient heroism unto death
that Mariam ultimately exemplifies, she ran the immediate risk of being
perceived as a Salome, setting the world upside down in her pursuit of
divorce.

It is characteristic of the telling of Frances's story that her refusal to
have sexual relations with her husband should be characterised as 'a morbid
resolve' by one modern historian.[44] If Frances Howard had resisted her
initial arranged marriage, no doubt that would have been tolerable, even
praiseworthy; but once the marriage has taken place, then resistance to
her sexual appropriation by her husband is construed as unnatural. It is
not perhaps surprising to find this attitude persisting in modern times,
since only in 1991 has the offence of marital rape been recognised by the
law in England – but the underlying feeling that a woman ought to submit
to her husband's sexual desire (or tolerate his lack of it) is an important
strand in the nexus of assumptions which Frances Howard opposed by
prosecuting her suit for annulment. In the libel itself she attempted to
demonstrate the required passivity when claiming to have 'yielded herself
to his power' and 'offered herself and her body to be known'; and she had
also shown herself sensitive to accusations of 'disobedience' to her husband
(charges that, as we will see, were much more significant to the case than
they now might seem).

Canon law had long allowed that a marriage could be annulled on
grounds of impotence. Helmholz writes:

> Canonists distinguished several possible causes of the incapacity –
> lack of sexual organs, natural frigidity, 'quasi-natural' frigidity, and
> impotence caused by *maleficium* or *sortilegium*.

He continues:

> The libels in these cases followed a fairly standard pattern, on the model
> of the language of the decretals. The woman alleged a legitimate
> marriage, subsequent cohabitation (usually for the canonically pre-
> scribed three year period), the woman's desire to be a mother, and the
> man's inability to satisfy that desire. She asserted that as a consequence
> the marriage could not stand, and asked to be divorced.[45]

As the summary of Frances Howard's application given above shows, just
such a libel was presented in this case. Each stage of the hearings followed
the canonists' prescriptions, including the testimony of seven com-
purgators of the wife's kin and acquaintance, the oaths of both parties and
the examination of Frances's body. Whatever the true circumstances of

the family life of the Essexes, to secure a separation they must needs represent themselves to the court in a narrative determined by the law's demands.[46]

But though canon law provided the matrix for this suit, one of the reasons for the attention it provoked was that such hearings were extremely rare in England (in strong contrast to France, where, according to Pierre Darmon, 'from the sixteenth century onwards, the trickle of impotence trials took on the proportions of a tidal wave').[47] The lawyers in the case scrabbled around trying to find native precedents; part of Abbot's argument was precisely that the two precedents that were produced – of one Bury and of Henry VIII and Anne of Cleves – were less than convincing parallels. One reason for the paucity of cases was possibly that the difficulty of proof meant that the threat of collusion was high. Such suspicions were entertained of this case, as Chamberlain's remarks indicate:

> There was a divorce to be sued this terme twixt the earle of Essex and his Lady, and he was content (whether true or fained) to confesse insufficiencie in himself.[48]

Dunne responded to the suspicion by insisting in his treatise that Essex's contrary plea that the non-consummation of the marriage was the fault of his wife demonstrated the opposite:

> rather to the discoverie of the truth and to avoyd all suspicion of fraud and collusion in the parties it served to great purpose, for heereby the Lady was driven to make her proofe, and the Earles mynde fullie also appeared to bee opposite to the suite commenced.[49]

If agreement there had been in setting up the case, it was obviously very fragile.

The question of collusion is clearly very important, but attempting to decide where one stands on this matter brings in its train questions of central importance for this chapter. There are, I would suggest, a number of different ways of reading the story of this annulment, each of which begins from a different hypothesis:

1. It was entirely duplicitous, arranged by mutual agreement because the marriage had obviously failed.
2. It was arranged solely because of Frances's desire to marry Robert Carr; annulment for impotence was the only way out, and was reluctantly admitted by Essex, who then sought a counter-claim.
3. Essex was in fact totally impotent, and this was a contributory factor to Frances's falling for another, and the real cause of the suit. The

suggestion of *maleficium* causing selective impotence was to avoid shaming Essex.

4. The case as presented in court was the case as it stood in fact: that Essex experienced impotence only towards Frances, not least because of her hostility towards him.

The historian's choice from these alternatives has a profound effect upon the tenor of any subsequent narrative. Most have readily assumed that it was Frances Howard's sexual experience which needed to be disguised under the collusive proceedings. Few, it seems, have wondered whether it was Essex's impotence that had to be concealed.

Whilst Frances's letter to Turner already quoted might seem to suggest that the refusal to couple was hers alone, evidence does survive which suggests that Essex was in fact unable to consummate his marriage. Goodman wrote of 'the testimony of the minister of Chiswick, who was with the lady in her last sickness, when she was past hope of life, and speaking with her of this business, she did then protest upon her soul and salvation that the Earl of Essex was never her husband'.[50] At the time Northampton was more peremptory, when contemptuously alluding to 'my good lord the gelding', and commenting dismissively on the duel that Essex was to fight with Henry Howard (Frances's brother), who had insulted his virility:

> I hope god the just judge will assist the right quarrell. If my lord would drawe his sword in the defence of a good prick it wear worth his paines, but never to make such a poor puddinges Apology. I doo scarce perswade my self that a man can be saved that dies in the defence of an ille pricke and therefore the silly count needes a litany.[51]

One of the proofs offered at the hearings was that Essex had confessed his impotence before witnesses (Worcester, Knollys and Suffolk), but on the other side Abbot reported that:

> I was also by a good friend informed, that my lord of Essex, on that Sunday morning, having five or six captains and gentlemen of worth in his chamber, and speech being made of his inability, rose out of his bed, and taking up his shirt, did shew to them all so able and extra-ordinarily sufficient matter, that they all cried out shame of his lady, and said, That if the ladies of the court knew as much as they knew, they would tread her to death. (*ST*, 822)

If Essex were indeed only impotent towards Frances, then his display, of course, proved nothing either way. But Essex's second marriage collapsed, and there was suspicion that the child his wife Elizabeth bore after six years of marriage was in fact the product of her adulterous relationship with Sir William Uvedale. Furthermore, if one were disposed to believe the charge of impotence, one might see the endless series of quarrels and near duels in which Essex was involved as a displacement of anxiety about his virility into proofs of a masculine valour.

At the time it scarcely mattered what the truth of the matter was. Merely by raising the spectre of male impotence Frances Howard compounded the transgression against male authority that her initiation of the suit began. In alleging her husband's incapacity she challenged Essex's virility in more comprehensive terms than his mere inability to perform the sexual act. The author of *Truth Brought to Light*, for example, claimed that the world thought Essex 'was of an able body, and likely to have many children, and to undertake any exploit for the good of the commonwealth'.[52] The last clause of this comment, linking public potential to sexual potency, is revealing. This book was published during the Civil War, and felt the need to rescue the reputation of the Parliamentarian hero. But the Royalist Sanderson could turn the tables by recalling:

> Of him, common fame had an opinion, (grounded upon his own suspition,) of his insufficiency to content a wife; and the effects of this narration, with the sequell of his life, and conversation with his second wife, is so notorious, as might spare me and the reader our severall labours for any other convincing argument. But with his first, when both were of years to expect the event and blessing of their marriage-bed, he was alwaies observed to avoid the company of ladies, and so much to neglect his own, that to wish a maid into a mischief was to commend her to my Lord of Essex.[53]

Essex's impotence, like the sexual adventurousness of Frances Howard, is determined by the prior assumptions of commentators, and the needs their histories serve. But whatever the polemical use later made of Essex's impotence, it must be obvious that in 1613 the conduct of the trial was dictated by the need to contain the potential damage to the whole edifice of Essex's masculine honour which a belief that his prick was indeed a 'poor pudding' would bring about.

The allegation that Essex was impotent only towards his wife was greeted with incredulity at the time, though the condition is well-enough known to modern psychologists. Freud, claiming that it was one of the most frequently encountered psychiatric conditions, observed:

> This singular disturbance ... manifests itself in a refusal by the executive

organs of sexuality to carry out the sexual act, although before and after they may show themselves to be intact and capable of performing the act, and although a strong psychical inclination to carry it out is present.[54]

Freudians find the explanation in 'castration anxiety'; in earlier periods (and perhaps not much less plausibly) witchcraft was offered as a cause. Reginald Scot, in his *The Discoverie of Witchcraft*, writes:

> They also affirme, that the vertue of generation is impeached by witches, both inwardlie and outwardlie: for intrinsecallie they represse the courage, and they stop the passage of the mans seed, so as it may not descend to the vessels of generation: also they hurt extrinsecallie, with images, hearbs etc. . . . manie are so bewitched, that they cannot use their own wives: but anie other bodies they maie well enough away withall.[55]

Scot is sceptical of the power of witches in general, but there can be little doubt that a belief in selective impotence caused by charms or spells of one kind or another was widespread. Middleton's *The Witch* is instructive here.[56] In its main plot Sebastian has seen his affianced Isabella stolen from him by Antonio. To prevent consummation of their marriage he appeals to Hecate to provide a charm which will render Antonio impotent. Hecate offers him the skins of serpents and of snakes, assuring him:

> So sure into what house these are conveyed,
> Knit with these charmèd and retentive knots,
> Neither the man begets nor woman breeds;
> No, nor performs the least desires of wedlock,
> Being then a mutual duty. I could give thee
> Chiroconita, adincantida,
> Archimadon, marmaritin, calicia,
> Which I could sort to villainous barren ends;
> But this leads the same way. More I could instance:
> As the same needles thrust into their pillows
> That sews and socks up dead men in their sheets;
> A privy gristle of a man that hangs
> After sunset – good, excellent! Yet all's there, sir.
>   (I.ii.157–69)

The witches also provide another character, Almachildes, with a ribbon which, when possessed by a woman, will make her fall in love with him. In the subsequent action of the play both these charms function successfully. Antonio appears at the beginning of Act II calling for 'two cocks boiled to jelly' to try to restore his amorous appetite after his wedding-night failure, and Almachildes' ribbon persuades Amoretta and the Duchess successively to fall in love with him. Whilst the witches are presented with a comic exaggeration which may signal a certain scepticism on Middleton's part, the efficacy of their charms suggests at the very least an underlying anxiety about their power.

Though (or perhaps because) allegations of impotence by *maleficium* were rarely brought before the courts in England, the prevalence of such practices in France fascinated Sir Charles Somerset on his travels in 1611–12. He observed:

> There are a kinde of people here, which they call *Noueurs d'esquillette* that is, Tyers of points, which are witches; they are all over France, but especially in *Poitou*: they are for the most parte excommunicated every sonday. That which they doe by their enchantings, is that when they knowe of two that go to be married, they tye a knott as a terme it, which indeede is no other then to make the man unable to *solvere debitum uxori*, as long as he lives, that is, not to be able to gett his wife with childe, or to do the action with her, though they can doe it with anie other women; such, a man may see, is the malice of the divell, that he alwayes makes a man that he may doe that which is unlawfull, and seldome or never hindreth a man from that; though sometime as you see in this, he makes a man unfitt to performe that which is lawfull.[57]

This is just the condition of Middleton's Antonio, who continues to have a sexual relationship with his long-time whore, Florida. It is also the condition claimed by the Earl of Essex in his reply to the libel, when he responded that 'he believeth, that before and after the Marriage, he hath found an ability of body to know any other woman, and hath oftentimes felt motions and provocations of the flesh, tending to carnal copulation' (*ST,* 67).

Despite long legal tradition and the power of popular belief, Abbot wrote to the King expressing his doubts at the possibility of *maleficium* producing impotence, objecting that he could find nothing in the scriptures or in the early fathers to justify such a claim. This lack suggested to him that the charge of selective impotence 'was a concomitant of darkness or popish superstition', and therefore that those who lived in a time when the light of the gospel had broken forth 'should be free from this *maleficium*' (*ST,* 795). Abbot's argument reflected the strictly Biblical basis of his staunch Puritanism.[58] When the King replied he dealt brusquely with

Abbot's theological objections, and, as the author of *Daemonologie*, unsurprisingly maintained firmly: 'if the Devil hath any power, it is over the
flesh, rather over the filthiest and most sinful part thereof, whereunto
original sin is soldered' (*ST,* 801).[59]

Since Essex's sexual capability was the fundamental issue on which the
annulment turned, it might seem curious that no physical examination of
him was conducted. In French trials examination of both parties was
customary, and among the 'Doubts conceived out of the Fact and Process
in the Suit' was the question 'Whether my lord of Essex would be inspected
by physicians, to certify (so far as they can by art) the true cause and nature
of the impediment' (*ST,* 788). But though Essex was questioned about his
impotence, his body, unlike that of his wife, was not searched. In part, no
doubt, the reluctance to examine the Earl derived from the fact that canon
law did not demand such a physical examination, but left it open whether
the court should require it.[60] Equally it may have been that the bishops
were too embarrassed to proceed on this course. Abbot recalled:

> that my lord of Litchfield had put to him [Essex] certain questions, that
> four things were necessary in generation; 'membrum virile', erection,
> penetration, and 'ejaculatio seminis'; which, although they were then
> smiled at, and since that time much sport had been made at the court
> and in London about them; yet now our married men on all hands
> wished that punctually his lordship might have been held to give his
> answer unto them. (*ST,* 816)

Even this limited verbal examination, as Abbot rightly feared, provoked
ribald comment. Weldon later spoke of the 'bawdy bishops'; and an
anonymous versifier wrote disparagingly of Frances's examination, and
contemptuously of the bishops:

> This Dame was inspected but Fraude interjected
> A maide of more perfection
> Whome the midwyffes did handle whilst the Knight held the candle
> O there was a cleare inspectione
>
> Nowe all forraigne wrytters, crye out on those myters [mitres]
> that allowe this for virginitye
> and talke of Ejection and want of Erection
> O there is a sound dyvinitie.[61]

But it is surely of greatest significance that the block to a physical examination of the Earl came from *his* counsel. At one stage an examination of
the Earl and a trial 'whether they might carnally know one another' were

considered by the judges (*ST*, 824). One manuscript clearly states that it was the Earl's counsel who insisted that the impotence was a case of *maleficium*, and the writer continues 'yf the Erle had binne the partie to be inspected (which they denie) ther conjecture might have had the better shew, but thai denieng this . . . '.[62] At this point speculation takes over. Did the Earl not wish to be inspected lest his claim to be sufficient for other women be invalidated? Or, alternatively, would examination have threatened to expose the collusive practices of husband and wife?

Whatever the reason, the Earl's masculinity was not put to the test. William Terracae answered the objection that Essex had not been examined with the sensible observation that such a test would not work:

> For either shame then in the man, or feare
> (Such as yt is) maie in that part prepare
> So paralitick a dejection
> At such a cold and loathed search; as none
> Ought passe a faithfull verdict thereupon.[63]

Nonetheless, however reluctant the bishops might have been, the possibility of examination of the male is suggested in Jonson's *Epicoene*, when Truewit suggests to Morose that he can escape from his marriage by protesting his impotence. The ladies fear that there might be fraud, which Truewit answers suggesting 'if you suspect that, ladies, you may have him searched', to which Daw adds 'As the custom is, by a jury of physicians'.[64]

Who was pretending what, and whose face was being saved by the claim of Essex's impotence only towards his wife, can never be established with any certainty, though it seems to me that the hypothesis of Essex's actual incapacity is not without evidence to support it. But in challenging his potency, Frances Howard triggered a more general male anxiety which was bound to produce the hostile reaction to her that has been enshrined in all subsequent accounts. The nature of that anxiety, and the demons raised by a charge of impotence are, once again, most profitably to be discerned in consideration of literary texts.

Thomas Campion's lyric 'If any hath the heart' dramatises an incident of sexual failure. It concludes:

> A Love I had, so fayre, so sweet,
>   As ever wanton eye did see.
> Once by appointment wee did meete;
>   Shee would, but ah, it would not be:
>   She gave her heart, her hand shee gave;
>   All did I give, shee nought could have.

What Hagge did then my powers forespeake,
  That never yet such taint did feele?
Now shee rejects me as one weake,
  Yet am I all composed of steele.
    Ah, this is it my heart doth grieve:
    Now though shee sees, shee'le not believe![65]

The fact that the poet attributes his sexual failure to witchcraft provides additional evidence of the prevalence of belief in *maleficium* in the seventeenth century; but Campion is here reflecting the original from which his poem derives, Ovid's *Amores*, III.vi. In Marlowe's version the relevant lines read:

What, waste my limbs through some Thessalian charms?
May spells and drugs do silly souls such harms?
With virgin wax hath some imbas'd my joints,
And pierc'd my liver with sharp needles' points?[66]

The attribution of impotence to witchcraft has a long history, and is by no means specific to the early modern period, nor to Western Europe. The transhistorical and transcultural nature of the belief testifies to the way in which it figures a deep-seated and universal male fear. In Ovid's poem, more evidently than in Campion's recension of it, the fear of shame – and the compensatory boasting of othertime sexual prowess – are clearly delineated. But Ovid, unlike Campion, shifts the blame from himself to the woman. 'Well, I believe she kiss'd not as she should, / Nor us'd the sleight and cunning which she could', complains the poet.

The deflection of failure on to the woman is even more clearly marked in Thomas Nashe's poem of sexual failure, 'The Choice of Valentines'. Here the poet goes to a brothel for a tryst with his lady, but suffers from premature ejaculation. It is the 'comely swelling' of the woman's buttock which:

    makes the fruits of love eftsoon be ripe,
  And pleasure pluck'd too timely from the stem,
    To die ere it hath seen Jerusalem.[67]

His paramour then succeeds in raising 'it from his swoon', and a successful bout follows. The lover is thus presented as utterly at the mercy of the provocations of the woman, his sexual mastery dependent upon her ministrations. But worse is to follow, for the mistress remains unsatisfied, and concludes:

Adieu, faint-hearted instrument of lust,

That falsely hast betray'd our equal trust.
Henceforth no more will I implore thine aid,
  Or thee, or men, of cowardize upbraid.
My little dildo shall supply their kind,
  A knave that moves as light as leaves by wind,
That bendeth not, nor foldest any deal,
  But stands as stiff as he were made of steel,
And plays at peacock twixt my legs right blithe,
  And doth my tickling swage with many a sigh.
                                    (pp. 465–6)

Here, very explicitly, Nashe registers both male fear at the erratic performance of his sexual equipment, and the commonplace projection of
the blame on to female voraciousness.

In very general terms, the involuntariness of erection is construed as a
symptom of the irrationality of love. Since it is an *a priori* assumption that
reason is one of the fundamental principles of male identity, it must follow
that the uncontrollable behaviour of the penis derives from some external
force. On the positive side love strikes because of the ministrations of
Cupid, or is the consequence of womanly beauty; on the negative side
the blame for impotence is displaced on to the witch, or interpreted as a
mark of the insatiability of the female. It is entirely typical, therefore, that
Wilson should blame Frances for her husband's impotence in two quite
contradictory directions at once. He suggests that Forman, on Frances's
behalf:

> did use all the artifice his subtilty could devise, really to imbecillitate
> the Earl; for no Linnen came near his body, that was not rinsed with
> their *Camphire Compositions*, and other faint and wasting ingredients,
> and all inward applications were foisted on him by corrupted servants,
> to lessen and debilitate the *seminal operations*.[68]

But then he also claims that Frances obtained 'an Artifice too immodest
to be exprest, to hinder Penetration. And thus she tormented him, till he
was contented to let her steer her own course'.[69] Whether it was the
charms or the device that caused Essex's failure scarcely matters – what is
important to Wilson is that the fault is not Essex's.

If Frances Howard exposed herself to attack because of the threat her
suit offered to male potency, she by the same action rendered herself
vulnerable to another charge. In declaring her husband impotent she
was inevitably characterised as expressing a longing for sex, however
transmuted into the desire 'to be made a mother'. As Darmon comments:

Wives who embarked upon the adventure of an impotence trial automatically compromised themselves. Most often they were accused of succumbing to physical desire. According to Boyle's *Dictionnaire* (1715), it was damnation enough for a woman

> to confess publicly that she cannot contain herself. For every woman who institutes such proceedings does declare to all and sundry that she has such a defect.[70]

As he goes on, 'by an astonishing shift of responsibility, the women who complained of their husbands were seen as the ones at fault'. This shift is clearly related to the fear of female sexual desire which issues in diatribes against their insatiability. The author of *The House of Pleasure*, for example, launches in his final chapter into a vitriolic tirade, in which women are thus characterised:

> for inticements of the flesh and proneness to lust, of such an untamed and unbridled concupiscence, that they may well bee tyred, but never satisfied with the acte of Venerie.

And later he bitterly observes:

> howe quiet and merrie a man shal finde his wife, if he indevour to satisfie that which Solomon in the 30. of his proverbs saith hath never enough, and with many and often imbracings desire to fill the unsatiable gulfe of her wombe with endlesse copulations.[71]

Many literary texts, and much of the commentary on Frances Howard are founded upon such assumptions. But a little poem survives, in one manuscript associated with Frances Howard, which communicates the dilemma a woman faces:

> Whie should wee maides turne wives?
> but for exchange of lives,
> and unknowne ioyes to knowe.
> It is my hap so strange
> to wedde and feele no change.
> O love whie should men wooe,
> that knowe not how to doe
> the rightes that longe thereto.
> Wee wives that have such men
> Lett us turne maides agen
> And marri'd state forgoe
> And praiers to Cupid make

That hee would undertake
That noe such man should wooe
That knowes not howe to doe
The rightes that longe thereto.[72]

If this is an attempt to 'speak' Frances's plight, then it might be read sympathetically as part of the thin trickle of proto-feminist discourse in the early modern period. But it could just as easily have been read as confirming men's worst fears about women. (It is the same interpretative problem that we have already encountered in the speech of Opinion in the *Barriers*.)

By suing for divorce at all Frances Howard flouted the doctrine of wifely obedience, and by charging her husband with impotence she raised the fearful spectre of male inadequacy. At the same time her action in bringing matters to open court challenged the conventional requirement of female silence and chastity. The centrality of this dual requirement to the characterisation of the ideal female in the Renaissance has been often and thoroughly documented by feminist scholars in recent years. But there is a paradoxical aspect to this ideological enchainment. For, as scholars such as Stephen Greenblatt and Thomas Laqueur have shown, though chastity was demanded of women, this did not imply sexual passivity.[73] The belief that both male and female produced seed during intercourse required that both sexes experience sexual pleasure and simultaneous orgasm for fertilization to take place. But while this might seem to acknowledge women's sexual awareness as a fact, the control and subordination of their sex demanded that their bodies, biologically perceived as imperfect mirror-images of the male, should wait upon masculine heat to be stirred to life. Antony Stafford, for example, glossed the symbolism of Roman marriage in which fire and water were carried before the couple (as they were in *Hymenaei*) with the words:

> To the same ende did the Romanes of old, carrie before the married couple, fier, and water (the former representing the man; the later, the woman), what else signifying, then that the woman should expect till heate bee infused into her by her husband? it being as much against the nature of an honest spouse, as of the coldest water, to boile of her selfe.[74]

Women were expected to be sexually responsive, but only at the dictation of their husbands. For a woman to speak of desire for herself was to escape male control, her wayward mouth to become a sign of her wayward sex. As Peter Stallybrass observes, 'the connection between speaking and wantonness was common to legal discourse and conduct books . . . Silence, the closed mouth, is made a sign of chastity'.[75] In Chapter 2 the spectre of the gossips' meeting was briefly invoked. It becomes more pressingly relevant still to understanding the ways in which Frances Howard's libel for divorce could so easily be construed as a whorish self-speaking.

In Sir Kenelm Digby's strange semi-autobiographical romance, *Loose Fantasies*, the Queen, who has conceived an illicit love for Theagenes, is advised by her servant Lenana:

> I speake plainely Madame what I think, for although the straight and painefull attire of modesty which men have discourteously left to our share do oblige us to disguise our thoughtes when wee are in publicke; yet when wee are among our selves where wee may be confident, it were indiscretion in the highest degree not to putt off that combersome weede and lay it aside . . . and for that which is called honor although it be but a Chymaera fancied by ignorant fooles, yet since our indulgence hath bin such as to submitt our neckes to that yoke (through the craft and subtilty of men) I thinke we give way enough unto it if what wee do according to this true and naturall doctrine born with us, be governed by discretion, and accompanyed with caution and secrecy.[76]

In Digby's work, this denial by women of male power over their private words and conduct is a sign of villainy. But in Marston's *The Wonder of Women, or the Tragedy of Sophonisba*[77] an analogous complaint is offered by the unambiguously virtuous heroine. Sophonisba, awaiting the arrival of her bridegroom Massinissa, speaks to her maid, Zanthia:

> I wonder Zanthia, why the custom is
> To use such ceremony, such strict shape,
> About us women. Forsooth, the bride must steal
> Before her lord to bed; and then delays
> Long expectations, all against known wishes.
> I hate these figures in locution,
> These about-phrases forced by ceremony.
> We must still seem to fly what most we seek
> And hide ourselves from that we fain would find.
> Let those that think and speak and do just acts
> Know form can give no virtue to their acts
> Nor detract vice.
>
> (I.ii. 6–17)

When her husband finally appears she continues:

A modest silence, though't be thought
A virgin's beauty and her highest honour;
Though bashful feignings nicely wrought
Grace her that virtue takes not in, but on her;
What I dare think I boldly speak.
After my word my well-bold action rusheth;
In open flame then passion break!
When virtue prompts, thought, word, act never blusheth.
Revenging gods, whose marble hands
Crush faithless men with a confounding terror,
Give me no mercy if these bands
I covet not with an unfeigned fervour;
Which zealous vow when ought can force me t'lame,
Load with that plague Atlas would groan at, shame.

                                                        (I.ii. 43–56)

In these speeches Sophonisba articulates exactly the perils which await the woman who makes known her desires. It is an absurd charade, in which men recognise women's sexuality, and want them to express it, but at the same time demand their co-operation in a fiction of maidenly modesty that is to be discarded with their clothes. As Dympna Callaghan puts it:

> Female sexual initiative is regarded as a kind of "natural" deviance, simultaneously feared and expected, both aberrant and typical, and regarded as synonymous with the desire to control men ... Female sexual initiative, like female government is regarded as grotesque.[78]

It has been a powerful and persistent mode of control down to the present day – and one may see something of its power in the 'real life' of the seventeenth century in the letters of Maria Thynne. She wrote to her husband:

> My best beloved Thomken, and my best little Sirrah, know that I have not, nor will not forget how you made my modest blood flush up into my bashful cheek at your first letter, thou threatened sound payment, and I sound repayment, so as when we meet, there will be pay, and repay, which will pass and repass, *allgiges vltes fregnan tolles*, thou knowest my mind, though thou dost not understand me. Well now laying on side my high colour, know in sober sadness that I am at Longleat, ready and unready to receive thee, and here will attend thy coming. [The letter then turns to matters of business. She ends:] Even so, being as melancholy as a red herring, and as mad as a pilchard and as proud as a

piece of Aragon ling, I salute thy best beloved self with the return of thine own wish in thy last letter, and so once more fare ever well, my best and sweetest Thomken, and many thousand times more than these 1 000 000 000 000 000 000 000 000 00 for thy kind wanton letters

Thine and only all thine
Maria[79]

Her desire shines through the letter, but even in this private correspondence modesty must prevail and Maria resorts to a bogus foreign language in order to speak bawdily. The flame in her cheeks is represented by her as a response to the wantonness of her husband's writing, rather than owned as her longing. In a later letter we see an even clearer internalisation of the prescriptive model of female behaviour when she writes:

My best Thomken, I know thou wilt say (receiving two letters in a day from me) that I have tried the virtue of aspen leaves under my tongue, which makes me prattle so much, but consider that all is business, for of my own natural disposition I assure thee there is not a more silent woman living than myself.[80]

Maria Thynne's letters speak a determined, lively, witty character. But yet a perceived need for restraint imposes a self-censorship lest her language transgress the stereotypes of female virtue.

These texts graphically illustrate the assumptions which Frances Howard challenged by demanding the right to sex, and to make a new choice of marriage partner. Having proclaimed her husband's sexual incapacity, her unruliness was almost inevitably construed as indicative of her own unchastity. As Lisa Jardine observes of Renaissance drama in general:

the male characters ... perceive free choice on the part of the female character as an inevitable sign of irrational lust, and as the inevitable prelude to disorder and disaster.[81]

The response to dramatic characters is exactly paralleled by the response to Frances Howard's actions.

Thus far I have focused upon the challenges that Frances Howard's suit posed to a patriarchal culture. These same attitudes colour the perception of the other main action in the hearings, the examination of Frances's body. The legal reason for a physical examination was to rebut Essex's counter-claim that it was an impediment in her that prevented sexual intercourse. But those who gleefully reported on the episode later were transparently interested in it as a test of Frances Howard's sexual innocence – an innocence which they were predisposed to disbelieve and culturally unable to imagine.

Not least, the search of Frances, whereas her husband was not examined, is a striking demonstration of the way in which a double standard of sexual morality operates. Abbot reported that the King 'constantly professed, "That he believed that my Lord of Essex was impotent for a woman". He told us, "that some of the earl's friends had put a woman to him, and he would not touch her" ' (ST, 814). Neither the King nor Abbot demonstrates any sense of outrage at this course of action. What, on the other hand, might Abbot have said if Frances's supposed inability had been tested by 'putting a man to her'!

There were those in the seventeenth century who objected to the double standard.[82] Counter-arguments might come from tainted sources, such as the whore Cataplasma in The Atheist's Tragedy who encourages Levidulcia's adultery with the words:

> Methinks 'tis unjust
> That a reproach should be inflicted on
> A woman for offending but with one,
> When 'tis a light offence in husbands to
> Commit with many.
>
> (IV.vi. 28–32)

But many divines made the same point, as John Donne did in his 1621 marriage sermon:

> The body is the temple of the Holy Ghost; and when two bodies, by mariage are to be made one temple, the wife is not as the Chancell, reserv'd and shut up, and the man as the walks below, indifferent and at liberty for every passenger. God in his Temple looks for first fruits from both.[83]

And one C.N. in his An Apology of Women put the matter powerfully:

> Doe they [men] not observe houres, dayes, and all occasions, to batter the walles of their chastity? And what will not importunity and opportunity effect? which as they aggravate the fault in the agent, so they extenuate, though not excuse it in the patient. Certainly if they should use the like meanes, to obtaine men, a Nay would bee as seldom as treason in the mouthes of most men. Yet so injurious are the censures of these our times, that if a Jove vanquish but, or vitiate, or in vanquishing, viciate a silly Io, a grave Cato a light or tender virgin, black

infamy shall overcloud, and brand her reputation, not once touching his.[84]

Voices such as these, however, were powerless against the mechanisms which demanded chastity from women, but not from men.

It is this very investment in female chastity which demands that virginity must have an objective and examinable existence, whereas male potency was apparently thought altogether too erratic and fragile a thing to be available to demonstration. So Frances Howard was examined by two midwives and four matrons selected from a panel of six midwives 'whereof two to bee midwives practised about the deliverie of noble woemen' and ten noble matrons, 'woemen fearinge God and Mothers of children'.[85] A collective modesty descends upon the report of these inspectors – the *State Trials* version says they delivered their 'secret Reasons, etc. which were not fit to be inserted into the Record'. In Abbot's account doubt is immediately cast on the competence of the inspectors, as he recalls:

> yet my lord of London told us openly, "That he being with them, found that the ladies knew not well what to make of it; that they had no skill, nor knew not what was the truth; but what they said was upon the credit of the midwives, which were but two, and I knew not how tampered with." (*ST*, 807)

In another manuscript, however, we find a record that:

> the midwifes ... do likewise testifie that thai fownd her straight as a child of ix or te[n] yeares owld. Which containing as much as modestie might sh[ow?] thoughe uttered but uppon beleefe yet for the reson therunto adjoined maketh as substantiall proofe ... as th[e] law requireth.

And later the objection that the matrons did not inspect is answered:

> not the midwifes onlie but the ladie matrones also did inspicere thowghe the midwifes proceded further then the rest, as it was convenient for their science and knowledge in those affaires, yea and for the danger also that might have insued if the matronnes and the midwifes had used ther handes, obstetrix velut explorans sive malevolentia, sive inscitia, sine casu dum inspicit perdidit, saies S. Augustine.[86]

The possibility that the examination for virginity might of itself destroy the 'evidence' upon which a claim for its existence could be based is problematic enough. In this particular case it is compounded by the fact that the midwives were being asked both to ensure that there was no obstruction to intercourse, and yet at the same time, presumably, that the hymen which guaranteed virginity was still unruptured. Dunne, or whoever compiled this manuscript, is trying very hard to counter the doubts about the inspection, but he is struggling with an impossibility – for, as some even at the time recognised, there can be no certainty in such inspection anyway.

Chamberlain reported the virginity test in these terms:

> the Lady hath ben visited and searcht by some auncien Ladies and midwifes expert in those matters, who both by inspection and otherwise find her upon theyre oath a pure virgin: which some Doctors thincke a straunge asseveration, and make yt more difficult then to be discerned.[87]

One medic who cast scornful doubt upon virginity testing – and especially upon the abilities of midwives to conduct such examination – was Laurent Joubert, whose *Popular Errors*, published in France in 1578, ran through many editions – and was especially famous (or notorious) for its chapter 'Whether there is certain knowledge of the virginity of a maiden'.[88] Despite his being engaged in professional in-fighting, trying to dismiss the claims to professional competence of mere women as opposed to male doctors, he has many telling criticisms to make of the various signs, likely and unlikely, that were held to constitute evidence of virginity – including the presence of the hymen (which he disputes) and claims for narrowness of the vagina as indication of inexperience. Chamberlain's Doctors presumably shared Joubert's opinions.

But whatever the scientific trustworthiness of the inspection, and whatever the legal necessity for its taking place, as Darmon observes of the French trials, 'Inspection . . . constituted a respectable front for the play of an unacknowledged libido and exacerbated voyeurism'.[89] The reporting of the examination of Frances Howard's body seems to have been somewhat shamefaced, but the French were less inhibited. The French jurist Anne Robert left an account of an inspection, carried out by both midwives and male physicians:

> A maid is obliged to lie outstretched to her full length on her back, with her thighs spread to either side so that those parts of shame, that Nature has wished to conceal for the pleasure and contentment of men, are clearly visible. The midwives, matrons all, and the physicians, consider these with much earnest attention, handling and opening them. The presiding judge adopts a grave expression and does hold back his laughter . . . The surgeon, holding an instrument that is fashioned expressly for the purpose . . . or with a male member made of wax or other matter, explores the entrance to the cavity of Venus, opening,

dilating, extending and enlarging the parts. The maid abed does feel her parts itch to such a degree that, even if she be a virgin when examined, she will not leave other than corrupted and spoiled.[90]

This description brings out clearly the kind of voyeuristic, pornographic imagination that coloured contemporaries' perception of Frances Howard's examination, especially after the Overbury revelations. The later stories that another woman had been substituted for her derive from the same foundation. Weldon's account is typical:

The lady of Essex, for modesty sake, makes humble suit to the reverend bawdy bishops, (who were also plotters in this stratagem,) that she might not appear barefaced for blushing; but desired to come vailed with a taffity over her face. This by all means was thought so reasonable, for a pretty modest lady, that the bawdy bishops, and pur-blind ladies, which had forgotten modesty themselves, could not think it worthy the denial. One mistris Fines, near kins-woman to old Kettle, was dressed up in the countesses cloathes, at that time too young to be other then virgo intacta, though within two years after, had the old ladies made their inspection, the orifice would not have appeared so small, to have delivered such a verdict as they did, and a just one upon their view; though upon some of their knowledges it was not that lady they were to give verdict upon. If any make doubt of the truth of this story, the author delivers upon the reputation of gentleman, he had it verbatim from a knight, otherwise of much honor, though the very dependency on that family may question it, which did usher the lady into the place of inspection, and hath told it often to his friends in mirth.[91]

The tendentiousness of Weldon's account becomes clear at the end – this is a story for men to giggle about over a drink. (Sanderson's attempt to refute the charge, also claiming the authority of an eye-witness report, which insisted that there was only one door, and that no substitution was possible, is so much less fun.)[92] But Weldon's narrative also encapsulates the impulses that launch and perpetuate such stories. Frances Howard cannot be a virgin (he's heard the evidence of the Overbury trial, besides which it is impossible that any court lady of nineteen can have preserved her virginity). The modest veil (which one might think a reasonable demand) becomes then a sign of that ever-present male anxiety, that women's sexual experience cannot be safely construed from appearances. A further factor is the way this all-female jury is parallel to the womanly space of child-bed, which, as is apparent in the top left-hand corner of the 'Tittle-tattle' picture (Plate 14), is construed as a place of gossip, and therefore untrustworthy.[93] It is, however, absolutely vital to Weldon's view of female sexuality that though he has attacked the reputability of the midwives by suggesting that they had their 'spectacles ground to lessen, not to make the letter larger' he cannot surrender the hope that virginity can in fact be established. The substituted girl must, therefore, have been a 'real' virgin (though characteristically the possibility of her long continuance in that state is ridiculed).

In Osborne's 'factional' play the underlying values that determine this story are even more visible. Turner has great difficulty in finding a virgin to take Frances's place:

> *Turner*   I have turn'd o'er so many female manuals as might furnish a cabinet for the great Turk, but find them either marked by their own fingers or adulterated with marginal notes like books at the second hand, not possible to pass undiscovered amongst any but scholars, and such as go drunk to bed. (IV.i.163–9)

The one that is finally to be substituted is, we are told, 'As entire as Eve was before she waked her husband or turned costardmonger to the serpent' (V.iv.5–6). The recollection of the Fall is sufficient testimony to Osborne's belief that sexual transgression is a given of female nature (recalling De Flores in the passage quoted earlier, p. 78). But it is in the description of Frances's examination given by the servants Bess, Nan and Tankard the butler that we most clearly discern Osborne's values:

> *Bess*   How did the Lady Frances behave herself in the hands of the bawdy searchers?
> *Nan*   She lay flat upon her back like a tumble-stone with her face covered. Where, after the Knight had laid her evidence bare, he spent some time in discoursing of the largeness of the margent, but, when he came to take measure of the diameter, which he did with his pick-tooth, he found it not to exceed that of a small thimble. The same was averred by the rest . . . who concluded her free from any masculine conjunction whatsoever. (V.vi.1–13)

The female servants confess themselves amazed that any could be a virgin at her age, and then discuss their own deflowerings. By making the inspectors male, and having the proceedings recounted by servants who have been peeping through the door, Osborne intensifies the male voyeurism that the historical inspection was bound to generate. This play is remarkably uncensorious about the sexual duplicity of women (as befits a dramatisation which calls itself a tragicomedy, and ends before the murder of Overbury), but the examination of Frances Howard's body could raise darker resonances.

Juries of midwives were but rarely called on to conduct examinations of virginity; one of their more frequent tasks was the examination of suspected witches for the telltale mark of their infamy.[94] Karen Newman cites one mid-century clergyman's account of searchers who:

> having taken the suspected witch . . . placed [her naked] in the middle of a room upon a stool, or Table, crosse-legg'd, or in some other uneasie posture, to which if she submits not, she is then bound with cords; there is she watcht and kept without meat or sleep for the space of 24 hours.[95]

The overlap between the searching of the female body for its violation of the norms of chastity and the hunt for the witches' mark of transgression is disturbing. Newman observes that 'all those behaviours transgressing traditional gender codes were conflated', and cites from *The Witch of Edmonton* the very pertinent recognition by the witch, Mother Sawyer, that her accusation 'is only part of a larger animus against all women':

> *Mother Sawyer* A Witch? who is not?
>   Hold not that universal Name in scorne then.
>   What are your painted things in Princes Courts?
>   Upon whose Eye-lids Lust sits blowing fires
>   To burn Mens Souls in sensual hot desires:
>   Upon whose naked Paps, a Leachers thought
>   Acts Sin in fouler shapes then can be wrought.[96]

In the subsequent trials Frances Howard's power 'to bewitch any man' becomes an essential ingredient in the narrative built up to convict her. But even at the time of the annulment, since *maleficium* was alleged as the cause of Essex's impotence, there is indeed a sense that the jury of midwives and matrons were already conflating the two issues and searching the body of Frances for signs of her witchery.

It was not only men who were anxious about virginity, for women too internalised male expectations. In Massinger's *The Renegado*, for example, Donusa is in worried dialogue with her maid:

> *Donusa* And could thy friends
>   Reade in thy face, thy maidenhead gone, that thou
>   Hadst parted with it?
> *Manto* Noe indeed. I past
>   For currant many yeeres after, till by fortune,

> Long and continewed practise in the sport
> Blew up my decke. A husband then was found out
> By my indulgent father, and to the world
> All was made whole againe.

Donusa is fearful that her own misdemeanour will be discovered, but it is Manto's confidence that loss of virginity is undecipherable until pregnancy declares it to the world which is truly threatening to a male audience.

The Changeling offers a more complex treatment of the same subject. Beatrice-Joanna, having surrendered her virginity to De Flores, and fearful that she will be found out on her wedding-night by Alsemero, agonises:

> There's no venturing
> Into his bed, what course soe'er I light upon,
> Without my shame.
>   (IV.i.11–13)

Her husband-to-be has no such confidence in his ability to discern a virgin, and carries around a box of medicines, including virginity-testing potions. Beatrice-Joanna discovers the box, and persuades her maid Diaphanta to take the potion in order to discover its effects. Diaphanta duly gapes, sneezes, laughs and falls into a melancholy; and Beatrice-Joanna, thus instructed, is able to feign the symptoms when Alsemero checks her out. She is, however, still not confident that she can deceive him on her wedding-night, and persuades Diaphanta to take her place in the marriage-bed.

Middleton's attitude to the virginity test (like his attitude to witchcraft discussed earlier) is by no means clear. Scepticism about such potions there certainly was. Joubert ridicules them in his *Popular Errors*:

> Tests are also given to find out if the maiden is a virgin. Give her a little powdered lignum aloe to drink or eat; if she is a virgin she will piss immediately. Item: put on hot coals some broken patience dock leaves, and have the maiden smell the smoke; if she does not bepiss herself she is not a virgin; likewise if she does not become pale from patience dock flowers. All these tests are ill founded and one ought not to pay them any attention whatsoever.[97]

Middleton, however, seems content to accept the efficacy of the test, while at the same time demonstrating that no matter how careful a man might be, he is doomed to deception. Alsemero is ridiculed for his excessive trust in external signs, but deeper anxieties are raised by the fact that he also conspicuously fails to recognise that he has been on the receiving end of a bed-trick.

Bed-trick scenes in fiction always play dangerously along a precipice; in Shakespeare's *Measure for Measure* and *All's Well that Ends Well*, for example, they are a daring plot device to bring good out of ill, though even here the very plausibility of substitution both demeans the individuality of the women and unsettles the certainty of the men who 'know' them. In Sidney's *Arcadia* the old King, Basilius, thinking he has had a night of passion with a young girl, when he has in fact slept with his own wife, waxes lyrical about the novelty, and cries out 'O who would have thought there could have been such difference betwixt women!'.[98] At one level he is transparently foolish, but at another, the easy transferability and unrecognisability of female bodies hints at a profound male fear. (A fear whose flip side is the repertory of jack-the-lad jokes which vary on the theme 'you don't mind the mantelpiece when stoking the fire'.)

The virginity-testing motif in *The Changeling* may well have been suggested to Middleton by the annulment hearings nearly a decade earlier, but as Margot Heinemann rightly says 'It is not so much a question of topical allusion, but rather of social patterns and sensibilities'.[99] One might add that Middleton is also relying upon the appeal of a popular literary motif to his audience. This works in reverse, of course. By going into her physical examination veiled, Frances Howard invoked the literary plot-motif of the bed-trick, and not surprisingly Weldon and others were only too delighted to read it as such. It imports into the narrative that male scepticism about female sexuality which seeks to allay their own deepest fears with a mastery achieved through the knowingness of contempt.

Frances Howard's defiance of the whole nexus of assumptions about female sexuality, wifely duty and silent endurance could end only in her censure. Whatever the truth about her sexual experience or her husband's impotence, it was inevitable that she would be blamed, and that blame would issue in the familiar male guise of vilification of her as a whore. William Terracae, with some justice, if not much tact, insisted that the virginity test was an irrelevance, since the trial was of Essex's virility, not Frances Howard's virtue:

> so that
> (had she not bene a virgin found) praie what
> Had this reliev'd in his case? or made good
> His want, if she upon the search had stood
> Faultie in such a shame, when He to Her
> Who should, could not, the lawfull Act preferre?[100]

But to make such a case was to protest in vain. Though Frances Howard brought the petition against her husband, it was – and still is – she who endured the greater trial.

Terracae usefully brings us back from the consideration of the wider questions of cultural and sexual politics to the detail of this particular case, and it is on representations of the divorce hearings themselves that I want to concentrate now. Various satirical poems on the divorce found their way into commonplace-books up and down the country. Though there is uncertainty in dating such texts, there is a revealing contrast between verses which seem to have been written before and after the Overbury trials. I have argued, for example, that assumptions about voracious female sexuality lurk underneath the annulment hearings. After the evidence of the murder trials such attitudes are given untrammelled expression. A poem alleged to have been found in Sir Nicholas Overbury's study describes Carr's rise to power and then continues:

> When hee was at this Huffe of pride
>   Come listen to me, and you shall heare,
> Hee wanted a hackney for to ride
>   And to serve his Turne for other geare
>
> Hee lighted upon a lusty filly
>   Come listen to me and you shall heare,
> Shee had a Marke, underneath her belly
>   That serv'd his Turne with other geare.
>
>   . . .
>
> A tougher Jade was n'er bestridden
>   Come listen to me and you shall heare,
> Sheel jerk and bound when shee is ridden
>   And serve the Turne for other geere.[101]

The poem continues interminably in the same vein, insisting throughout in very direct terms upon Frances's sexual performance. By contrast some verses which may well have been composed before the murder hearings seem to accept Frances Howard's claim of Essex's impotence:

> Lady changed to Venus Dove
> Gently guid your Car of love
> Lett your sport both night and day
> Be to make your Carr away,
> Make it knowne you meet at last
> A Christmas Car-all that surpast.

Plantes enough may hence ensue
Some-are-sett where none ere grewe
Some-are-sett and some are layd
If none stand, God morrowe Mayde.[102]

This is very much a down-market version of the defence of the match that we will be considering in the next chapter. The hope of children, central to the application for the annulment, is alluded to, and the onus is on Carr to prove himself more of a man than Essex had been. Another widely circulated epigram is rather more ambiguous:

Theare was at Court a Ladye of late
That none could enter shee was soe straight
But now with use shee's growne so wide
Theare is a passage for a Carre to ride.[103]

It is not clear whether the 'use' has been by Carr himself, before or after the marriage, or whether others have played their part. But what is unequivocal is the implied contempt for the female body. This is even more transparently the case in the following verses:

From Catherines docke there launched a pink
Which sore did leake but did not sinke
Ere while she lay on Essex shore
Expectinge rigging yard & store
But all disaster to prevent
With winde in poope she sayld to Kent
At Rochester she anker cast
Which Canterburie did distast
But Winchester with Elyes helpe
Did drawe to shore the Lyons whelp
She was weak sided and did reel
But Some are sett to mende her keele
To stop her leake & mende her porte
And make her fit for any sporte.[104]

In this epigram, if anywhere, is unambiguous evidence of the kind of scandal the annulment hearing generated even before the later revelations. Central to the poem is a picture of woman as 'leaky vessel', in need of stanching. It is part of the standard currency of Renaissance misogyny. Gail Paster has finely demonstrated the continuity between medical theory and the representation of 'female self-control in a form – a leaky form – obviously related to talkativeness, but far more shameful'.[105] Perhaps most pertinently for this poem, she draws attention to the 'famous iconographic depiction of female virginity as a sieve that does not leak, an allusion to the Vestal Virgin Tuccia', and points out that 'if not-leaking becomes something of a mythological miracle reserved for a long-gone Roman lady and the occasional virgin queen, then leaking remains the normal punitive condition for women'. In the poem Frances is placed in this 'normal' condition. She is 'leaky' before she starts out, and it is the job of men to 'rig' her properly and stop her leakiness. Essex's 'yard' has been found wanting, but Carr's sexual possession of her will repair her, if not restore her reputation. In this epigram Frances is wilful, but dependent on men, incontinently leaky, but when 'stopped' good only for sexual sport. (The joke in the opening line is also relevant. St Katherine's dock was an area notorious for brewhouses and taverns, and therefore a haunt of prostitutes, but Katherine was also the name of Frances's mother.)

The speed of Frances's remarriage was enough to suggest that the divorce had been arranged for that purpose, even if the extent of her previous meeting with Robert Carr were not known. The general accusation of lechery was therefore easy to make, and in one verse this is the charge levelled at both Robert and Frances:

> Letchery did consult with witcherye
> how to procure frygiditye
> Upon this grounde a course was found
> To frame unto a nullatye
> And gravitye assuming lenyte
> gave strength to this impietye
> hoping thereby a way to spye
> to rise to further dignitye
> But whats the end both foe and frend
> Cry shame on such austeryte
> And book and bell do dam to Hell
> the Lord and Ladyes lecherye[106]

Something of the same moral disapproval of the couple, and of the bishops, runs through the comments of Sir John Throckmorton. On 27 May, writing to William Trumbull, he says:

> I hear a speech, and it is written also, of their annulling the marriage between the earl of Essex and his lady. The ground I know not, but am sorry to hear it questioned. God will punish, I fear me, and that sharply our land for these crying sins.[107]

By 22 June he has heard of Carr's presence as future husband, and when in September he reports the possible duel between Essex and Henry Howard he concludes:

> The quarrel is deadly being grounded upon the business of the earl's lady. Thus you see the little care taken at home of all things; our government as well ecclesiastical as politic will become a scorn and byword to all nations.[108]

These comments and the preceding poem represent the kind of attitude that Abbot's commentary on the divorce hearings, with its self-congratulation for principled opposition and assertion of great popular support for his position would lead us to expect was universal.

Just as spicier narratives have consistently been preferred to soberer judgements, so it has been easier to assume universal disgust than to consider the substantial evidence that many contemporaries were not unduly troubled by the divorce. The Reverend Thomas Lorkin, for example, writing to Sir Thomas Puckering on 8 July, reports events without any moralising gloss, even when retailing the suggestion that if the sentence is given in favour of Frances 'it is generally believed that a match shall be concluded between my Lord of Rochester and her: thereby to reconcile him and the house of Howard together, who are now far enough asunder'.[109] Lord Fenton's comments we have already sampled (see p. 83). He seems to have been convinced throughout that 'for certaine it wilbe a nulletye'. In his letter of 20 May he suggests that it was Southampton and Pembroke who persuaded Essex to retract his admission of impotence.[110] But by August Southampton himself, the most loyal follower of Essex's father, wrote to Winwood:

> For the Business it self, I protest I shall be glad, if it may lawfully, that it may go forward; though of late I have been fearful of the consequence, and have had my fears increased by the last letters which came to me.[111]

Exactly what consequence Southampton feared is not made clear, but one might suspect that it was the political realignment that would follow on the remarriage to Carr. It is vital to remember that even when contemporaries were shocked by events, they were not necessarily scandalised by exactly the same aspects of the case as modern historians. So it is in Chamberlain's objection to the divorce. He wrote, on 10 June:

> Yet some lawiers are of opinion that yf she will take her oath that he is impotent towards her, yt will serve the turne, wherof yt is thought she will make no bones, as presuming that she is provided of a second, which I shold never have suspected, but that I know he was with her

three howres together within these two dayes, which makes me somwhat to stagger and to thincke that great folkes to compasse theyre owne ends have neither respect to frends nor followers.[112]

There is little moral disapproval here of a sexual kind; what upsets Chamberlain is the disloyalty of the leading actors to their clientage.

Another cause for censure of the annulment was the King's intervention in the case and his packing of the commission with two extra judges bound to vote in favour. (After the divorce the son of Bishop Bilson, one of the two late-added commissioners, was knighted, and suffered under the nickname 'Sir Nullity Bilson' to the end of his days.) Even though this is an objection we might still find well-founded, it is one which must be kept distinct from the moral opprobrium that is routinely visited on Frances Howard herself. Paradoxically, in view of the injustice of seventeenth-century law to modern eyes, the King may even have been thought to do well to overturn it, whatever his motivation in doing so.

In order fully to comprehend what was at stake in the annulment hearings and the controversy they provoked it is absolutely essential to separate out the different elements that have engendered hostile reaction. A brief return to *The Changeling* makes the issues clearer. In that play there is a contrast between the main plot concerning Beatrice-Joanna, and the subplot of Isabella. Both women come under male pressure, and, as Christina Malcolmson puts it in her discussion of the play: 'whereas a morally weak woman like Beatrice-Joanna can become a monster, a strong woman like Isabella can fully protect her integrity'.[113] In her analysis this contrast illustrates the difference between 'aristocratic degeneracy' and the 'virtuous middle-classes' (an argument which echoes Margot Heinemann's view of the play). There can be little doubt that some such contrast is in Middleton's mind; there can be little doubt, too, that such a perception informed a common reading of Frances Howard's conduct, and that Middleton was reflecting that response in his play. But when Malcolmson imports this understanding of Frances Howard's career to substantiate her reading of the play her argument turns the 'background' of the divorce and murder hearings into a schematic narrative in which its various issues are conflated and simplified. Malcolmson is a subtle literary critic who necessarily relies on a briefly sketched history to provide the launch-pad for discussion of the play. I am working the other way round, and would argue that the events of Frances Howard's life are complex and ambiguous, but that once they are turned into the narrative of history, then it is the simplified outlines of literary texts such as *The Changeling* which provide the matrices within which her story can be expressed and comprehended.

Whereas, in the end, Malcolmson tends to agree with Middleton's representation of the Frances Howard story, I would see it as expressive of the nexus of attitudes and assumptions Frances Howard confronted. Though the legal processes were questionable, it does not follow that Frances Howard had no case. Though there is little doubt that Frances Howard was only able to bring the suit because of the eminence of her own family and the political position of her intended husband, it does not follow that hostility to her class should be merged with hostility to her sex, as it is in Middleton's play and many other fictional and historical accounts.

In the course of this chapter it has, I hope, become clear that the reading of the annulment is no simple matter. In the first place, there is substantial testimony that it was by no means as universally detested at the time as most later commentators have maintained. Furthermore, where there was opposition it was in no small measure to the political consequences of the remarriage, rather than to the annulment in itself. But thirdly, and perhaps most significantly, it is the fear of female sexual self-expression which underlies, unacknowledged, much of the commentary on the divorce. Abbot's strongest moral argument against allowing the annulment was his alarm at what the consequences of permitting it would be. He protested:

> For as soon as this cause is sentenced, every man who is discontented with his wife, and every woman discontented with her husband, which can have any reasonable pretence, will repair to me for such nullities. (*ST*, 811)

He is echoing an argument that was used repeatedly, both of this case in particular and of permission for divorce and remarriage in general. With tedious repetitiveness authorities adjure their readers to 'mind the gap' that permitting any divorce would open up. Abbot argued that if the marriage of Robert Devereux and Frances Howard were compelled to continue:

> all the inconvenience doth redound but to one person ... if the disagreement never be appeased, it is no more but one lady doth want that solace which marital conjunction would afford unto her; which many a good woman is enforced to endure, and yet commits no sin, neither labours to violate the laws of the church ... Let a woman do that in modesty, which others are enforced to do out of necessity; and let her expect God's leisure in fasting and in prayer, and in other humiliation. (*ST*, 857)

The final sentence reveals what is really at stake. For Abbot, as for so many others for so many centuries, the preservation of the institution of marriage is more important than what kind of marriage it is. The 'humiliation' of women is a necessary consequence of the determined preservation of the principle of hierarchy for which marriage was symbol, and through which, in practice, it was articulated and enforced. The persistence of attitudes in essence the same as those expressed by Abbot is self-evident. As a legal historian put it: 'The most striking feature of the history of divorce law has been the continuity of legal theory and the reluctance to liberalise existing divorce laws or even to make the existing law more accessible to the majority of the population'.[114]

Confirmation of this continuity is to be found in a book published in 1811 entitled *A full account of the curious and interesting proceedings instituted in Doctor's Commons by Rachel Dick against her husband the Rev. William Dick for a Nullity of Marriage on the grounds of Impotency.* Its foreword is especially revealing:

> The precedents of seeking a dissolution of the marriage knot but upon a plea of impotency, are very few; so that it may well be questioned whether, when preferred, it does not arise less from any real cause that the woman may have to complain of her husband's deficient powers, than from a propensity to change, for the purpose of indulging and gratifying her own carnal desires; and it is not a little worthy of remark, that in almost every instance where the wife has so complained, she has eventually turned out a woman of abandoned meretricity. (pp. 3–4)

In this publication, and as evidence of these assertions, the case of Essex and Frances Howard is recounted. The (in?)appropriately named Reverend Dick rebutted his wife's charges, and the annulment was not granted. But the assumptions that power this preface about female duplicity, changeability and sexual voraciousness are precisely the same assumptions that two hundred years before animated the hearings of Frances's suit, and, sadly, nearly two hundred years later, are largely replicated in most accounts of that suit.

Chapter 4

Interlude: Celebration

On 26 December 1613 Frances Howard married Robert Carr, now Earl of Somerset, in what was the major court event of the Christmas season. Chamberlain in a letter to Alice Carleton provides a description of the occasion:

> The mariage was upon Sonday without any such braverie as was looked for, only some of his followers bestowed cost on themselves, the rest exceeded not either in number or expence. She was married in her haire and led to chappell by her bridemen a Duke of Saxonie (that is here) and the earle of Northampton her great uncle. The dean of Westminster preached and bestowed a greate deale of commendation on the younge couple, on the Countesse of Salisburie, and the mother-vine (as he termed her) the Countess of Suffolke. The Dean of the chappell coupled them, which fell out somwhat straungely that the same man, shold marrie the same person, in the same place, upon the self-same day (after sixe or seven yeares I know not whether) the former partie yet living: all the difference was that the Kinge gave her the last time, and now her father. The King and Quene were both present and tasted wafers and ypocras as at ordinarie weddings.[1]

Chamberlain is disappointed at the lack of expenditure on wedding outfits (though not, interestingly, much troubled by the bride's appearing 'in her haire' as a sign of virginity). But if there was not much expense on the clothes of the bridal party, conspicuous consumption was to follow. The couple received gifts from courtiers great and small. Chamberlain estimated their value as £12,000, while Thomas Penruddock told the Earl of Arundel that the offerings 'from all persons of quality' were 'esteemed to be no less worth than £30,000 in plate and jewels'.[2] Everyone judged it in their best interests, whatever scruples they might have had, to perform the obligation of honouring the marriage of the King's favourite, from whom benefits could be expected in future to flow. There was considerable expenditure, too, upon the entertainments for the marriage. On the wedding night Campion's *Somerset Masque*[3] was performed, to be followed the next evening by *A Challenge at Tilt* delivered by two Cupids, scripted by Jonson. Two days later Jonson's *The Irish Masque* occupied the evening, and then on 1 January 1614 the challenge of the Cupids was taken up in a tilting. The King requested a repeat of *The Irish Masque* on 3 January, and the following night the Lord Mayor, Thomas Middleton, was coerced by the King into entertaining the couple. (He had at first protested that his house was not big enough, only to be told to command the biggest hall in town and get on with it.) At least one play, and a *Masque of Cupid* by the mayor's namesake were performed. (Middleton's masque, most regrettably, is lost.) The festivities were rounded off on Twelfth Night by Gray's Inn's offering of *The Masque of Flowers*,[4] funded at a cost of £2,000 by Francis Bacon. Poets also offered gifts of verse. Jonson wrote a poem 'To the Most Noble, and Above His Titles, Robert, Earl of Somerset';[5] William Alabaster composed an Epithalamium in Latin.[6] Terracae's poem on the nullity was probably completed before the marriage, but later in 1614 Chapman published his defence of the annulment and remarriage, in his long poem, *Andromeda Liberata*.[7]

The orgy of expense and gift-giving at this marriage has usually been taken to demonstrate the corruption and hypocrisy of the Jacobean court, and to exemplify the subordination of principle to self-interest that the whole system of patronage required. Though recent scholarship has done much to make the nature of a patronage culture more fully understood,[8] the prevailing judgement is that the line between acceptable conformity to the system and degrading corruption was frequently transgressed in the Jacobean court, and never more than on this occasion. The literary compositions generated by the wedding have come in for especial censure from critics. In this chapter I want to consider the texts themselves for what they can tell us of attitudes to the marriage at the time of its solemnisation, but first it is necessary to examine the sources and consequences of this hostile critical reaction. The adverse commentary on the poems seems to derive from a number of different impulses which need to be distinguished one from the other.

In the first place, though literary historians have explicated the theory and practice of panegyric poetry and have for many years attempted to situate the poets within networks of obligation,[9] there remains an underlying embarrassment with the whole genre. In our own age the public poetry of praise (except of the decently dead) seems absurd, and the office of Poet Laureate an institutionalised joke. Our cultural preconceptions about the nature and function of poetry are affronted by the spectacle of Renaissance writers using their work as currency in the soliciting of favour, however much we may intellectually understand their situation. In the case of this wedding it is as if the rain of material gifts is considered merely venal, where the betrayal by Donne, Jonson and the rest of their poetic vocation is an unforgivable mortal sin.

The second reason for anxiety in confronting the poetry of praise is an extension of the first. Such poetry raises problematic questions about the relation of 'fact' and fiction, historical background and literary foreground. The 'old–New-Critical' emphasis on literature as the embodiment of permanent, transcendent truths that stand above and beyond any historical context has been dethroned, but adherents of more recent critical theories, including some varieties of 'historicism', are often equally uneasy with any attempt to appeal to a material and particular reality. Their theories require that there can be nothing that stands outside the constructions of language, nothing that is unmistakably prior to the literary text. Panegyric poetry, however, entwines the realms of imagination and material reality. It points unambiguously and unavoidably at the world outside itself and engages with its contemporary political scene in detailed and often complex ways. Theorists who prefer grand designs to minute examination of particulars become impatient, and rest content with a broad-brush background.

The third problem has to do with the circumstances of the Carr/Howard marriage itself. As William McClung and Rodney Simard note, in speaking of Donne's 'Eclogue':

> Neither the murder of Overbury . . . nor the passion between Somerset and Lady Essex seems adequate to account for the continuing deprecation of this poem and its author on the basis of the historical circumstances surrounding its composition.[10]

They see the excess of spleen as deriving from a 'displacement of homophobic feelings into overwrought accounts of the supposed adulteries and homicides of the famous pair', noting the suppression of all mention of Somerset's relationships with the King and with Overbury. The thesis is a bold one, but it has to be said that there seems to have been remarkably little concern with this issue at the time. Campion, for example, blithely includes in his masque the lines:

> Some friendship betweene man and man prefer,
> But I th'affection betweene man and wife.
>
> (p. 274)

As with so much of the poetry we will be considering in this chapter, one blenches at what Campion might have thought of these lines once it became known that Carr's friend had been murdered in order that the marriage could proceed. But he is self-evidently not concerned about any homosexual relationship which might have subsisted between Carr and King or Carr and Overbury. It seems to me that there is a more obvious source of the excessive distaste, one that Heather Dubrow suggests when she remarks that 'the fears of sexuality, especially female sexuality, that attended on weddings found their objective correlative in the reputation of the bride'.[11] Her analysis of such suppressed anxiety in the epithalamic genre as a whole is persuasive, but I would suggest that Frances Howard is not the 'objective correlative', but rather the product of that hostility.

Animosity against her (and therefore against those who wrote in praise of her) derives most obviously from a conflation of responses to the annulment and remarriage with those elicited by the later-revealed murder of Overbury. Annabel Patterson, for example, prepares the ground for a discussion of Donne's 'Eclogue' in these terms:

> We know that Donne had by this time already profited from the greatest scandal of James's reign, in which Frances Howard's divorce from the third earl of Essex and remarriage to Robert Carr, earl of Somerset and still the reigning favorite, was accomplished at the cost of Sir Thomas Overbury's life.[12]

The introduction of the murder at the end of this summary indicates how a lack of scrupulousness about the precise awareness that poets like Donne might be supposed to have had can fatally colour everything that follows. Since almost all critics also assume that an adulterous relationship between the couple was public knowledge in 1613, they are compelled to the position that the poets must have chosen to shut their ears and avert their moral gaze in order to praise Frances Howard. Since most critics have an investment in the defence of their authors' integrity they then search for the criticism that must, somehow, be present in the texts.[13] At the simplest level such a strategy is not even necessary, since there is plenty of evidence that the writers were not in possession of this later-acquired knowledge. Jonson's poem to Somerset, for example, includes the lines:

> May she whom thou for spouse today dost take
> Out-be that wife in worth thy friend did make.[14]

His allusion here to Overbury's poem 'The Wife' must indicate that he had no suspicions of murder. Later revelations meant that Jonson (unsurprisingly) did not include this poem in his 1616 Folio. But yet in that collection Jonson did choose to reprint all the masques written for both of Frances Howard's marriages.

This different response to texts that one would suppose were equally tainted by their circumstance reveals that whatever difficulties modern readers have with panegyric poetry, Renaissance poets themselves wrestled with its problematic nature. The standard defence in classical and Renaissance theory was that such poetry offered an explicitly idealised picture of its subject in order to educate him or her into recognition of the roles they should attempt to fill. If the person praised did not in actuality live up to the poet's image then the fault lay in him or her, and not in the poet. This is the argument of Jonson's epigram 'To my Muse', which concludes with the lines: 'Whoe'er is raised / For worth he hath not, he is taxed, not praised' (p. 224). In 1614, however, Jonson confessed to Selden:

> I have too oft preferred
> Men past their terms, and praised some names too much;
> But 'twas with purpose to have made them such.
> Since being deceived, I turn a sharper eye
> Upon myself, and ask to whom, and why,
> And what I write? And vex it many days
> Before men get a verse, much less a praise;
> So that my reader is assured I now
> Mean what I speak, and still will keep that vow.
>
> (pp. 331–2)

If this recognition prompted him to suppress the poem to Carr, Jonson must have felt that the aspiration of the masques to embody more general truths meant that they could transcend their particular occasion. He was content merely to remove from their headings any specific references to the people for whom they were written. (One must wonder, incidentally, whether Ted Hughes would identify with Jonson's difficulties after having published his laureate poems, including those in praise of the marriage of Sarah Ferguson and Prince Andrew, and of the children of the Prince and Princess of Wales, some few months before the couples separated and were overwhelmed with scandal.)

Reading these poems aright is, then, a complex matter. I am not suggesting that modern disgust should be contested simply by turning the background from black to white, arguing only that it was perfectly possible to think better of Frances Howard in 1613 than was later the case (important though that argument is). The poets, after all, were themselves aware of the scandal that the events had occasioned, and in almost all of these works they make it their business to confront contemporary gossip. At the same time, their own attitudes were necessarily shaped within the same forces that produced that sense of outrage, making their negotiation with it extremely complex and precarious. But before turning to detailed analysis of the poems two issues need to be clarified. The ability of writers to respond to the marriage was affected by purely practical problems, which should not be overlooked. More important, perhaps, is the setting out of the position each of them occupied in the political world of 1613.

It might easily be taken as a sign of authorial evasion that two of the masques for the occasion actually contain very little direct application to the marriage. But in the case of *The Masque of Flowers* the dedication to Bacon suggests that an earlier intention for all four Inns of Court to get together to provide a masque had proved unworkable, since the costs were beyond them, their resources having been eaten up by the lavish entertainments for Princess Elizabeth's marriage in February 1613. The Grayans were left with but three weeks to mount their show, which explains its rather routine nature. (Middleton's *Masque of Cupid* was produced even more quickly, if Chamberlain's assertion that they only had 'fowre dayes warning' be credited.[15] It must have been an 'off-the-peg' piece, and can scarcely have had much verbal material – one reason perhaps, why it has not survived.)[16] Jonson's *Irish Masque* might also have been significantly affected by circumstance. On 11 November 1613 Chamberlain wrote:

> The mariage was thought shold be celebrated at Audley-end the next weeke, and great preparation there was to receve the King, but I heare that the Quene beeing won and having promised to be present, yt is put of till Christmas and then to be performed at White-hall.[17]

It seems to me probable that Jonson's Irish project was already in his mind by the time that the change of plan became known. The events in Ireland which underlay his choice of subject had rumbled on through the spring and summer of 1613, and his story, of a group of Irish gentlemen losing their fine masquing apparel at sea on their way to the English court, could easily be modified by suggesting that the reason they came was to honour the marriage, rather than directly to pay tribute to the King. It is significant that this masque, like Jonson's offering the previous year, *Love Restored*, was limited (and therefore cheap) in its scenic demands, and was to be performed by a very similar cast of second-rank court figures, chosen for their prowess as dancers rather than their nobility. The state of court finances had demanded a cut-back in expenditure, and it seems to me most plausible *The Irish Masque* was originally intended to be the principal

entertainment for the Christmas season (Campion's masque was presumably largely financed by the Suffolks and the participants themselves).[18]

Even in the case of Donne's 'Eclogue', where the poet apologises for
the lateness of his tribute, the delay, usually read as indicating Donne's
uneasiness with the whole affair, could have had a pragmatic cause. As
Bald points out:

> One reason why [Donne] did not have an epithalamion ready for
> Somerset's marriage, but had to write it after the event, may have been
> that he was ill . . . As far back as September 1613 Donne had had eye-
> trouble.

He cites a letter written at Christmas complaining:

> It is one of my blinde Meditations to think what a miserable defeat it
> would be to all these preparations of braverie, if my infirmity should
> overtake others: for, I am at least half blinde, my windows are all as full
> of glasses of Waters, as any Mountebanks stall.[19]

It is tempting to see Donne's troubled eye-sight as all too appropriate for
the blinkered vision of events he is assumed to have had; but before
taking off into ingenious critical exegesis it is as well to acknowledge the
significance of mundane practicalities in determining what was written.

The most urgent reality which pressed upon the poets, however, was
their own particular situation in the world of patronage. In the eighteen
months or so before the wedding the outline of court politics had been
thrown into confusion by the deaths of the Earl of Salisbury and Prince
Henry. The great offices of state remained unfilled, and Henry's court, a
focus of artistic patronage, was dissolved. As we have seen, the
Carr/Howard marriage itself implied significant shifts in the balance of
political power. In this fluid time, when no one could quite answer the
question 'who's in, who's out?', the extravagance of gifts of all kinds is
primarily a mark of a collective anxiety. Of the poets whose works we
will be considering only Campion, perhaps, was clear about his position.
As a long-time client of Sir Thomas Monson, who had owed allegiance
to the Howards for many years, he had benefited from Jonson's absence
earlier in 1613 by being asked to provide the wedding-night masque for
the marriage of Princess Elizabeth. He had followed that up with *The
Caversham Entertainment*, offered shortly afterwards to Queen Anne at the
seat of Thomas Howard's son-in-law. Clearly he had pleased his patrons,
and it is not surprising that he should be entrusted by them with the
wedding-night masque for their daughter. Campion responded with a

work which takes on the problems surrounding the marriage with a political directness not matched in any other text.

The authorship of *The Masque of Flowers* is not known, but its financial backer, Francis Bacon, had an equally clear motive for its sponsorship. Carr had been influential in securing Bacon's promotion to the Attorney-Generalship earlier in 1613, and this work was a simple (if expensive) thank-offering. (It is revealing that the dedication of the work to Bacon should speak of it being presented 'in honour of the marriage and happy alliance between two such principal persons of the kingdome as are the Earl of Suffolk and the Earl of Somerset'.[20] Frances disappears from sight – the 'glue' once again between male alliance.)

Alabaster is a rather shadowy figure. He had made multiple conversions to and from the Roman Catholic church, after starting his career as chaplain to the second Earl of Essex. At about the time of the marriage it would seem that he had finally and firmly committed himself to the Anglican church, and found favour with King James. Since it is unlikely that Robert Carr could read the difficult Latin of Alabaster's poem, it is most probable that it was aimed at pleasing James rather than his favourite.[21]

Jonson's position was much more problematic. As David Riggs points out, the Earl of Northampton was his 'deadly enemy', and he had 'recently been cultivating the rival faction headed by Pembroke' so that 'it is hard (though just possible) to believe that he felt much enthusiasm for the burgeoning alliance of Somerset and the Howards'.[22] As the pre-eminent court poet Jonson had little option but to furnish appropriate celebration, but he must have felt awkward in appearing so to shift allegiance. His readiness to triumph over the fall of Somerset and celebrate the restoration of Pembroke/Sidney influence in *The Golden Age Restored* (1616) suggests that he had been careful to mind his back in 1613.

Donne, meanwhile, was pursuing his perpetual struggle to find the patronage that would secure the court employment from which his injudicious marriage over a decade earlier had excluded him. Robert Carr seemed a possible avenue for his political ambitions because Donne already had friends amongst the Scottish contingent at court in James Hay and Sir Robert Ker, a second cousin of the favourite. He had declared himself ready to write a treatise in defence of the nullity – and was, in the event, to secure significant reward from Somerset, for whom he began collecting together his scattered poems with a view to publication.[23] Donne's poem is the most obviously troubled of all the offerings we will be considering. The 'Epithalamion' addressed to the couple is prefaced by a pastoral dialogue between Idios ('one's own', or 'pertaining to oneself') and Allophanes ('appearing otherwise'). In their exchange the poet (as 'Idios') tries to justify his absence from court at the time of the marriage. Both David Norbrook and Annabel Patterson argue convincingly that this part of the poem expresses Donne's own deeply divided attitude to the court, and the tensions this generated in him as he pursued his secular ambitions.[24] The prologue is by no means irrelevant to the Carr/Howard marriage, since Donne's praise of 'A Court, where all affections do assent / Unto the King's' (ll. 76–7) blithely overrides the scorn generally felt for those commissioners, especially the added bishops, who had so readily conformed themselves to the King's will. But the general political uncertainties which suffuse the poem need to be distinguished from any particular moral objections that Donne might or might not have had to the marriage.

Chapman presents the saddest picture of all. He seems to have had a positive genius for picking losers as his patrons. As A.R. Braunmuller sums up his career: 'Essex was executed; the new scholar-prince, Henry, died just as the poet completed the *Iliad* translation and anticipated future support; Carr was accused, condemned, jailed, and never restored to favour'.[25] Of all the works to be considered *Andromeda Liberata* is the most extreme in its apologia for the couple. If this is a mark of Chapman's desperation in pursuit of a patron, it is nonetheless the case that of all the poets under consideration only he remained loyal to the Somersets after their fall from grace.

Whatever differences there were between the poets, on one strategy they were all agreed. Every work contains within it some celebration of the love that the couple show for one another. Campion prefaces his text with a Latin epigram which, translated, reads: 'That true marriages may endure, you must lead the wedding procession with two torches: Hymen must hold one torch, and it is best that Love hold the other' (p. 267). Jonson concludes *A Challenge at Tilt* with a speech by Hymen praising marriage 'when the contention is not, who is the true love, but (being both true) who loves most... This is a strife wherein you both win, and begets a concord worthy all married minds' emulation, when the lover transforms himself into the person of his belov'd, as you two do now' (ll. 198–203). Chapman gives his hero, Perseus, a hymn to love (ll. 283–344) and celebrates the love of Robert and Frances under the guise of Perseus and Andromeda in emphatic terms:

> In mutuall love
> One onely death and two revivalls move:
> For her that loves, when he himself neglects
> Dies in himself once, In her he affects
> Straight he renewes, when she with equall fire

Embraceth him, as he did her desire.
(ll. 469–74)

Such sentiments are not exactly unexpected in works praising a marriage, but in this case they corresponded to reality. Whatever else one may think of Frances Howard, of her obsessive love for Robert Carr there can be very little doubt. More than this, however, the conventional hymns to love acquired particular force in this case since they stand as a kind of retrospective apologia for the failure of the loveless, arranged marriage which had preceded it. But once the poets moved beyond this point, they inevitably became embroiled in matters much less clear-cut.

Frances Howard wore her hair freely flowing at the wedding as a sign of her virginity. When Wilson later described the scene he wrote:

She thinking all the World ignorant of her sly practises, hath the impudence to appear in the habit of a Virgin, with her hair pendant almost to her feet; which Ornament of her Body (though a fair one) could not cover the deformities of her Soul.[26]

She is immediately accommodated to the figure of Webster's *White Devil*, or Spenser's false Florimell, her fair outside concealing the inevitable truth of female deceitfulness. Though Wilson is writing in knowledge of later revelations the attitude he represents was undoubtedly to be found at the time. But Wilson's comments perfectly illustrate the double-bind in which Frances Howard found herself. If she had not been married 'in her hair', then that would have been tantamount to admitting that the annulment was a fraud; if she was, then immediately ribald tongues could wag. The poets who wrote in praise of the marriage found themselves in that same double bind. Some of the poets chose to confront these suspicions directly.

William Terracae seems to do so with astonishing tactlessness when he dedicates his poem to Frances Howard in these terms:

And you (faire Maddam) in like Goddnes rest,
So shall you shyne with all those graces blest,
That star-like crowne the Trueth; and shall obtrude
To shame, both Envie and the Multitude.
    As for those frailties, that may shade thy Presence
(Those Adventitiall, not of thy true Essence,
And wher is that Composure framd of blood
And flesh, that may make boaste of simple good?)
Heaven will not like a feind-like liverd man
Light those, and hide in Mistes Cimmerian

Thy naturall vertues, but quite Opposite
The worst extinguish, and the better light.[27]

It is easy to assume that the 'frailties' to which he refers concern Frances
Howard's amatory past. The poem as it progresses, however, suggests that
her blemishes are not sexual transgressions but her subversions of good
order in frowardness and 'disobedience, and unharty showes / Of dutious
spousall Love unto her Lord' (fol. 12ᵛ). It is a useful reminder that even if
poets register doubts about the marriage, the grounds of their unease
might not be quite what we might now anticipate.

But poets did address the question of Frances Howard's chastity. William
Alabaster appended two English poems to his Latin Epithalamium, and in
the one offered to Frances wrote:

A rose to spring uppon a courtly plaine,
    Wher glories son doth warme a tender brest,
    And wordes like windes, doe virgin leafes unvest,
And yet to keep unblowne the bud of shame:
    Is such a patterne of transcending fame
    And of another age, that tw'er a paine
To seeke to parallel this rose againe:
    Since nature now few worthy workes doth frame
It seames that vertue gaspeth unto death,
Which in thy chastnes drew so longe a breath.[28]

Alabaster chooses to celebrate Frances Howard by insisting that she has
held on to her virtue when, in this fallen age, few women can withstand
the assaults of the court. He thus bravely inverts one of the assumptions
which, as we have seen, helped to consolidate Frances's representation as
a flighty woman. But Alabaster's poem, like Frances's conduct in wearing
her hair down, is victim of a double bind. Whilst it can be read as a
recognition and contradiction of negative characterisations of the bride, it
is easy for the sceptical critic to see the poem as expressing its author's
'real' anxiety about her 'actual' conduct through an anxious denial of what
he feared to be true.

The force of such scepticism to generate negative readings of the texts
can be seen in the case of a few lines in Donne's 'Epithalamion' where
the bride is addressed:

    Powder thy radiant hair,
Which if without such ashes thou wouldst wear,
Thou, which to all which come to look upon,
Art meant for Phoebus, wouldst be Phaëton.

                                        (ll. 142–5)

Heather Dubrow, convinced of Donne's knowledge of Frances Howard's dubious morality, says:

> On one level, these lines merely refer to a common method of adorning the hair, but it is surely no accident that ashes are traditionally associated with penitence. This passage subtly but unmistakably warns the bride that only repentance will preserve her from danger: she must control her passions ... lest she destroy and be destroyed as tragically as that arrogant young astronaut Phaëton.[29]

It is an ingenious reading. But if one assumes that Donne could honestly have believed that Frances Howard was actually a virgin, then the 'ashes' take on a rather different significance. Jonson, as we have seen, explained the ashes in the hair of the bride as a symbol of her entrance into the matron's state (see p. 21). From this element of Roman iconology, one might argue, Donne constructs a compliment to Frances Howard's beauty in which the tempering of the glory of her hair required by the marriage ceremony is represented as necessary to prevent her *appearing as* (not *being*) a Phaëton to those who watch her. The threat the poem speaks of is to the audience who might be consumed by the splendour of her chaste display, not to her. The reading of these lines crucially depends upon whether one is attempting to excuse Donne by insisting that he included coded criticism within his poem, or whether one is proceeding on the assumption that he could legitimately, and in good faith, be seeking to defend the bride against the accusations he knew to be in the air. There are few details in the poem that are not substantially affected by the critic's starting point. The question is graphically focused in Donne's statement that the couple 'their bodies never yet had seen'. Dubrow calls it 'the most outrageous lie of the poem' (p. 185); but, as we have seen, Donne may well not have had any reason to think his assertion to be untrue.

It might seem that the writers would be on safer ground in directing attention to the future rather than to the past. So Campion includes this dialogue in his masque:

3   What good can be in life,
    Whereof no fruites appeare?
1   Set is that Tree in ill houre,
    That yeilds neither fruite nor flowre
2   How can man Perpetuall be,
    But in his owne Posteritie?
Chorus   That pleasure is of all most bountifull and kinde,

That fades not straight, but leaves a living Joy behinde.

(p. 275)

These lines emphasise the rightful desire of a woman to be able to have children which formed the central justification of the annulment, and grafts that defence into the conventional epithalamic promise of progeny.

Alabaster similarly, if more pointedly, urged the couple to look towards the future, when he wrote:

> May the chaste turtle-dove not teach you lessons in fidelity, doves in the murmurings of lovers, ivy in intimate embraces or conch-shells in kissing; let each be an example of love to the other, so that the husband may quickly make you a mother from a maid, and you may quickly welcome him as a father from a husband.[30]

There might not seem to be anything controversial here, but when Chapman seemed to be making the same kind of statement he ran into enormous problems.

Andromeda Liberata narrates the rescue of Andromeda by Perseus from the rock to which she had been tied to propitiate a monstrous whale which threatened her parents' kingdom. In the course of the poem Chapman characterises the rock as 'barraine' (l. 143), and later suggests that those who prevent generation are 'homicides':

> For who belov'd, not yeelding love againe,
> And so the life doth from his love devide,
> Denies himself to be a Homicide?
> For he no lesse a Homicide is held
> That man to be borne lets, then he that kild
> A man that is borne.

(ll. 488–93)

Even before the poem was published it would seem that there was some fear that it might give offence. Uniquely amongst all works entered in the *Stationer's Register*, no less than four Privy Councillors licensed the work, including the Earl of Suffolk.[31] Whether it was the printer, or Suffolk, or even Chapman himself who were worried, the outcome justified any anxiety. Later in the year Chapman was forced to publish a defence of the poem, which he claimed had been 'maliciously misinterpreted', and from the 'Free and Offenceless Justification' it is apparent that the lines which caused offence were those quoted above. Some took them to refer to the Earl of Essex as the 'barren rock', and applied the lines on homicide either to the Earl, or else to the bishops who had opposed the annulment.

Chapman struggled to claim that his contemporaries had misread his text. He ingenuously argued that the image of a barren rock could not be applied to a living figure, and tried to turn the comments on homicides into a compliment to Essex, arguing:

> I condemne
> As churlish *Homicides*, who will denie
> In love twixt two, the possibility
> To propagate their lives into descent
> Needfull and lawfull, and that argument
> Is *Platoes*, to a word; which much commends
> The two great personages, who wanting th'ends
> Of wedlocke, as they were, with one consent
> Sought cleere disjunction, which (with blest event)
> May joine both otherwise, with such encrease
> Of worthy Ofspring, that posterities
> May blesse their fautors, and their favoures now:
> Whom now such bans and poisons overflow.
>
> (ll.106–18)

There is an unmistakable air of panic in Chapman's self-justification. Whether he really thought that the passages in the original poem meant what he later said they did, or whether he had merely believed that he could get away with an implied slur on Essex's virility, is open to debate. It is ironic, however, that a poem which, as we shall see shortly, is itself devoted to discussion of opinion and interpretation should have been vulnerable to the variable interpretations of its original audience.

This brings us to the most important feature of a number of these works. The writers, aware of the gossip and rumour that surrounded the wedding, chose to confront it directly and, in the case of Campion and Chapman, to turn it into their central subject. But Donne, too, has a passing comment on this matter. In a stanza headed 'Equality of Persons' he writes

> But undiscerning Muse, which heart, which eyes,
>   In this new couple, dost thou prize,
>   When his eye as inflaming is
> As hers, and her heart loves as well as his?
>   Be tried by beauty, and then
> The Bridegroom is a maid, and not a man.
> If by that manly courage they be tried,
> Which scorns unjust opinion; then the Bride

> Becomes a man. Should chance or envy's art
> Divide these two, whom nature scarce did part?
> Since both have both th'inflaming eyes, and both the loving heart.
>
> (ll. 116–26)

Of this passage Dubrow says:

> Most obviously, they justify the bride's divorce and subsequent remar-
> riage. Lines 124–5 state explicitly what the rest of these passages imply:
> those events are nature and, indeed, virtually inevitable. It is telling,
> too, that Donne associates harmony between man and woman with
> the destabilization of gender. But it is equally telling that in this
> quotation . . . traditional assumptions about gender, though questioned,
> are ultimately supported and maintained. Courage is in this instance
> associated with the woman and beauty with the man, but the poem
> does not deny that these generally are and should be male and female
> qualities respectively . . . Here, as in American politics of the 1980s,
> anxieties generate a reassertion of conventional and conservative values.
> (pp. 187–8)

I would argue that the lines are much more powerful than this. As we
have seen, Frances Howard's confrontation of patriarchal attitudes was a
major factor in determining the hostile reaction her divorce suit provoked.
Later she was to be represented satirically as of a 'mannish' nature in the
Haec Vir pamphlet, typifying the dangers of female transgression. If the
print reproduced as Plate 6 does depict Frances Howard as the figure
waiting for cure by Doctor Panurge, then the same point is being made.
In this context, for Donne to attribute 'manly courage' to her 'scorn of
unjust opinion' is a clear-eyed contradiction of those values and the force
they had in determining the nature of the 'opinion' ranged against the
bride. It seems to me that Dubrow is wrong to see this passage as a
reinscription of patriarchal values; it is her conviction of Donne's prior
anxiety and the couple's guilt which makes this move necessary, rather
than anything in the text that compels the reading.

In Donne's poem 'opinion' is but briefly invoked, whereas Campion's
Somerset Masque is comprehensive in its address to the political and moral
questions raised by the marriage, and in its confrontation of the issue of
gossip and rumour. The masque divides into two sections, the first set on
the sea coast, the second in London. It opens with four Squires explaining
that twelve Lords who had set out from the four corners of the earth to
honour the marriage had been overcome at sea by the enchantment
of Error. In an extended, but entirely visual series of antimasques the

consequence of the domination of Error is exhibited in disordered dances of winds, elements and continents. The antimasques are dispelled by the appearance of Eternity with the three Destinies carrying a tree of gold, accompanied by Harmony and nine musicians. The Queen is invited to take a branch from the tree in order to release the Knights. As soon as she does so the scene changes to London, and the masquers dance in honour of the marriage. After the revels, in a brief coda, twelve skippers appear from four barges, dance and exit, leaving the Squires to compliment the King and usher in the wedding night.[32]

The whole device is grounded upon the power of false fame to paralyse those who would offer tribute to the couple. The First Squire tells how the Knights set forth, and continues:

> Deformed *Errour*, that enchaunting fiend,
> And wing-tongu'd *Rumor*, his infernall freind,
> With *Curiositie* and *Credulitie*,
> Both Sorceresses, all in hate agree
> Our purpose to divert.
>
> (pp. 269–70)

As the antimasque unfolds, Campion's strategy declares itself. Error is dangerous not only in itself, but because the confusions it breeds can be seen as an analogy of a much wider collapse, as winds, elements and even continents dance, one after the other, 'in a strange kind of confusion'. The juxtaposition of these dances means that analogy becomes cause; the continents are in confusion *because* of Error's machinations. Campion magnifies the danger of false fame in order the more completely to demonise it. It is a typical ideological mystification, since it buries the particular underneath the power of the generalised image, and substitutes juxtaposition for logical sequence.

The *Somerset Masque*, however, is not just a glorious cover-up. What gives Campion's work its most daring quality is that the power of enchantment is destroyed by the Queen. The Tree of Grace and Bounty is set before her, and she is invited to take a branch from it:

> Since Knights by valour rescue Dames distrest,
> Let them be by the Queene of Dames releast:
> So sing the Destinyes, who never erre,
> Fixing this Tree of Grace and Bountie heere,
> From which, for our enchaunted Knights we crave
> A branche, pull'd by your Sacred Hand, to have;

That we may beare it as the Fates direct,
And manifest your glory in th'effect.

(p. 273)

One can only imagine with what gritted teeth Anne performed the
ceremony (or with what bated breaths the audience waited to see what
she would do), but by displacing the praise of the King to the end of
the masque, and putting the Queen centre-stage, Campion forced the
confrontation of present political realities. The argument the masque offers
is ultimately circular: scandal about the marriage threatens the court, but
because the court, in the person of Queen Anne, accepts the marriage,
therefore the scandal is misguided; but Campion lacked nothing in bravery
in moving back from the generalities of the antimasque to this very specific
focus on the precise politics of the moment.

It is certainly possible to argue that, despite its aggressively positive tone,
the masque registers an underlying insecurity on the part of the writer.
The fact that Campion grounds his invention 'upon enchantments' seems
incautious, particularly in view of the presentation of paralysed knights,
some of them encased in golden pillars. This might seem uncomfortably
close to the Earl of Essex's plight, impotent because of witchcraft. It could
be suggested too that Campion's choice of the Virgilian *Fama* as the model
for Error is open to misconstruction. In the *Aeneid* Fame's reports of the
illicitly consummated love of Dido and Aeneas were, after all, true.
Undoubtedly the masque does carry within it some unease. But at the
very least one would have to accept that Campion was not simply shutting
his eyes to the issues, and that, in the state of knowledge in 1613, he
mounts as good a case as could be expected.

Campion's defence was, of course, conducted by and in the presence
of most of the major participants: the couple, the King and Queen, family
(many of whom performed in the masque) and opponents alike (Pembroke
and Montgomery were also among the masquers). Chapman's *Andromeda
Liberata* stands in a different relationship to the scandal that it, like Campion's masque, tries directly to confront. The poem is offered 'To the
Prejudicate and Peremptory Reader', and though the preface is (like the
poem itself) obscure and crabbed, it seems that Chapman is addressing
himself generally to those who have complained of the match. His ideal
reader is one who might, unawares, have let the 'common surfet' of
opinion taint his views, but who will learn from the poem and enlist in
support of the match.

The dedication to the Earl and Countess of Somerset begins roundly:

As nothing under heaven is more remov'd

From Truth & virtue, then *Opinions* prov'd
By vulgar *Voices*: So is nought more true
Nor soundly virtuous then things held by few.

(ll. 1–4)

Chapman encourages his patrons with a self-confirming syllogism:
many say nasty things of you, but the many are always deluded, and
therefore the few who defend you must be right. The élitism of
this passage is very characteristic of Chapman's intellectual position
throughout his writings, and is not perhaps very appealing to modern
taste. But when he addresses Frances herself one can see the positive
possibilities contained within it.

And you, most noble Lady, as in blood
In minde be Noblest, make our factious brood
Whose forked tongs wold fain your honor sting
Convert their venomd points into their spring:
Whose own harts, guilty of faults faind in yours,
Wold fain be posting off.

(ll. 160–5)

Chapman first of all recognises that malicious gossip has its root in the
faction of the court. (In the preface he observes that '*Truth* is never
the fount of *Faction*'.) Secondly, and more interestingly, he observes the
possibility that the scandal is generated out of the guilt in the minds of
opponents. Both of these perceptions are developed and enriched as the
poem progresses.

The story of the poem is, as Chapman said, an allegory of the situation
of the Somersets as he saw it. Andromeda is Frances, prey to the monstrous
whale which symbolises the false rumour occasioned by the envy of the
gods for her beauty. Perseus, her rescuer, is Robert, motivated by love to
defend her and release her from her imprisonment. How much further
one can push the detail of correspondence between story and situation is
by no means clear. So, for example, the chronology of events in the poem
could be taken as significant. Andromeda is victim of defamation and
bound to the rock before Perseus hears of her or comes to her defence.
She actually tries to persuade him not to marry her, for otherwise his
reputation will be dragged down with hers. This might suggest that
Chapman, like others at the time, believed that the attachment between
Robert and Frances followed rather than caused the separation from Essex.
But to read the allegory so literally is perilous. Chapman's complaint when
he was forced to defend the poem against attackers was precisely that a

'malicious reader by straining the Allegorie past his intentionall limits, may make it give blood, where it yeeldes naturally milke, and overcurious wits may discover a sting in a flie' (pp. 329–30). So, for example, one must imagine that Suffolk cannot have considered that comment on his own conduct was intended when Andromeda is represented as being exposed to the monster by the will of her father.

Whatever the significance of narrative detail, the thematic congruence between Chapman's poem and Campion's masque is strong. Like Campion, Chapman magnifies the evil of rumour until it becomes a symptom of a potentially fatal corruption of the whole society. Andromeda is offered as a sacrifice to lift the threat of the monstrous whale from the whole kingdom. The amplification of the danger of scandal is, of course, particularly useful as a strategy in confronting the particular issues of this marriage, but both the poets are able to mount this argument because issues of honour, reputation and defamation did have very wide resonance in their society.

Shakespeare's *Othello*, for example, is founded upon the ramifications of codes of honour for both men and women. One of the bitterest ironies in the play is that it should be the false-speaking Iago, the contriver of defamation, who delivers the lines:

> Good name in man and woman, dear my lord,
> Is the immediate jewel of their souls.
> Who steals my purse steals trash; 'tis something, nothing;
> 'Twas mine, 'tis his, and has been slave to thousands.
> But he that filches from me my good name
> Robs me of that which not enriches him
> And makes me poor indeed.
>
> (III.iii.160–6)

But the most comprehensive examination of the question, and an undoubted influence upon Chapman's poem, is the Sixth Book of Spenser's *The Faerie Queene*. In this book the poet sets out to exemplify the virtue of Courtesy, and the quest of its central figure, Sir Calidore, is to destroy the Blatant Beast. This enemy is the personification of malicious rumour, whose mouth is thus described:

> And therein were a thousand tongs empight,
>   Of sundry kindes, and sundry quality,
>   Some were of dogs, that barked day and night,
>   And some of cats, that wrawling still did cry,
>   And some of Beares, that groynd continually,

And some of Tygres, that did seeme to gren,
And snar at all, that ever passed by:
But most of them were tongues of mortall men,
Which spake reprochfully, not caring where nor when.

And them amongst were mingled here and there,
The tongues of Serpents with three forked stings,
That spat out poyson and gore bloudy gere
At all, that came within his ravenings,
And spake licentious words, and hatefull things
Of good and bad alike, of low and hie.[33]

Spenser insists that:

No wound, which warlike hand of enemy
Inflicts with dint of sword, so sore doth light,
As doth the poysnous sting, which infamy
Infixeth in the name of noble wight:
For by no art, nor any leaches might
It ever can recured be againe.

(VI.vi.1)

Chapman develops Spenser's image by his insistence on the way such scandal is a projection of the minds of the spectators on to those they malign, so that 'this sweete Ladies exposure was / Of all these moodes in men the only glass' (ll. 215–16). He thought of his poem as providing the cure that Spenser feared impossible, claiming that the 'chiefe object' of his poem was 'to revive / By quickning honor, in the absolute best' (ll. 635–6).

Throughout his career Chapman was sensitive to misinterpretation and misconstruction of his work. Like Jonson he was torn between the need to please his readers and contempt for their capacities when they failed to respond as he felt they should. If there is a rather unappealing élitism, even egotism about the stance his poem takes, it means, nonetheless, that Chapman has a real sense of the fragility of meaning and interpretation. This surfaces particularly in the defence of his poem, where he stubbornly claims 'I might reasonablie & conscionablie [be] master of mine own meaning'. There is, then, a revealing similarity between the work he hoped his poem would do in clearing the reputations of Frances and Robert, sullied by the vile imaginings of the vulgar, and the defence he was forced to mount of the work itself. He protests plaintively: 'doth any rule of reason make it good, that let the writer meane what he list, his writing notwithstanding must be construed *in mentem Legentis*? to the intendment of the Reader?' (p. 330). In struggling with questions of truth, meaning and interpretation, Chapman's *Andromeda Liberata* examines the issues that are at the heart of this study. For just as he was aware of the precariousness of textual signification, Chapman was alert to the difficulty of 'reading' human individuals. In *The Tragedie of Chabot, Admirall of France*, a play which it has been plausibly argued is about the Earl of Somerset,[34] a minor figure, Asall, is asked what he thinks of Chabot's worth. He responds:

> As of a Picture wrought to opticke reason,
> That to all passers by, seemes as they move
> Now woman, now a Monster, now a Divell,
> And till you stand, and in a right line view it,
> You cannot well judge what the maine forme is,
> So men that view him but in vulgar passes,
> Casting but laterall, or partiall glances
> At what he is, suppose him weake, unjust,
> Bloody, and monstrous, but stand free and fast,
> And judge him by no more than what you know
> Ingenuously, and by the right laid line
> Of truth, he truely, will all stiles deserve
> Of wise, just, good, a man both soule and nerve.[35]

These observations develop the same concerns Chapman had addressed in *Andromeda Liberata*. Chapman anticipates modern critics in making the anamorphic portrait a symbol of the precariousness of interpretation, but unlike them still wishes to retain the possibility that there is a right way of looking, one position from which the true character of the person may be understood. Readers of *Andromeda Liberata*, he must have felt, simply refused to take up that 'correct' point of view.

If Chapman's work offended Essex and his followers, Jonson's *A Challenge at Tilt* also ran into difficulties. Like the *Barriers* he had written for Frances Howard's first marriage, this work was intended to dramatise the political harmony that was hoped for as a consequence of the marriage. John More, for example, had written optimistically that: 'Here is a general reconcilement made between my ld. of Howard and my lords of Pembroke, Southampton etc. in this conjuncture'.[36] When the combatants took the field the Howard family fought in the colours of the groom, while Pembroke and Montgomery fought in the bride's colours. Thus were the political hopes vividly embodied in the 'cross-dressed' combatants. But the Agent of Savoy reported that 'Many lords have been invited to a certain tilt, but many of them have refused because they are relatives of the Earl of Essex, and others have excused themselves, not being part of this [Howard] faction.'[37] The harmonious surface of the printed text conceals a dissonance that would have been sharply apparent to the original spectators, who were as aware of who was not taking part as of those who were present.

For contemporaries the celebrations of Frances Howard's marriage may have rung hollowly – especially for those who saw a threat to their own political futures in the conjunction. But for others, perhaps including those who wrote poems and masques to honour the match, it was possible to rejoice, and to do so with a clear conscience. Modern critics have perhaps been less than even-handed in their judgements, being rather too ready to side with the opposition, and too eager to assume the worst of Frances Howard herself. Of course, once Overbury's murder was revealed in 1615, the poets must have felt embarrassed to varying degrees. As we will see in the next chapter, however, that revelation is itself rooted in factional politics, and ambiguous to the modern historian.

Chapter 5

The third trial: Murder

In 1614 Frances Howard stood on top of the world. Her marriage had harnessed Robert Carr to the Howards, and her family prospered. In 1615 Roger Wilbraham summed up their position:

> [Suffolk] Lord Treasurer; his son-in-law, the Earl of Somerset, Lord High Chamberlain and the most potent favorite in my time; Lord Knollys, another son-in-law, Treasurer of the Household and by his favor made Master of Wards; the Earl of Salisbury another son-in-law; the Lord Walden, his eldest son, married to the heir of the Earl of Dunbar, another of the chief favorites of King James; all the younger sons married to livings of £1,000 and more; the Chancellor of Exchequer and many other officers placed by his means and his son-in-law Somerset's, that great favorite.[1]

But even as Wilbraham was writing this letter the series of revelations that were to culminate in the trials for the murder of Thomas Overbury was beginning to unfold. A summary account of the events is the necessary prelude to this chapter.

Overbury had been committed to the Tower on 21 April 1613 for his refusal of an ambassadorial post offered to him by the King. It is very likely that he was the victim of a 'set-up' contrived by the earls of Northampton and Suffolk, with Carr's complicity, to ensure that he would be safely out of the way during the annulment proceedings. Overbury knew too much of Carr's dealings with Frances, and, motivated by a deep political hostility to the Howards, he opposed the match with a fervour that could make him dangerous. It cannot have been difficult to secure the King's compliance, for James was no friend of Overbury's, resenting his influence over the favourite. Having secured his imprisonment, it was essential for the Howards to control his communication with the outside world, and they moved quickly to replace Sir William Wade as Lieutenant of the

Tower with someone whom they knew would prove amenable to their designs. Sir Gervase Elwes was installed on 6 May (though he still had to pay £2,000 for the privilege of obtaining the post), and the following day Richard Weston, a former servant of Anne Turner, was recruited as Overbury's keeper, at the instigation of Frances Howard.

While in prison Overbury became ill. He may actually have been sick before his incarceration, since he claimed that he had turned down the embassy because of an illness.[2] It is certain that once in the Tower he decided (perhaps with Carr's encouragement) to take emetics to aggravate his condition in the hope of persuading the King to clemency. He wrote to Carr: 'then will I use this vomitt four dayes after, which will be a new occasion for you to be importunate to send me into the country to save my life'.[3] As the months passed his illness grew worse, despite the attentions of distinguished physicians, including the King's own doctor, Dr Mayerne. He died on 14 September 1613. An inquest was conducted by Robert Bright, one of the coroners of Middlesex (somewhat irregularly, in that a City of London coroner might have been expected to perform this duty, the results of which were never presented at the King's Bench) and Overbury's stinking body, covered in sores and blisters, was huddled quickly into its grave. Chamberlain delivered this epitaph upon him:

> Sir Thomas Overburie died and is buried in the Towre. The manner of his death is not knowne for that there was no body with him not so much as his keper, but the fowlenes of his corps gave suspicion and leaves aspersion that he shold die of the poxe or somwhat worse: he was a very unfortunat man, for nobody almost pities him, and his very frends speake but indifferently of him.[4]

All then went quiet. But during the summer of 1615 rumours of foul play began to circulate openly. Exactly how suspicions were raised is a matter of some conjecture. The trigger may have been the confession of an apothecary's apprentice who had supposedly been hired to administer a fatal clyster (enema) to Overbury. This apprentice, named by a later writer as one William Reeve, had allegedly been spirited abroad, and having fallen ill, repented of his deed and confessed it to William Trumbull, the British Resident in Brussels, who communicated his news to Secretary Winwood. Whether or not Winwood received such a confession, he seems to have been the man responsible for initiating further investigation when he responded to the Earl of Shrewsbury's recommendation of Sir Gervase Elwes by suggesting to the King that there were questions to be answered about Elwes's past conduct. James in turn commanded Elwes to set down all he knew in writing, and on 2 September he complied, saying he was pleased to do so for 'the discharge of my owne conscience, and the clearinge of my owne poore creditt in the worlde'.[5] In this letter Elwes maintained that on one occasion he had encountered Weston carrying Overbury's supper, and was asked by him 'whether he should nowe give him that which he had or no'. On discovering that Weston referred to a small phial of liquid, Elwes claimed that he dissuaded Weston from administering what he suspected to be poison, and so terrified him with God's eternal judgement that he extracted a promise to forestall any subsequent attempts upon the prisoner's life. Elwes affirmed, however, that Weston had subsequently confessed that Overbury was murdered by a clyster administered by an apothecary's servant who had been corrupted by a bribe of £20.

On receipt of this letter the King appointed Lord Chief Justice Coke to investigate further. Weston was the first to be questioned, and though he at first protested his innocence, as examination succeeded examination he implicated in turn the apothecary James Franklin, Anne Turner, the Countess of Somerset and Sir Thomas Monson. The King was sufficiently worried by the evidence to appoint Ellesmere, Lennox and Zouche to serve as Commissioners with Coke in further sounding the depths of the case. Somerset himself was beginning to panic, and on 13 October 1615 left the King (then at his hunting lodge at Royston) to return to London, where he made frantic efforts to search for any letters that might be incriminating. On 17 October the Earl and his wife were confined to their houses, and soon committed to closer imprisonment; Robert to the Tower on 2 November, Frances, because she was pregnant, to be carefully watched at Lord D'Aubigny's house at Blackfriars.

Meanwhile, on 19 October, Richard Weston was brought to trial at the Guildhall. Asked whether he were guilty or not, Weston cried out 'Lord have mercy upon me, Lord have mercy upon me', but refused to plead. This refusal threatened to bring the whole proceedings to a halt. Since Weston was accused as the principal, no action could be taken against any other person suspected of being an accessory before the fact unless and until he had been found guilty. It was immediately suggested that Weston must have been nobbled by the Howards to stand mute, and he was threatened with the usual penalty for such obstinacy, the torture of *peine forte et dure*. This meant exposure naked in a public place, where he would be slowly pressed to death by weights laid upon him, and denied anything but bread and foul water during his ordeal.[6] The threat failed to persuade Weston – but Coke, in an astonishing move, asked Sir Lawrence Hyde nonetheless to outline the prosecution case. Hyde accused Weston of administering poison, concealed in tarts and jellies sent by the Countess to the prisoner. When all the evidence had been presented Weston was returned to the Tower and sundry divines, including Lancelot Andrewes, were sent to urge him to change his mind. Their persuasions were at first in vain, but finally Weston agreed to stand trial, a decision which, according to one manuscript, 'made the sheriffe leape halfe out of his skin with joy, and put him out of breath untill he had blased the newes'.[7] On Monday 23 October the trial went ahead, and the evidence was presented a second time, with the additional testimony of Sir David Wood, who deposed that he had been approached by the Countess to do away with Overbury for a fee of £1,000 before his imprisonment. The jury swiftly adjudged Weston guilty. As was to be customary in these proceedings, his execution was delayed until godly confessors had been able to 'instruct him for his soul's health' (and, it was hoped, elicit further incriminating evidence). At his execution on 25 October a number of gentlemen, including Sir John Lidcote (Overbury's brother-in-law), Sir John Holles and Sir John Wentworth (both supporters of the Earl of Somerset) disrupted proceedings by demanding of Weston as he stood on the gallows whether or not he had really poisoned Overbury. Some of them were to suffer imprisonment for their temerity in so appearing to question the King's justice.

After Weston's execution enquiries continued apace, and on 7 November Anne Turner was brought to trial. During her arraignment 'evidence' was produced of the sorceries of Forman, including models of naked human figures and sundry other exhibits, 'att the verye instant of shewinge whereof, there was a cracke from the scaffold, and suche a feare, tumulte, confusion and crye amonge the spectators, and in the hall everye man fearynge hurt, as yf the divell had bene raysed among them indeed'.[8] Turner protested her innocence, but was condemned, and, like Weston, consigned to the attentions of clerics before her execution. During the course of conferences with Dr Whiting in prison she confessed her guilt, and when finally brought to execution on 14 November, made a notably pious end.

Two days later Sir Gervase Elwes, the ex-Lieutenant of the Tower, was brought to the Guildhall. Of all the accused Elwes was the most highly educated and articulate, and he vigorously defended himself, claiming that he had, as far as he knew, deterred Weston from continuing with the plot, and protesting that no guardian could make provision against a suborned apothecary. One observer suggested that he 'spake so well for himself that for two hours no man thought he should have been found guilty'.[9] But Coke had a trick up his sleeve. At the very end of Elwes's defence he suddenly produced a new piece of evidence. He claimed that Franklin (the apothecary held responsible for providing the poisons) had, in an agony of conscience, voluntarily offered that very morning a new confession. Franklin said that he had been asked to read aloud to the Countess a letter from Elwes because she could not decipher the Lieutenant's handwriting herself. In this letter Elwes had written of Overbury that 'the more he is cursed, the better he fareth', which, to Coke's ears anyway, implied his complicity with a murder plot. At this Elwes was silenced, and a guilty verdict followed as a formality. Coke adjured the prisoner: 'spend your short time of life faithfully and fruitefully, and discover all the rest of this plott. You have wounded this common wealthe by concealment. You shall repaire it againe by discovery'.[10] In the event very little that was material to Coke's purpose was elicited. At his execution on 20 November Elwes made a notably full 'scaffold speech', but one which still fell far short of naming the Earl of Somerset or his wife.[11]

If Franklin had hoped that his confession might help him avoid prosecution he was to be disappointed. On 27 November he was in turn brought to trial at Westminster. After his inevitable conviction he manifested a conspicuously 'pressable' conscience, and confessed anything and everything to Dr Whiting. Especially important was the way he seems to have found 'the soft place in Coke's head', as James Spedding put it,[12] in suggesting that the poisoning of Overbury was but an outcrop of a dreadful conspiracy to undermine the realm. He came to execution on 9 December, when, according to one observer, he behaved 'in so strange fashion . . . that all men thought him either madd or drunke'.[13]

On 4 December, between Franklin's trial and execution, Sir Thomas Monson had been arraigned. Though Monson had been involved with the placing of Elwes in the Tower, not even Coke's ingenuity and determination could produce a convincing case against him of any further involvement. The King himself recognised the flimsiness of the evidence and ordered that the trial should not proceed. Coke managed nonetheless to use the occasion both to vent abuse of Monson for his Catholicism, and very injudiciously to hint that Prince Henry had been poisoned. Monson was returned to the Tower without trial and released the following year.

After these hectic two months there was a hiatus. Frances had been delivered of a daughter on 9 December, but proceedings against her and her husband were considerably delayed. They were indicted in January 1616, and Frances confessed to her guilt on 12 January, though insisting that her husband was not implicated. Robert stubbornly refused to bow to the King's will, despite the inducement of a possible pardon if he proved tractable. The main reason for the delay was the poverty of real evidence against Carr, and the consequent need to pursue all possibilities, including suspicions of complicity in taking bribes from Spain. In the event evidence of such action was not forthcoming, and in May 1616 the long-awaited trials finally went ahead. The prosecution was entrusted to Francis Bacon, an altogether subtler performer than the bullying Coke. Frances's trial on the 24 May, however, left little room for Bacon to demonstrate his skills. Her plea of guilty meant he only had to summarise the course of events as established in previous trials. No witnesses were summoned nor were any readings of examinations and confessions necessary. After the Attorney General's speech Frances was asked:

> what canst thou now say for thyself, why Judgment of Death should not be pronounced against thee?

To which she replied:

> I can much aggravate, but nothing extenuate my fault: I desire mercy, and that the lords will intercede for me to the king. (This she spake humbly, fearfully, and so low, the Lord Steward could not hear it, but Mr Attorney related it.)
> *Mr Att.* The lady is so touched with remorse and sense of her fault, that grief surprises her from expressing of herself; but that which she hath confusedly said, is to this effect, That she cannot excuse herself, but desires mercy. (*ST*, 957)

In this account the Lord High Steward, Ellesmere, signifies that the Lords will mediate with the king, in view of her humility and grief. In another report Frances was 'weeping bitterly' as she spoke, and

> the Lord Steward, commending the Kings wisdome and justice accompanied with mercy and princely care that noe suggestion could take hold of him against his nobilitie or other ... he with compassion pronounced the formall sentence given in cases of felony.[14]

The following day Robert Carr made an altogether more defiant appearance before his judges. Maintaining his innocence throughout the long day's hearing, he was nonetheless convicted and sentenced to death. In the event neither the Earl nor Countess were brought to execution. They were imprisoned in the Tower until, in 1622, they were released to live a retired life. Frances was pardoned within two months, whereas Robert had to wait for his formal pardon until a few months before the King's death in 1625.

This series of events marks the climax of the story of Frances Howard. The dominant picture of Frances Howard's character and conduct that has survived to the present day is largely constructed from the information provided during the sequence of trials. But, of course, these nuggets of information do not come down to us stamped with a guarantee of authenticity; they were narrated for a purpose, the purpose of securing a conviction, and they are mediated through the minds and pens of lawyers and reporters. As an essential first step the nature of this varied evidence must be considered. It may be helpful to separate the testimony into what might be termed its archaeological layers.

The bottom layer, and that which might be assumed to be nearest the 'facts', is made up of the pre-trial examinations of accused and witnesses. By no means all of the 300 or so interrogations Coke claimed to have conducted survive. Some of those that are missing are amongst the most important, including examinations of Weston, Turner and Franklin that were alluded to at their trials but now are lost. Perhaps most significant of all the absences from the point of view of this study is any written record of the confession that Frances Howard herself made to Lord Fenton and the Earl of Montgomery. The problem, however, is not just the incompleteness of this layer of evidence. Barely any of the depositions that do remain are verbatim records of interviews. One or two are written by the deponents themselves, but most of them are in the hand of their inquisitor, Lord Chief Justice Coke. In recent years the accuracy of police records of interrogation has come under ever-increasing suspicion, with first tape-recording and now video film being required to guarantee that evidence has not been tampered with, or suspects browbeaten. How much trust, then, can be placed in these testimonies, which were collected and often transcribed by the same man who was to act as chief prosecutor in the subsequent trials? We cannot know what threats or promises Coke made to elicit these statements, though the relentless bullying which characterised his court-room manner suggests that he was unlikely to have been the gentlest of inquisitors. Coke's own sensitivity on the matter is revealed when he reports to the King that in Weston's second trial:

> all the confessions and testimonies were redd dystinctly and plainely, and he openly and frely acknowledged all his confessions to be subscribed by his marke and that they were all true and were taken with mildenes and gentle meanes without any threateninge or hard woord.[15]

Of Coke's industry in compiling information there can be little doubt. He pursued every lead with relentless enthusiasm, and in the absence of any investigative police force he was necessarily reliant upon hints and suggestions, whatever their source. The anonymous note which implicated Mrs Thornborough (see p. 49), or the pointing finger of less than disinterested participants, such as the displaced Lieutenant, Sir William Wade, or the Earl of Essex, led to an ever-widening circle of interrogation.[16] It was not only the solicitation of information from dubious sources that rendered some of the testimony suspect. Somewhat surprisingly to modern eyes, prosecutions were begun long before the cases against all those alleged to be involved were complete. Gervase Elwes was not removed officially from his post at the Tower until after Weston's trial, and the Earl and Countess were not examined until very late in the year. As one trial succeeded another, therefore, Coke attempted to squeeze further evidence for the trials still to come by 'pressing the consciences' of each of the convicted criminals as they awaited execution. It was reported of Weston, for example, 'that he knewe nothing further, but if hee could remember any thinge before his deathe, hee would reveale it, and if hee could call to mynde any thinge that might breede probable suspicion, hee would signifie it'.[17] More chillingly, Anne Turner, in conference with Dr Whiting her confessor, was asked whether Sir Thomas Monson's 'hand was not in this business' to which she replied 'if you will have me say so I will'.[18] Particularly cynical was the treatment of Franklin. This apothecary was not only the most loathsome of those accused (Anne Turner pleaded that she should not be executed on the same day as him, for 'he is so foule'),[19] he was also a transparently compulsive liar, willing to respond to inquisition with the answers he felt his examiners demanded. Coke himself recognised that Franklin was 'a man *sub acto ingenio et summa nequitia*, and for these wayes of wickedness knoweth verie much', but he delayed his execution because he 'beginneth to make a greate discovery against others'.[20] Three days earlier Coke had written to the King that Franklin 'was not proceaded withall untill he had discovered sufficient matter against the Earle of Somerset'.[21] Carr, in Coke's eyes, is already guilty, and Franklin is pressured to declare, or invent, anything that will serve to ensure the Earl's conviction. If the record of pre-trial examinations is suspect, how much less reliable must the testimony seem that was extracted under the shadow of impending execution.

The evidence generated by interrogations is, then, mediated through Coke's urgent desire to secure conviction, and transmitted to us mainly in his script. Matters are further complicated as we move to the next 'layer' of witness, the accounts of the trials themselves. Andrew Amos long ago drew attention to the fact that comparison of the surviving interrogations with the reports of their use in the actual trials suggests that the prosecution regularly read out only parts of the confessions to the jury, suppressing information that might seem to cast doubt upon the guilt of the accused. He fulminates:

This process of garbling evidence was, in effect, equivalent to manu-facturing it: so that prisoners were not convicted upon the testimony of witnesses, but such testimony served only in the nature of a raw material for the ingenuity of the prosecuting counsel to fashion and varnish as they pleased.[22]

That such practices were commonplace cannot be doubted, but they are extremely difficult to demonstrate by comparing the trial records with the depositions, since the accounts of the trials are by no means unanimous in their testimony. The editors of the *State Trials* may have selected the most frequently encountered manuscript versions as the basis of their publication, but they did not always choose the most substantial accounts, nor necessarily those which might seem closest to the event.

How these various accounts were produced is by no means clear. There were shorthand writers in the early seventeenth century, as Webster's *The Devil's Law Case* indicates. As a trial is about to begin, the following dialogue takes place:

> *Sanitonella*   Do you hear, officers?
>   You must take special care that you let in
>   No brachygraphy men to take notes.
> *First Officer*   No Sir?
> *Sanitonella*   By no means;
>   We cannot have a cause of any fame
>   But you must have scurvy pamphlets and lewd ballets
>   Engendered of it presently.[23]

But a note at the end of one manuscript account of Weston's trial suggests a commoner proceeding. The writer says 'These are such notes as I could take while I stood thir in the Courte & my servant then writ out in hast without tyme to con[fer?] then with any other. Yet have I adventured to lett you see them as they are'.[24] The account collected by William Davenport in Cheshire of Weston's trial is subscribed by one James Brerebry: 'I was one of Westons jurie at his trial which causeth mee to write more particularlye then otherwyse I could have done'.[25] Stuart audiences were habituated by their education to listening to sermons on Sunday, taking notes, and then presenting a resumé in class the following day. The records we now have represent various stages along the road from notes taken at the trials to fully written-up accounts, supplemented by memory and produced after consultation with others. The variability of these accounts sets a problem for the historian seeking to recover the 'facts' of the hearings. But none-theless it was from such reports that contemporaries derived their understanding of the proceedings. Manuscripts turn up in repositories all over the country, in the great houses of courtiers as well as amongst the muniments of country gentlemen.[26] Their function was much more like that of a newspaper than that of a modern trial transcription and it is in that light that they must be read.[27]

It was not only the narrators of the trials who imposed a particular view upon the events they recorded. These reporters were already under the sway of the lawyers, who throughout the sequence of hearings were attempting to construct a narrative that would convince the jurors and the world beyond the court-room of the guilt of the accused, and, especially, of the complicity of the Earl and Countess of Somerset. This, then, constitutes the third layer through which the story of Frances Howard is filtered. In generating their account of events the prosecution had a formidable ally in the legal system itself. We are nowadays accustomed to the idea that a trial is a place where narratives offered in turn by prosecution and defence lawyers compete with one another, each seeking to persuade jurors of their plausibility. In the seventeenth century there was no such contest. Defendants were not represented by lawyers in court; they could not produce their own witnesses nor could they cross-examine those for the prosecution. Silent during the greater part of the hearing, the accused were almost always denied pen and ink to take notes of the charges and evidence produced against them in order to prepare the one speech they were permitted. (An exception was made for Robert Carr, but such help was forbidden to Gervase Elwes.)[28] Elwes himself eloquently summed up the difficulties that he faced as he began his speech in his defence:

> Your Lordship observed from your own Experience, how tender a thing happens sometimes in the course of an Evidence against a prisoner at the Barr. He is to answer on the sudden to Multitudes of particulars laid to his charge, having no knowledge before he come there, what will be said against him; nor may have any Councell against the King to defend him; nor is admitted to write anything for his Memory; nor may answer to the pointes as they are objected untill all are inforcit and burdend upon him: Beside the Distraction of his Mind by the sense of his Distress and Grief for his Wife and Children to be left desolate and cast upon the world, which may bereave him of himself and utterly disable him to answer for himself. Your Lordship said, that such a Man being innocent might be condemned.[29]

The words are a powerful and moving articulation of the utter vulnerability of the accused in a seventeenth-century English trial.[30] They also serve as a reminder that the narrative which the trials make available to subsequent historians is one dictated almost entirely by the prosecution lawyers.

Lawyers impose a view of events upon their audience; and this holds as true for modern practitioners as for Coke and his associates. As Anne Worrall suggests, in court:

> a privileged discourse is constructed from the broken utterances of the powerless; discontinuity is rendered continuous, contradiction rendered coherent, and fragmentation rendered unified. A grid is placed over the circumstances and emotions of the defendant and a recognizable reading obtained.[31]

A major constituent in the construction of this 'reading' is the creation and manipulation of the characters who people the plot the lawyers want to tell. Bennett and Feldman suggest that in the modern court-room:

> jurors are bombarded with invitations to stereotype defendants, victims, and witnesses. These incitations are, in effect, pressures for jurors to make connections that are, perhaps, satisfying, familiar, or pleasing – connections that may be stronger than the facts, norms, or logic of the matter would suggest.[32]

Things were no different in the seventeenth century. One example of such stereotyping is the fluctuating representation of Overbury's character. At the trial of Richard Weston, Mr Warr spoke of the dead man, 'much commending his singular honest and virtuous conversation; affirming, That he was addicted to no dishonest actions' (ST, 919). Having served its purpose as instigator of pity in the jury in the early trials, this characterisation was unceremoniously dumped by Bacon when he came to prosecute Robert Carr. He then described Overbury as 'of an insolent thrasonical disposition', and said he 'had little that was solid for religion or moral virtue, but was a man possessed with ambition and vain-glory', and concluded that 'howsoever the tragical misery of that poor gentleman ought somewhat to obliterate his faults … Overbury was naught and corrupt, the ballads must be amended for that point'.[33] To create a convincing story for the peers who were Robert Carr's judges Bacon required a different story from that which would satisfy the citizens of London who were the jurors at the earlier trials. The sentimental characterisation could scarcely be sustained before those who would have known Overbury well, and many of whom would have been alienated by him.[34]

But if the characters are turned into stereotypes, and if a 'grid' is imposed upon their story, from whence did the lawyers derive their models of what constituted a persuasive narrative? This question brings us to the topmost 'layer' of the archaeology of the narrative of the trials. Lawyers, even now, will readily admit that in their persuasive arts they draw upon literary techniques that have a continuous history from classical times onwards;[35] but if one suggests that they come to their brief with prior assumptions about what makes a convincing story, or with an eye on the fable they might be able to construct in court, they become as cross as a rudely propositioned maiden aunt. Like historians rushing back to the safety of 'the archive' they claim that they are entirely governed by the 'facts' at their disposal. Their separation of the 'ornament' of persuasive language from the 'true' facts which are elaborated upon is impossible to sustain, in the seventeenth century or at the present day. It is at this point that the analogy of archaeological layers breaks down – for this topmost 'layer' must, logically, already have shaped Coke's approach to the exam-inations which constituted the first level. There is a circular negotiation between event and cultural assumptions as they are encoded in surviving texts which makes it difficult or even impossible to break through and to declare with certainty that the murder was or was not done. The uncer-tainty is one common to the juror in a modern court-room and the historian alike – though both must, of necessity, come to some sort of hypothesis about the 'truth' that lies behind the narratives upon which they adjudicate.

In turning to the trials themselves, the first requirement is to place them in their political context, since there are strong arguments for saying that the hearings were precipitated primarily by political or factional considerations. Just as Frances's first marriage was politically motivated and her second was politically captured, so it is possible to argue that, whether she committed murder or not, she came to court because the confluence of events made the accusation convenient, and practically possible to pursue. Even the fact of her trial for murder is the consequence of male political rivalry.

Her husband's power and influence derived entirely from the affection in which the King held him. In late 1614 the opponents of Robert Carr took the risky step of introducing George Villiers to the court as a competitor for the King's attention. Throughout the early part of 1615 rumour and speculation about the waxing and waning of favourites was rife. Robert Carr failed dismally to handle the situation with any grace, tact, or even instinct for survival. Far from making the compromises that would have seen him retain influence, if not his central place in the King's affections, he stormed and ranted at the arrival of Villiers, and uttered vague threats against the King. James wrote him long letters in the early part of 1615, warning him to moderate his behaviour or risk losing favour,[36] but he took no notice; and it was at this strategic moment that

Winwood, Abbot and Pembroke, the same men who had insinuated Villiers into the court, suggested that the Overbury affair merited further investigation. Their political motivation was obvious to foreign observers. Francesco Quaratesi, secretary at the Tuscan embassy, reported:

> The faction opposed to the Lord Treasurer and Lord Chamberlain [Suffolk and Somerset] (who are presently the Archbishop of Canterbury, Secretary Winwood, the Earl of Arundel, the Earl of Pembroke, mylord Fenton Montgomery [sic] the new favourite of the King George de Villiers and some others, have now brought again to light this thing done long ago, and have had a witness questioned, who testified how the above-mentioned Overbury died because of the poison given to him in some medication, and this on behalf of the Earl of Suffolk and of the Countess his wife.[37]

As the trials proceeded so the glee of Somerset's political opponents became ever more conspicuous. Sir John Holles, a client of Somerset, had in July 1615 protested his constancy:

> My Lord of Summersetts respects to me made me his servant at the time of the day when every one rejoyced in his sunshine, and shall I with the butterflies be blown away with the puff of this westerly wind?

By November, writing from the prison where he had been placed because of his questioning of Weston at his execution, he bitterly observes of Lord Chief Justice Coke:

> his heaven is heer, and he is wonderfully fattned with the success, and glory of his employment. Pembrok expects to be chamberlain, and Villars a baron, and Master of the hors, what other chipps be gathered from the fall of this great oake, I know not, every bird of them will carry sum straw, or other to his nest, or els have they laboured in vayn.[38]

How right he was can be gauged by the comments of Sir John Throckmorton, observing events from Flushing. He wrote to Viscount de L'Isle on 8 November – before Carr had even been indicted – saying 'I trust that this great mans fall will rayse your Lordship and some of your nobell freinds to your just and worthy demerites'. Two days later he was making his own pitch, when he observed 'Undoubtedly their will be by this mans fall manye good things in his Majesty's guifte again. I beseach your Lordship, take this occation of my service at this time to move for sumthing for me unto his Majesty'.[39] That many suspected factional motivations for the trials is evidenced by Coke's speech before he pronounced Weston's death sentence, in which he found it necessary to protest that 'there is no practice or conspiracy in prosecuting of the business' (*ST*, 929). But, as S. R. Gardiner trenchantly observed: 'In those days a criminal prosecution was the readiest way of waging political warfare'.[40]

A great deal was at stake in these trials. Once James realised how closely they threatened Somerset and his wife he protested his earnest desire to have the matter sounded to the bottom. Gondomar reported:

> The King and the Earl of Somerset, either because they considered this a thing which it was impossible to prove, and which would be more likely to leave Somerset with credit and victory, and which would also bring credit to the King as being just in desiring the investigation (or for some other reason), took the resolution that he [Elwes] should be brought to justice; and so the King made in the Council a great protestation before God of his desire to see justice done, and that neither his favourite, nor his son himself, nor anything else in the world, should hinder him; and with the good pleasure of the Earl of Somerset, he named for the investigation my Lord Coke, Chief Justice of England, who was the creature and intimate friend of Somerset, but a man of high spirit, eloquent, and desirous of credit with the people; and this, together with the pressure of Somerset's enemies, made him, in no more than three days, turn round, and become excited and bloodthirsty in the investigation, withdrawing himself from Somerset and his friends, and ceasing to give them information of what he was doing.[41]

Whatever the King's private thoughts, once the process was under way it was absolutely necessary to the favourite's enemies that nothing should prevent them reaching their true goal, the destruction of the Earl. All the early trials, and even the conviction of Frances Howard herself, were but stepping stones on the path to the achievement of this aim.

It was for this reason, if for no other, that Weston's standing mute at his first trial provoked Coke into the legally discreditable tactic of outlining the case against him, though he had made no plea. The Lord Chief Justice, in setting out the charge to the Grand Jury, had already exhorted them 'to do justice in presenting the truth, notwithstanding the greatness of any that upon their evidence should appear to be guilty of the same offence' (*ST*, 912). In one manuscript account he responded to Weston's refusal to plead with the words:

> This is but a Machivilian tricke to save certaine accessories by whome it seemeth yow have binne dealt with this to doe ... but itt saves not them: your great lord and your lady are nowe committed in safe custody

as yow are: is there anie doubt but that if ever there bee a Parliament, they wilbee proceeded against according unto Justice.[42]

When Sir Lawrence Hyde opened the case, he immediately 'charged the countess of Somerset and the earl to be principal movers unto this unhappy conclusion' (*ST*, 915). At the end of this non-trial Coke produced 'two sheets of paper' wherein the King had ordered him to administer impartial justice, and celebrated the fact that notwithstanding 'the many favours and honours which his majesty had bestowed on the lord Somerset, and his nearness to his person, by reason of his office, yet he had committed him prisoner . . . and also had committed his lady' (*ST*, 922).

Coke himself was aware that he might have overstepped the mark, both in proceeding with the evidence and in making the King's instructions public, as an anxious letter sent that night to the King demonstrates. But he pointed out in extenuation 'with what great applause your Majesties princely zeale of Justice herein was of all the hearers accepted'.[43] Coke knew very well what he was at, and if part of his aim was to begin to weave the net which would entrap the Somersets, he was also trying to ensure that the King himself could not back out of his commitment to pursue the case to the end. The double success of his strategy may be judged by the response of one witness of the trial. He first bluntly affirmed: 'altho he [Weston] remained mute he was condemned as guilty in the judgement of all the hearers *& the acessories also*' [my italics] and went on to give an account of Coke's praise of the King's justice:

> with teares in his eyes partly for joy of it and partlie (as it seamed) for feare of his majesties daunger if such damnable practise wer not pre-vented. He concluded with a prayer for his Majesties preservation, every mans hart in that great assembly answering his therein; and such was the generall rejoycing for that dayes proceiding as all did magnifye his Majestie and many wer hard say that it was one of the happiest dayes that they had seene.[44]

As the trials proceeded, so the guilt of the Earl and Countess of Somerset was remorselessly insisted upon, even though at this stage they had been neither examined nor charged. Just as in her marriages Frances Howard had been the 'glue' to bind factions together, so the demonstration of her guilt supplied the lever for political opponents to bring down her husband.

The arraignments of the Countess and Earl of Somerset provoked unparalleled public interest. Sir Charles Mountagu wrote: 'Here is now such a hurrying to Westminster Hall to see the great lady arraigned as it distracts everybody's mind from anything else'.[45] There had never, he said, been 'such preparation in Westminster Hall for scaffolds as there is for this business'. Chamberlain also commented on the preparations for the trial, initially planned for 18 May 1616, but then deferred. He reported that a lawyer had paid ten pounds for places for himself and his wife for the two days, and 'fiftie pound was geven for a corner that could hardly containe a dousen'.[46] When the trials did finally begin there were 'more Ladies and other great personages then ever I thincke were seene at any triall',[47] and they included Frances's first husband, the Earl of Essex.

They were gathering for a spectacle, and as Chamberlain describes the preparation of 'the stage in the midds of Westminster Hall, with numbers of scaffolds round about', the theatrical dimension of the event becomes apparent. Francis Bacon also saw the trials as a species of theatre, when he wrote:

> For his Majesty's virtue of justice, in him so well attended, God hath of late raised an occasion, and erected it as it were a stage or theatre, much to his honour, for him to show it and act it, in the pursuit of the violent and untimely death of Sir Thomas Overbury, and therein cleansing the land from blood.[48]

This sense of trials staging the theatre of God's and the King's justice was commonplace, but at the same time it has considerable force in the context of this investigation. It suggests powerfully the interrelationship of theatrical and judicial narratives, in that the goal Bacon envisages of 'cleansing the land from blood' is exactly that end to which so many Renaissance tragedies tend, when in their grisly conclusions a medicinal 'bleeding' restores the kingdom to health. It indicates also the way in which the participants in the trials (and in executions which followed) felt themselves to be engaged in a public performance, with all that entailed.

The expectations that the crowds brought with them as they assembled for the trials were similarly conditioned by a sense of theatrical anticipation. They came because the accused were of the highest rank, and presented the standard cautionary spectacle of medieval and Renaissance tragedy, the fall of a person of high place. In the case of Carr the story was even more piquantly one of rise and fall. His career was summarised in an epigram:

> When Carre in Court at first a Page began,
> Hee sweld, and sweld into a gentleman
> And from a gentleman and bravely dight
> Hee sweld, and sweld till he became a Knight

At last forgetting what he was at first
Hee sweld into an Earle and then he burst.[49]

This anonymous verse emphasises that the animosity directed at Carr was
not simply motivated by his power, but by the fact that he owed that
power entirely to the King's personal favour. Whilst it was accepted that
kings might have favourites, the opposition of the Essexians to Carr
derived in no small measure from the contest between the old nobility,
claiming power by right of birth, and the upstart and alien favourite. Sir
John Throckmorton, when first he heard of the proceedings, wrote: 'I
beseach you that I maye be favoured to heare of this beusynes from you:
for I long to see the prosperity of our Aentient Nobillity, your Lordships
most nobell freinds, which will never be as longe as the uthers stand in
their strenth'.[50] It is a topic which Marlowe's *Edward II* had dramatised a
quarter of a century earlier. The play is structured upon the struggle
between the claims of the hereditary nobility to exercise power as of right
and the influence of the favourite Gaveston over the homosexual king.[51]
In a dialogue between the Mortimers, father and son, the Elder Mortimer
points out:

The mightiest kings have had their minions;
Great Alexander lov'd Hephaestion,
The conquering Hercules for Hylas wept,
And for Patroclus stern Achilles droop'd.

His son retorts:

   this I scorn, that one so basely born
Should by his sovereign's favour grow so pert,
And riot it with the treasure of the realm.[52]

In another widely circulated epigram the class-based bitterness at Carr's
rise emerges equally clearly:

Poore pylot thou art like to loose thy pinke
And by the lack downe to the bottome sincke
Thy landes are gone, alas they weare not thyne
Thy house like wyse another saies is myne
Now wher's thy witt? alas its two yeares dead
And whear's thy wife? another did her wedd
Art thou a man, or but some simple part?
Nothing thyne owne but thy aspiring hart;
Rawley thy howse, and Westmorland thy landes
Overbury thy witt, Essex thy wife demaundes.

> Like Esops Jay each Bird will have a feather
> And leave thee naked oppos'd to the weather.
> But yet thy frendes to keepe thee from the cold
> Have mued thee upp in Londons strongest hold.[53]

The vindictive delight evinced in this epigram at the stripping of Carr's power and possessions must have been echoed in the response of many of those who turned up with such anticipation to the trials.

On a more general level the trials confirmed in the minds of auditors what they already believed of the court, that it was an immoral and villainous place. This posed something of a problem for the prosecutors, in that the mud could so easily stick to the King himself. When Coke and Bacon lauded James's desire for justice during all of the hearings they were engaged in side-stepping that dangerous threat. The desperate need to put a positive gloss on events is manifested also by Ben Jonson's choice of topic for the masque for the Christmas season 1615/16.

The Golden Age Restored dramatises the return to Britain of Astraea, the goddess of Justice.[54] Performed between the first set of trials and the arraignment of the Somersets, the work had obvious topicality. In the opening speech Pallas praises James, in the figure of Jove, who

> can endure no longer
> Your great ones should your less invade,
> Or that your weak, though bad, be made
> A prey unto the stronger:
>
> And therefore means to settle
> Astraea in her seat again.
>
> (ll. 7–12)

And towards the end of the masque, Astraea herself eulogises the court:

> What change is here! I had not more
> Desire to leave the earth before
> Than I have now to stay;
>
> . . .
>
> Of all there seems a second birth;
> It is become a heav'n on earth,
> And Jove is present here.
> (ll. 207–9; 213–15)

Jonson articulates the message James wanted to hear and to convey. The masque celebrates his impartial prosecution even of those closest to him and makes it serve as testimony to his reforming zeal and dedication to an ideal of justice. At the same time there is a specific subtext to Jonson's work. By the time this masque was performed, William, Earl of Pembroke was installed in Carr's place as Lord Chamberlain, and Jonson's narrative of an old gang of Iron Age conspirators being driven out by the returning masquers of the Golden Age had an immediate application to the change-over of political power (a shift that Jonson himself was no doubt glad to see). It is likely that Buckingham danced as one of the masquers; more surprising, and more significant is Quaratesi's suggestion that: 'in a few days there will be a beautiful ballet, whose 'head' (*capo*) is the Earl of Essex who is continuously seen at Court now, after having been constantly absent after the now Countess of Somerset repudiated him'.[55] The court audience in January 1616 can have been in little doubt as to the message they were being offered: the Essexians were back, taking their rightful place in the political hierarchy. In choosing to dramatise the myth of Astraea, Jonson selected one of the stories most often associated with the iconology of Queen Elizabeth, thus giving particular potency to the suggestion that the expulsion of Carr made possible a return to an earlier and better state.

If the high political significance of the trials was one reason for the great scandal they caused, the details of the charges also ensured their fascination. The heady mixture of poison and witchcraft with adulterous sex would make every tabloid newspaper editor's heart leap even today; but the response of the modern newspaper reader would have a significantly different foundation from that of the seventeenth-century auditor of the trials. The specific ways in which the cultural associations of poisoning and of adultery assisted in securing the conviction of the accused need to be considered carefully.

When Coke began the charge to the Grand Jury he aggravated 'the manner and quality of the murdering, in shewing the baseness of poisoning above all other kinds of murder' (*ST,* 911). Bacon, in the final trial of the series, returned to the subject:

> For impoisonment, I am sorry it should be heard of in our kingdom; it is not 'nostri generis, nec sanguinis peccatum;' it is an Italian comfit for the court of Rome. (*ST,* 970–1)

He went on to give three reasons for the especial heinousness of poisoning. First that 'it takes a man away in full peace', second that 'it is easily committed, and easily concealed; and on the other side, hardly prevented, and hardly discovered', and thirdly he argued that because of its randomness no man could be safe.

The prosecutors were well-advised to expatiate on the matter, for murder by poison raised a number of related, and deep-seated fears. Thomas Tuke published in 1616 his *A Treatise Against Painting and Tincturing of Women. Wherein the abominable sinnes of Murther and Poysoning, Pride and Ambition, Adultery and Witchcraft are set foorth and discovered*. It seems as if the author had begun to write an indictment of cosmetics, and then suddenly to have taken the opportunity offered by the Overbury affair to broaden his attack. He inveighs against poisoning in terms very similar to Bacon's:

> these Italian devises by poisoning are most vile and divelish, and they say, *An Englishman Italianated is a divell incarnated*. If these arts should come in once amongst us, who shal be secure? Here can a man see who hurts him, & how shal a man prevent the blow, if he see not the armes that strikes him. Yea here a man shal be made away under the pretence of friendship. (p. 50)

Samuel Rowlands makes similar points in the verse which accompanies 'The Poysoned Knights Complaint' (Plate 12). The secret operation of poison, in an age without much forensic medical skill, was no doubt a legitimate cause of fear. But if poison was difficult to detect, it was therefore all too easy to suspect. Prince Henry, Queen Anne and James himself were all thought by some to have met their deaths in this way. In the Overbury trials it was blithely asserted that because poisoning was difficult to prove, the prosecution lawyers were not called upon to demonstrate either that the dates they gave for Weston's attempts were accurate, or that he actually employed the poisons they laid to his charge (*ST*, 924). The gesture towards the covert menace of poison was enough to excuse the abandonment of any satisfactory criterion of evidence or proof. Bacon simply asserted: 'For the matter of proofs, you may consider that impoisonment, of all offences, is most secret, even so secret, that if in all cases of impoisonment you should require testimony, you should as good proclaim impunity' (*ST*, 971–2).

Other cultural resonances of poisoning assisted the prosecution further. Tuke's invocation of the Italianate nature of poisoning rested upon a view of 'foreigners' that is amply reduplicated in the drama of the period. In Middleton/Tourneur's *The Revenger's Tragedy*, Webster's *The White Devil* and *The Duchess of Malfi*, to name but three examples, poisoned skulls, pictures and books terrify and thrill the audience. But there is another dimension that has some significance for these trials. Coke, as part of the character assassination which was one of his standard procedures, accused both Anne Turner and Sir Thomas Monson of Catholicism. At Elwes's trial, according to one account, he claimed that the poisoning 'was a Popish roote, that greatnes should shelter this and obscure it', and went on to suggest that 'the nameing of poyson "letters" is a tricke of popish equivocation'.[56] Frances Howard herself was suspected of Catholic leanings. Robert Cecil in 1610 had written to his son, telling him that his wife and Frances, her sister, had taken communion at Hatfield that Easter 'which has stopped the mouthes of many malicious persons that speak their pleasure of their long forbearance'.[57]

The chain of association which linked poison to Italy and thence to Catholicism may well have affected the readiness of jurors and audience to accept the guilt of the accused. (It is significant in this respect that Robert Niccols claimed that Forman's house was a place 'where disloyalty did oft conceale / Romes frighted rattes, that over seas did steale'.)[58] Such paranoid fears even more obviously lay behind the suspicions of a global conspiracy that remarks during the trials helped to fuel. In one account of Elwes's trial Hyde is reported as saying:

> But the wickedness of poisoning, had it not been prevented in time although it began in Overbury, would have not ceased with his destruction; but that his Majesties person, the Queen, and the whole State should have felt thereof. It being devised in the Court God knows what it might have wrought in the Court.[59]

In Davenport's commonplace-book is a report of 'newse sent Sir Richard Aston in Januarie 1616', which suggests that:

> A child of Mrs Turners sister . . . as soone as it was borne should have bene brought to the countess of Somersett (who was said to be with child) and left with her whereuppon it should have bene geven out that the Countesse of Somersett was brought to bedd, and the Kinge, Queene, and Prince with as manie of the religiouse noblemen Knights and gentlemen of worth as could conveniently get together should have bene invyted to a great banquett and there they should have bene all poisoned.[60]

The letter goes on to claim that the 'nobles and papists of England' would then have raised arms, brought in the Spaniards and 'beaten downe the cittie'. That such nonsense could be given any credence is eloquent proof of the paranoia that accusations of poison could unleash, paranoia that Coke and Hyde were happy to feed.

A more restrained, but perhaps no less potent and significant remark

was made by Mr Warr, when he 'lamented the place from whence the
poison came, should be from the court, the place (said he) from whence
all men expect their safeties and protection' (*ST*, 928). At the beginning
of Webster's *The Duchess of Malfi* Antonio tells of his experience at the
French court:

> In seeking to reduce both state and people
> To a fix'd order, their judicious king
> Begins at home: quits first his royal palace
> Of flatt'ring sycophants, of dissolute
> And infamous persons – which he sweetly terms
> His Master's masterpiece, the work of heaven –
> Consid'ring duly, that a prince's court
> Is like a common fountain, whence should flow
> Pure silver drops in general: but if't chance
> Some curs'd example poison't near the head,
> *Death, and diseases through the whole land spread.*[61]

The simile which characterises the progress of corruption as a poison is
precisely that which lies behind Warr's comments, and it is the ease with
which the actual poisoning of Overbury could be hooked into common
perceptions of the court and of papist terrorism that helps to account for
the scandal the case caused, and the fears it aroused.

At the trial of Anne Turner the accusation that Frances Howard and
she had plotted with Forman to use poisons to render the Earl of Essex
impotent was added. A good deal of the 'evidence' produced on this
occasion, including the supposed effigies of a man and woman copulating,
'naked bellie to bellie and in a bestiall fashion',[62] was totally irrelevant to
the crime for which Turner was being tried. Its introduction was engineered solely to taint the characters of Anne Turner and Frances Howard
by invoking the cultural connection of poisoning with women. Though
in the seventeenth century it is the Italianate nature of the crime that is
more often stressed, the link between women and poison, later to become
a commonplace of detective fiction, was already available. Reginald Scot
claimed:

> As women in all ages have beene counted most apt to conceive
> witchcraft, and the divels speciall instruments therof: so also it appeareth,
> that they have been the first inventers, and the greatest practicers of
> poisoning, and more naturallie addicted and given therunto than men.[63]

The connection is generated in part by the analogy that could be drawn
between the way women's beauty is perceived as insinuating itself into
men's hearts and the secret workings of poison. Later in his treatise

Scot makes just this metaphoric transition when describing the venom proceeding from the fleshly attractions of the harlot:

> For her eie infecteth, entiseth, and (if I maie so saie) bewitcheth them manie times, which thinke themselves well armed against such maner of people. Hir toong, hir gesture, hir behaviour, hir beautie, and other allurements poison and intoxicate the mind. (p. 304)

The long title of Tuke's book makes the same identification, and when Nathanael Richards characterised the court as a place full of enticements to lust he made explicit a connection between women, lust, poison and the death of Overbury. Of court ladies he wrote:

>   their high Towring lofty daring Pride
> (*Like Lust restrain'd*) lives never satisfide.
> If checkt for it; straight swiftest *Mercury*
> Strikes dead th'opposing foe to Venerie:
> Like (sometimes) that sad most Lamented Knight
> Who di'd by a Tricke: in such wofull plight
> (By Sugar Candid Poysons) workt in Paste
> (*From Sinne and Murder sent*,) whose delicate Taste
> Under the fein'd pretence, of seeming good
> Consum'd and burnt, his vitall crimson blood.
> Such is the Mighty-Madams Murdring spight,
> Court Concubines ne'r kill, but with delight.[64]

The allegation of poisoning thus enabled the prosecutors to invoke in their audience a variety of deep-seated animosities – against the court, against Catholics, and against women. The easy slide from one resonance to another in the minds of the jurors in turn helped to close the net around the accused.

The second powerful ingredient mixed into Coke's speech to the Grand Jury at Weston's trial was the matter of adultery:

> He said murder was the worst [crime] as appered by the judgments of god threatened against it and by gods punishment upon David notwithstanding he repented of it (wheare by the way his Lo. pertinentlie noted that adultery did often produce murder).[65]

In one report of Elwes's trial we read of Coke letting rip on the subject:

> Beware of Adultery, bewarre of taking away of other mens wives. It hath bene pronounced by God himself, For the woman that thou hast taken thou shalt die the death. A man shall seldome see an Adultery of

> as high degree indeed, but accompanied with Murther. Example of David . . . [66]

The suggestion of a necessary sequence from adultery to murder was frequently made. In Webster's *The White Devil*, for example, Cardinal Monticelso pithily observes 'next the devil Adult'ry, / Enters the devil, Murder' (III.ii.108–9). In the Overbury trials the establishment of adultery as a prelude to the murder was of great strategic importance to the prosecution. They were, after all, confronted with a situation where, if Overbury's antagonism to the annulment and remarriage were to be suggested as the motive for his silencing, it was by no means obvious why, having mewed him up safely in the Tower, Frances Howard or her husband needed to do any more. Allegations of adultery could both supply a motive, and, more importantly, be deployed to stir up a tide of moral condemnation which could deflect such questions.

Adultery was considered, by the preachers at least, a moral crime of the utmost seriousness. Dod and Cleaver, for example, warned that if married couples 'deale unchastly, it is not only unjustly done in regard of themselves, but they forfeit their bond to God, even to the hazard of their salvations'.[67] When William Whately admonished newly married persons to avoid adultery, he hoped:

> they will never suffer any strength of desire, or violence of allurement, to cast them into so deepe a forgetfulnesse of the commandement of God, the lawes of their country, the light of their conscience, the covenant of their marriage, the person of their yoke-fellowes, the honour of their bodies and the safety of their soules; as to offend God, disobey the Magistrate, scandalize the Church, wrong the yoke-fellow, pollute their bodies and damne their soules.[68]

As Whately indicates, adultery was not considered solely to be a private, individual sin. If marriage was deployed as an image of the common weal, its fracture was an image of civil disorder.

It is not surprising, therefore, that the connection of adultery with murder should be made in this case, nor that poisoning should have been so often the imagined method by which discontented wives would do away their husbands. Margaret Ferne-Seed, arraigned for the murder of her husband in 1608, was alleged to have attempted poison before cutting his throat; Elizabeth Caldwell was ultimately persuaded by her lover, Jeffrey Brown, with the aid of the widow Isabel Hall, to attempt to poison her husband. (The plot misfired and she killed a child by mistake.)[69] The most famous cases, both of which were turned into plays in the early 1590s, were the murder of Anne Sanders' husband by her lover, George Brown (and again there is a persuasive widow egging the wife on), which became *A Warning for Fair Women*, and Alice Arden's murder of her husband in 1551 which was dramatised as *Arden of Feversham*. In the latter play Alice attempts first to poison her husband, resorting to physical violence when that fails.

Catherine Belsey has discussed these and other texts, pointing out how the fear of murder by wives seems to have increased in the last years of the sixteenth century, and arguing that this is a symptom of the instability in the ideology of marriage in the period.[70] It is a convincing argument, all the more so when one considers John Rainolds' depiction of the difficulty which a man living with an adulterous wife faces:

> And how can he choose but live still in feare and anguish of minde, least shee add drunckennesse to thirste, and murder to adultery: I meane lest she serve him as *Clytemnestra* did *Agammemnon*, or Livia did *Drusus*, or Mrs Arden did her husband?[71]

It was within this attitudinal context that Coke and Hyde developed their strategy. They knew exactly what they were doing in putting the adultery of Frances Howard at the forefront of their case. Although she was not accused of husband-murder, one of the effects of the evidence of her attempts to poison Essex was to conflate both crimes and to bring all the resonances of the ultimate female insurrection into play. It was convenient for their purpose, too, that Frances Howard should have the widow Turner as her confidante, since she fitted so easily into the stereotype of the lustful widow, familiar in misogynist writing, and often dramatised on the stage.[72] Like a Livia in *Women Beware Women*, or an Anne Drury in *A Warning for Fair Women*, Anne Turner could be figured as the experienced woman who leads the younger on the road to damnation (she was supposed to have tried out the love-potions first herself to secure the attentions of Sir Arthur Mainwaring, and it was she who was alleged to have acquired and tested the poisons destined for Overbury).

By far the most significant effect of the prosecution's presentation of adultery as the proximate cause of the murder was that such a charge profoundly determined the prevailing opinion of Frances Howard. A fictional example makes the point economically. John Rainolds published an enormously popular set of moral tales, *The Triumphs of Gods Revenge*, in a collection which expanded in size over the years. His *History XXVI* concerns a woman, Imperia, who loves Morosini, but is prevented by her father from marrying him; instead she is compelled to wed the aged Palmerius. When Morosini returns from his travels Imperia commits adultery with him, and they then conspire to murder her husband. Whereas at the story's opening the author pities Imperia, forced into this ill-assorted match, as soon as she gives in to her lover 'shee lost her honour, by committing this beastly sinne of sensuality and Adultery'.[73] She quickly becomes 'our lustfull and lascivious Imperia' (p. 355), and 'a dangerous Cockatrice or pernicious viper' (p. 358). Rainolds is capable of rather more sympathy when he observes 'at one time do I pitty both ther youth and folly, and hate their obscene affections each to other; and their foule crimes to God herein' (p. 356). He is prepared to blame the father for forcing the marriage and even to recognise the unfairness of expecting a woman to forgo sexual pleasure in marriage to an aged impotent; but nothing can wipe out the transformation in Imperia wrought by the sin of adultery.

The prosecutors played upon the judgemental attitudes represented in this fictional example to create the climate of feeling in which Frances Howard's guilt could be readily assumed. At Weston's trial Lawrence Hyde made every effort to brand Frances. He recounted the hostility between Carr and Overbury that developed because of his attraction to her. One report has him say that Overbury found Rochester 'lusting after a filthie woman another man's wife. Hee gave him good counsell: this Lord was angry and tolde itt his lewde woman for soe she was'. The writer comments approvingly on Overbury's reported remark 'will you never leave the company of that base woman (and so hee rightly tearmed her)'.[74] Hyde seems to have been worried lest he had gone too far in traducing Frances Howard, for in one account of Weston's resumed trial he is reported as beginning his address with the words: 'if any man or woman finde themselves agrieved with any termes that I shall use, let them understand it is not I that say they be base, lewde, or filthie; but if the matter touch them and prove them soe, let them looke to it'.[75] Any nervousness he may have felt had disappeared by the time Elwes came before him. One of the incriminating pieces of evidence was a letter written to him by Frances in which she asked the Lieutenant to change some tarts and jellies for others, telling him 'the tarts or jelly taste you not of, but the wine you may drink, for in it is no letters'.[76] It was suggested that by 'letters' Frances Howard meant 'poison' and that Elwes knew this code. In his defence Sir Gervase claimed that 'he knew nothing more by the Lady of Somersets letters, than that the Tarts should intercept letters; though he since thought, and now perceives 'tis otherwise.' But Hyde interrupted him and said 'Why should the Lady of Essex intercept Rochester's letters when she lay with him every night almost?'.[77] As we have seen (see p. 68), Northampton's letters imply very strongly that Frances and Robert kept apart during the divorce hearings – precisely the time when this letter was sent – and Hyde's blackening of the characters of the Somersets can have had little basis in fact. But accuracy mattered not a jot; it was vital to the case to establish the lustful, adulterous stereotype in the minds of all auditors.

When Bacon prosecuted Robert Carr he steered clear of this kind of abuse, but he suggested that Overbury's conduct fomented Frances's hatred 'in respect that he crossed her love, and abused her name (which are furies in women)' (*ST*, 974). It is subsidiary to Bacon's central purpose, since it is the Earl of Somerset who is his target, but his comment suggests the second dimension of the accusation of adultery laid at Frances's door. Whilst the prosecutors defamed the Countess of Somerset as an adulteress, at the same time they could present her fear of such defamation as the motivating force for her act of murder.

In so doing they were recognising a cultural imperative for a woman to preserve her honour intact. Moralists' advice to women continually insisted upon this necessity. Vives, for example, pithily observed that 'A woman hath no charge to see to but her honestye and chastyte. Wherefore when she is enfirmed of that, she is sufficiently appoynted'.[78] In the case of adultery, the double standard ensured the greater guilt of women. As Guazzo has it:

> Though the Husbande offende God as muche as the Wife, in vyolating the sacred bande of Matrimonye, yet the wife ought fyrmelye to print this in her harte, and to remember alwayes, that where the husband by this fault doth, according to the opinion of men, but a little blemish his honour, the wife altogeather looseth her good name, and remaineth spotted with such infamye, that she can never recover her honour agayne, neyther by any repentaunce, nor by amendmente of her life.[79]

Northampton's awareness of the importance and the precariousness of his niece's reputation is apparent in the letter quoted earlier, urging the couple to keep apart during the divorce hearings (p. 68). But concealment of a love affair is also standard literary motif with a long history. Catullus, translated by Jonson, asked 'Cannot we delude the eyes / Of a few poor household spies?'.[80] A poem attributed in one manuscript to Anne Vavasour, the long-time mistress of Queen Elizabeth's champion, Sir Henry Lee, movingly varies the topos to express the vulnerability of a woman in love with a man not her husband. The speaker addresses her lover, explaining why she seems distant to him in public:

> Thou seest we live amongste the lynxes eyes
>   that pryes and spyes eache pryvye thought of mynde

thou knowest ryghte well what Sorrowes may aryse
   yf once they chance my setled lookes to fynde.

. . .

we sillye dames that false suspecte doo feare
   and lyve within the month [mount] of envyes lake
must in our heartes a secrete moaninge beare
   farre from the shew that outwardlye we make.

Goe where I like I list not vaunte my love
   wher I desire ther must I fayne debate
one hathe my hand another hathe my glove
   but he my harte whom most I seme to hate.[81]

It was not enough merely to avoid the 'lynxes eyes'. As we saw in the last chapter, reputation is constructed in language, and honour based on what people say rather than upon actuality. Horatio in John Day's *Law Tricks*, for example, observes:

Her sexes credit, or discredit thrives
In th'outward shape and fashion of their lives,
And be a womans vertue nere so strong,
Her honour's weighed upon discourses tongue.
Be her name sullied, were her thoughts as bright
As Innocence, the world would count her light.[82]

All too often, however, a woman was denied the possibility of her own speech in order to defend herself. In the 52nd Novell of the First Book of Painter's *Palace of Pleasure* a princess of Flanders repels a nocturnal assault, but when she thinks of telling her brother her maid advises her to keep silent, since:

the brute [rumour] will runne that he hath had his pleasure upon you. And the greatest numbre will say, that it is very difficult for a Gentleman to doe such an enterprise, except the Lady minister some great occasion.[83]

The depressing similarity of these attitudes to those still articulated in the courts during cases of rape is striking.[84]

As Moll Cutpurse observes bitterly to Laxton, who 'thinks each woman thy fond flexible whore':

How many of our sex by such as thou
Have their good thoughts paid with a blasted name

That never deserved loosely or did trip
In path of whoredom beyond cup and lip?
But for the stain of conscience and of soul,
Better had women fall into the hands
Of an act silent than a bragging nothing.[85]

Shakespeare's great plays of sexual jealousy, *Othello*, *The Winter's Tale* and *Cymbeline*, dramatise the power of words and false report to threaten their heroines. Many women, for instance, must have echoed Hermione's recognition of her powerlessness in the face of male fantasy, when she cries out to her husband 'My life stands in the level of your dreams' (*The Winter's Tale*, III.ii.80).

That women of the seventeenth century had thoroughly internalised these demands, and were sharply aware of the need to preserve their reputation, is reflected in the frequency with which they brought actions for defamation at the ecclesiastical courts. As J.A. Sharpe and Martin Ingram have demonstrated,[86] women of all social classes in significant numbers were prepared to turn to the courts to clear their names of sexual slander. It is significant also that the majority of such cases were brought by wives, rather than by unmarried women, suggesting 'that the maintenance of sexual honour was more important after than before marriage'.[87] For her imputed adultery Frances Howard suffered the satirical abuse of anonymous rhymesters, as we have seen. In this respect also she endured no more than many of her more lowly born sisters. Libels on women's conduct were circulated orally, scattered randomly abroad, or affixed prominently to buildings.[88]

But if Frances Howard shared the common lot of women in her society, her social status gave a particular inflection to the damage her honour would sustain because of the accusation. Mason commented that a fornicating man 'wrongs the woman which hee polluteth, and brings a perpetuall disgrace upon her, and this disgrace redounds to her father, her friends, and the whole familie'.[89] In Painter's 45th Novell from the First Book the Duchess of Savoy is wrongly accused of adultery. She does not fear to die 'were it not that by my death I shoulde leave an eternall blot to my good name, and a perpetuall heritage of infamie to my house and kindred'.[90] When, in *The Winter's Tale*, Hermione stands accused by Leontes, she, too, speaks of her honour in familial terms:

> For behold me,
> A fellow of the royal bed, which owe
> A moiety of the throne; a great king's daughter,
> The mother to a hopeful prince, here standing

To prate and talk for life and honour, fore
Who please to come and hear. For life, I prize it
As I weigh grief, which I would spare. For honour,
'Tis a derivative from me to mine,
And only that I stand for.

(III.ii.36–44)

The prosecutors in the trials were acutely aware of the way accusation of Frances Howard could seem to be traducing the honour of her family as a whole. Lawrence Hyde employed the image of the rotten branch which might be profitably hewn from the family tree, and Francis Bacon that of the individual corrupt seed of the pomegranate to insist that they aimed only at the daughter, not the rest of her family.

She, like any member of a family such as hers, would have felt intensely an aristocratic pride of birth. Quaratesi brings out this quality in his story of what happened when Coke went to question the Countess. According to him Frances observed:

'this Cook would like to turn everybody into soup.' And going to meet him she asked him: 'What do you want from me?' 'I came here to question you,' the Judge answered. 'You have dishonoured me publicly,' she added, 'and now you come here to question me?' 'No, madam, you have dishonoured yourself,' the Judge added, 'when you rejected your first husband.' 'Come, now, don't think that with your tricks and stratagems you can do to me what you did to those poor simple people whom you had executed. Go away, my life is ready any minute for the King's order; do the worst you can.' And having said that, she retired without being questioned.[91]

Arrogance there is, undoubtedly; but this picture of the arch-bully Coke being imperiously dismissed by Frances has a strong appeal. She must have recognised that the lawyers had left little of her reputation intact, and must have known the likely outcome – but she still clutches the rags of her honour to her and turns upon the enemy.

Quaratesi, viewing the trial as a foreigner, was obviously dismayed that the Countess of Somerset 'has been very badly treated publicly in the words of the Chief Justice of this kingdom, although she was not present'. He adds a revealing further piece of information, that 'as the testimony of a witness concerning the Countess's honour was being read by a clerk in a very low voice so that only the Judges could hear it, the Chief Justice ordered that it should be read aloud, saying that it did not matter since she was a rotten branch of an otherwise noble plant and trunk'.[92] In such a climate as this the suggestion that Frances Howard was driven to murder by the need to protect her honour and to revenge herself upon an individual who had impugned her virtue would have been very persuasive. In a neatly devised fashion, then, the prosecution both managed to abuse Frances Howard's honour, and at the same time to imply that defending that honour motivated her to murder.

The case against the Countess of Somerset was strengthened by the revelation that she had attempted to procure the services of Sir David Wood to assassinate Overbury before he was imprisoned. The episode also provides a sidelight on the question of honour. Coke had been told by Lord Fenton that David Wood might have useful information,[93] and he was examined on 21 October, in between Weston's two trials. Sir David alleged that Frances Howard, having heard of a quarrel between himself and Overbury, offered him £1,000 to get rid of their enemy. Wood replied that Overbury 'had refused to come unto the feild', and said he would do nothing unless Robert Carr would guarantee his safety. When Frances Howard could not produce this assurance, but promised that she would see him safely conveyed away, Wood 'tould hir that he might be accounted a great foole, if he upon a womans words should goe to Tibourne'.[94]

What is interesting about this testimony is that Wood's own determination to revenge the insult Overbury had offered him in a duel does not provoke censure. Though duelling was officially forbidden, honour quarrels between men, often prosecuted abroad, had reached a peak in 1613, when, as Lawrence Stone puts it, 'it looked as if the English nobility, like fighting cocks in a ring, were about to indulge in wholesale mutual slaughter'.[95] The Roaring Girl, Moll Cutpurse, dressed in man's clothes, can fight and wound Laxton in defence of women's honour, but she is explicitly an aberrant exception, a comic transgressive figure. For other dishonoured women there were but two alternatives, to suffer in silence, or to visit revenge upon themselves by taking their own life. Lucrece by her suicide becomes the truly heroic female, passive and quiescent; Frances Howard, on the other hand, by attempting her own revenge becomes the type of the malicious woman.

The prosecutors interwove the accusations of poison and of adultery and dishonour with considerable skill. Their task was made easier by the way these charges could both be accommodated to, and strengthened by, the claim that, in the words of Lawrence Hyde, this crime was the result of 'implacable malice, being the mallice of a woman'.[96] The idea that women are especially prone to extreme and unreasoning malice was a commonplace. Sampson Price, preaching at Paul's Cross in 1616 and citing Ecclesiasticus 25.13, maintained 'There is no love stronger then the love of a woman. *It is strong as death*: and no wickednesse like the wickednes of a wicked woman'.[97] Rainolds prefaces his series of narratives with a discussion of Ambition, Revenge and Murder which 'have ever prooved fatall crimes to their undertakers', and argued 'Nowe as they are powerfull in men, so they are (sometimes) implacable in women, who (with as much vanity as malice) delight in these sinnes'. Of his first story he says 'I wish the event of this History would give the lye to this ensuing position, that there is no pride nor malice to that of a woman', and tells us that in his second story we may see 'the old phrase made good and verifyed: That there is no affection or hatred to that of a Woman: for where they love, they love dearely; and where they hate, hate deadly'.[98] Painter makes a similar claim in his story of the Countess of Celant (Second Book, Novell 24):

> When a woman is disposed to give herselfe to wickednesse, hir mynde is voyd of no malyce or invention to sort to ende any danger or perill offered unto hir. The facts of one Medea (if credit may be geven to Poets) and of Phaedra... wel declare with what beastly zeale they began and finished their attempts: the eagles flight is not so high, as the foolyshe desires, and conceiptes of a woman that trusteth her own opinion, and treadeth out of the track of duety, and way of wysedome.[99]

Painter's final comment brings out the underlying conviction that once a woman steps outside the proper confines of patriarchal control then there is nothing to limit her innate wickedness.

The belief that women do not possess the rational control to regulate their own behaviour might be thought specific to this period; but, in however transmuted a fashion, similar suppositions have conditioned attitudes to female criminality down to the present. As Anne Worrall observes:

> Criminality is still assumed to be a masculine attribute and women criminals are therefore perceived to be either 'not women' or 'not criminals'.[100]

Ann Jones has amply documented the way in which the second of these perceptions often prevailed during the nineteenth century. Women who by all presumption of evidence had killed their husbands (often with poison) were acquitted because male jurors could not contemplate the possibility that their image of ideal womanhood could be so totally shattered.[101] In the Renaissance, however, it was the opposite pole which dominated. Beard, for example, wrote: 'If these and such like cruelties as we have spoken of before, be strange and monstrous for men, what shal we then say of wicked and bloudie women, who (contrarie to the nature of their sex) addict themselves to all violence and bloudshedding'.[102] Shakespeare's Lady Macbeth and Queen Margaret, for example, are women whose extreme violence is explicitly linked to their denial of their femininity. In Painter's story of Didaco and Violenta (First Book; Novell 42), Violenta is deserted by Didaco, who bigamously marries another; she exacts what might seem a justified revenge, but is characterised as one who 'fed her bloudie and cruell harte with none other repaste but with rage and disdaine'. When she commits the murder she is 'inchaunted with wrath, rage and furie like another Medea' and not content with killing her husband tears out his eyes, tongue and heart and throws them into the street. She is finally beheaded 'not only for that she had presumed to punishe the knights tromperie and offence, but for her excessive crueltie doen upon the dead body'.[103] In the next story, 'A Lady of Thurin', the Duke punishes his adulterous wife by imprisoning her in a room with the dead body of her lover; and, though his behaviour is remarked as rather cruel, he is not brought to justice for his actions. Male revenge is legitimate, female revenge a mark of dangerous excess. (One might note, in passing, the depressing continuity of this disparity registered in the different sentences handed down to men and women in cases of domestic violence even today.)[104]

Historians were quick to entrench the idea of Frances Howard as just such a monster of excess in common perception. Wilson characterised her as 'another Alecto' who 'drove furiously, her Chariot having two wheels, which ran over all impediments: One was, to sue a Divorce betwixt her and her Husband . . . The other was, to take away Overbury, the blemish in her Eye, and that laid such a stain upon her, that nothing but his blood could expiate.'[105] Sir Simonds D'Ewes spoke of the murder as having been brought about 'to satiate the implacable malice of one cruel murderess';[106] in Weldon's account she is described as Herodias.[107] Two centuries later the same assumptions condition Amos's characterisation of Frances as 'a Countess, whose vice and sorceries, according as lust and vengeance prompted, confirmed the experience of history, that the very few bad women whom the world has seen, have been the worst of God's creatures'.[108]

Every society finds it necessary to demonise murderers by insisting that their actions are the consequence of irrationality or evil. To admit that such action might be a logical response to, or even worse, a necessary consequence of the dominant values of society would be too unsettling to contemplate. This construction of 'the criminal' operates, of course, on men as well as women; nonetheless it is evident from Hyde's attack that there was a particular potency in invoking the horror of implacable female malice. Part of the force of this characterisation depends upon the fact that female villainy can be represented at one and the same time as aberrant, and yet typical. One of the most widely circulated of all the satirical epigrams on the Overbury murder is this:

> A Page, a Knight, a Viscount and an Earle
> All those did love a lustfull English girle
> A match well made, for shee was likewise fower
> A wife, a witch, a poysoner, and a whore.[109]

There is a neatness in this epigram, bringing together the rising fortunes of Carr with the declining moral standards of his wife; but its popularity must surely also have derived from the way that the concluding line is a variation upon a standard misogynist characterisation of woman's life-history. Indeed, so potent is the grid from which the epigram derives that in one transcription, with scant regard for history, the stereotype re-emerges:

> A Page, a Knight, a Viscount and an Earle
> Did lately mary with an English Girle –
> A mayd a wife a widow and a whore
> Whoever saw so cross a match before.[110]

The interplay between the matrix, already hostile to women, and the version which characterises Frances Howard's transgression is an apt parallel to the way in which the lawyers invoked and manipulated those stereotypes which would make their case as persuasive as this epigram was popular.

Having been routinely characterised during the early trials as the implacable murderess, suddenly, at her own trial and in the subsequent hearing of her husband, all is changed. In his speech at Frances's trial Bacon addressed the assembled peers: 'I know your Lordships cannot behold her without compassion. Many things may move you, her youth, her person, her sex, her noble family; yea, her provocations, (if I should enter into the cause itself), and furies about her; but chiefly her penitency and confession'.[111] On the following day, in setting out the evidence against Somerset he observed that he 'fell into an unlawful love towards his unfortunate Lady, then Countess of Essex'.[112] This amazing volte-face was partly a consequence of Bacon's own style replacing that of the aggressive Coke; it was also undoubtedly influenced by the fact that the jury of peers was very different from those of the previous trials – they would have expected due acknowledgement of family and rank. But the chief reason, as Bacon himself said, was that Frances Howard had confessed her guilt.

In exactly the same way, once Anne Turner, the other woman in the case, had confessed her guilt then the response to her is transformed. Her trial was designed to prove her a witch, and Coke summed up by telling her 'that she had the seven deadly sins: viz. a whore, a bawd, a sorcerer, a witch, a papist, a felon, and a murderer, the daughter of the devil Forman' (*ST*, 935). Justice Crook, calling the crime 'the most haynous and hatefull offence that hath happened in this our times', and telling Turner 'there is no pretence of excuse against such a cloude of witnesses, wherein you are encompassed', adjured her to confess and to repent.[113] This she did, so enthusiastically and comprehensively that her execution produced a powerful response. John Castle, writing to James Miller, described the scene:

> Since I saw you, I saw Mrs Turner die. If detestation of painted pride, lust, malice, powdered hair, yellow bands, and all the rest of the wardrobe of Court-vanities; if deepe sighes, teares, confessions, ejaculations of the soul, admonitions of all sortes of people to make God and an unspotted conscience alwayes our friends; if the protestations of faith and hope, to be washed by the same Saviour, and by the like mercies that Mary Magdalen was, be signes and demonstrations of a blest Penitent, then I will tell you, that this poore broken woman went *a cruce ad gloriam*, and now enjoyes the presence of hirs and our Redeemer.[114]

There are two reports of her scaffold speech amongst the State Papers,[115] and Thomas Tuke hoped that 'her words might take impression in those that heard them, and her example serve others for instruction'.[116] At least two broadsides survive, one entitled 'Mistress Turner's Repentance', the other reproduced as Plate 7. In the next trial, that of Elwes, Coke himself cried out that 'shee that was before an example of wickednes was nowe become a zealous perswader to Christian pietie, and goodnes'.[117]

A number of different issues are raised by the way the characters of both women were transformed. Most immediately it is further evidence of the way in which 'character' in the trials, and in seventeenth-century society and fiction in general, was not read as being constituted out of a unified and continuous 'personality'. These two women occupy two consecutive spaces – of monstrous female and of penitent sinner, eliciting quite contradictory responses. Feminist critics have argued that such switches were especially typical of the representation of female characters. Catherine Belsey, for example, maintains that women 'were only inconsistently identified as subjects in the discourses about them which circulated predominantly among men'.[118] Though her argument seems persuasive, the discontinuity of identity in female characters is different in degree rather than kind from the representation of male figures. More roles are available to men, so that transitions move in smaller stages than in the great leap from one side to the other of the binary characterisation of women as virgins or whores, but the basic perception of identity as constituted out of a series of discrete roles which might overlay one another, but are not integrated by an inner core of 'selfhood' is constant across the gender division.[119]

Whatever the larger argument, the response to male or female criminals at the moment of execution always had the possibility of sudden revaluation of the victim. Weston and Elwes, as well as Turner, made a 'good' end; Franklin did not. What makes for a different response in the surviving record is partly whether the convicts put on a 'good performance', but mainly whether or not they confessed and exhibited penitence on the scaffold. The work of Michel Foucault has focused attention on these matters in recent years. Put very reductively, his argument is that confession involves the penitent being persuaded to constitute his or her sense of self within the language that is provided by the machineries of power, both secular and religious. Execution, in his theory, is a mechanism of state theatre, called to demonstrate the power of authority upon the body of the guilty. The dying speech brings the two together as it registers the subjects' internalisation and acceptance of their participation in the ritual which, in turn, the state co-opts as reinforcement and justification of its actions.[120]

The confessions and scaffold speeches of the participants in the Over-bury murder do much to bear out these views. Elwes spoke as follows:

> I will speak nothing of myne innocence, but here will submitt my selfe to the Kinge, the lawe, and to God; the Kinge herein is just, and the lawe hath justly condemned me, I will ripp upp my self, and leave nothinge unsayed may make me seeme vile, for doe you thinke I stande upon credit, I will not staine myne owne soule to conceale anie thinge, and not to ripp yt upp, for if I should, I think I should never see God, face to face.[121]

From the perspective of the authorities his speech makes a satisfying acknowledgement of guilt, and his language of 'ripping up' his own conscience betokens a sense that his confession and speech participate in, and endorse the ritual of execution shortly to follow. The process of Anne Turner's confession can also be seen as conforming to the Foucauldian hypothesis. In the course of her conversations with Dr Whiting while awaiting execution she confessed her guilt, further implicated the Countess, and surrendered her Catholicism to the state religion, agreeing to take communion for the first time in her life, and saying afterwards 'I thank god and you for the comfort I have received for this good work of yours todaye; my conscience is much more eased than it was'.[122] When she came to execution she even more clearly identified herself with her fate, when saying that though she endured 'a shamefull death, yet shee acknowledged gods mercye in it; for by that meanes *she came to know her selfe*, and was made truely penitent'.[123]

Confessions such as these, therefore, served the state both practically, in that further details might aid future prosecutions, and also at a more symbolic level in the spectacle they offered to the populace at large, both as a deterrent to crime (most scaffold speeches included advice to the onlookers to avoid the sins for which the accused suffered) and an endorsement of the machineries of power. The Foucauldian hypothesis, however, has been strongly challenged by Thomas W. Laqueur, who argues that, especially in England, the spectacle of execution was much less closely controlled and much more anarchic than Foucault allows.[124] I would want to suggest that there is a further problem in that the political and religious dimensions of this drama of confession and execution have perhaps been too readily elided by writers in a secular age.[125]

It is vital to recognise that the soliciting of confession in the seventeenth century pointed above the authority of King and state to the over-arching judgement of God. When Sir Henry Montague addressed a group of men found guilty of murder he began: 'so wee hartily desire of God, that your condemnation may not bee of death unto death, but rather a meanes to a better life'.[126] Throughout the long speech which follows he makes a consistent distinction between the judgement of the courts which they have already undergone, and the judgement of God which they must yet face. It is true that Montague brings both together in his insistence that:

> Godly sorrow breeds Repentance; and true Repentance expresseth itself in the hearty confession of sin: and true confession is not forced, but voluntarie: not only of what apparent evidence wrings from us, but what is secret, and only knowne to our selves and unto God. (p. 56)

The fact that God knows it all already, making complete confession necessary, was a convenient instrument for the state to use in soliciting the further evidence it desired from the convicted – and we have seen how Turner, for example, was coerced into saying what her confessor would have her say. So too, in Montague's advice we may see the way in which confession does indeed demand the subject's production of itself in terms given by authority. He says:

> my advice unto you is, that you would erect a judgement seate in your owne soules, judging yourselves by the evidence of your owne consciences, that so you may not be judged of the Lord. (p. 54)

But if religion could be co-opted in the service of the state, there was always the possibility that it might lead the convict's mind in a significantly different direction, and might, indeed, even threaten the state's authority. Foxe's *Book of Martyrs*, after all, celebrated repeatedly the executions of those who consistently refused to admit the authority of their executioners. The self produced by the Puritan examination of conscience, the auto-biographic self that Elwes, like so many others, narrated in the course of his scaffold speech, could by that very act of self-examination place itself in opposition to the state in whose name the sentence of death was executed.

In Castle's account of Anne Turner's execution he turned her into a Christlike figure. In the broadside, 'Mistress Turner's Repentance', the Doctor who accompanies her encourages her as she views the scaffold:

> On a Tree
> Dyed our Redeemer; hee that dyed for thee,
> And all repentant Sinners. For the way,
> It makes no matter (greatly) how we pay
> This debt of Life, so Heaven assurance give,
> That when we dye, a better life to live.
> Fire, Water, Torture, any way, 'tis well
> *To goe to Heav'n, ev'n by the Gates of Hell.*

The invocation of the parallel with Christ is, one would have thought, rather perilous; it was certainly in the interests of authority to make sure that the penitent thief on Calvary was uppermost in the audience's mind rather than Christ, crucified for refusing to accept the authority of the state. Foucault recognises that 'the condemned man found himself transformed into a hero by the sheer extent of his widely advertised crimes, and sometimes the affirmation of his belated repentance',[127] and allows that this indicates that the literature of crime might therefore become 'a sort of battleground around the crime, its punishment and its memory'. But perhaps it should also be allowed that in securing the confession of the criminal, and in encouraging the scaffold speech of repentance, those in authority were confessing themselves also to be subject to the prior and absolute demands of religion.

When the Duke in *Measure for Measure* refuses to despatch Barnardine because he is not in a fit state to go to his execution, being drunk and totally unrepentant, he says that 'to transport him in the mind he is / Were damnable' (IV.ii.65–6). Foucauldian critics see in Barnardine an almost heroic declaration of the limits of the state's power to coerce confession.[128] In these lines, however, the damnation the Duke fears is not Barnardine's, but his own, should he be guilty of sending a soul to hell. The urgent pressings of conscience demanded for the convicted not only procured useful evidence and persuaded the condemned person to validate the authority of the state; they were also required to appease its guilt. It is significant in this regard that the entire second half of *A Warning for Fair Women* is organised around the persuasion of Anne Saunders to confess her crime, and whilst there is very little emphasis upon the way this will confirm the justice of the state, there is a great deal about the salvation of her own soul. This brings out the anxiety on the part of those who coerce confession, an anxiety which turns to relief when the convict falls into line.

In their speeches as they stood on the edge of eternity the condemned sought to give retrospective shape to their lives. Elwes, for example, not only confessed the sins of gambling and sabbath-breaking; he also spoke of 'Gods great mercy, in bringing me hither, for I might have died other wise accidentally... in my synnes unexpected of, But nowe I dy comfortably'.[129] The crowds seem also to have needed the sense of completion and narrative roundedness that execution brought to the moral tale. The response of those who attended executions so enthusiastically must, as Laqueur argues, have been very mixed. Even when they sighed and wept over the penitent convict, however, their feeling seems to have been that of Moll Cutpurse: 'Confession is but poor amends for wrong / Unless a rope would follow' (*The Roaring Girl*, III.i.118–19).

The ballads and other writings that followed these executions quickly slotted the stories of Weston, Elwes and Turner into conventional narrative frames. In the case of Weston and Elwes the moral most often drawn was that of the dangers of the desire for gold and of trusting in those of high place. In Robert Niccols's *Sir Thomas Overburie's Vision* Weston speaks to the audience:

> To you therefore that hunger after gold,
> To you, whom hope of great mens grace makes bold
> In any great offence, henceforth let me
> For evermore a sad ensample be.[130]

Elwes had given the lead himself to such a reading of his plight in his execution speech. He warned his auditors 'for feare of great persons not to do the like' as he had done.[131] The hint was picked up enthusiastically by Niccols, by the author of *The Bloody Downfall of Adultery, Murder, Ambition*, and in the broadside reproduced as Plate 12. As Linda Peck demonstrates, these writers were latching on to a pervasive, and therefore persuasive, topos in interweaving religious and courtly discourse about court corruption.[132] They echoed, too, the common depiction of the hired assassin in contemporary drama, as Martin Wiggins has recently shown.[133]

In the case of Anne Turner, there was a similar suggestion that her motivation was greed and false trust; in her confession to Whiting she 'with greate passion said oh my Lady Somerset, oh my Lady Somerset woe worth the tyme that I once knewe her, my love to them and to there greatnes hathe brought me to a dogged death'.[134] Much more appealing in her case, however, was the chance to turn her death into a sermon on the downfall of vanity. Anne Turner introduced the fashion of yellow starch for ruffs and cuffs to England. At her execution her executioner wore yellow starched cuffs, a gesture which not only terminated the fashion but also gave direction to the moral spectacle. The ballad reproduced as Plate 8 typically represents her fall as the consequence of a female over-fondness for pleasure and superficiality. The morals drawn from all of these stories have as a common subtext mistrust of the court, of its vanity and of its duplicity, though the particularities are interestingly gendered.

The moral to be drawn from Frances Howard's story was rather different. By confessing her crime and remaining modestly silent during her hearing, she conformed herself admirably to the female stereotype of obedient passivity. Anne Haselkorn comments on the penitence that adulteresses conventionally display in the theatre:

> The repentance is designed to punish the female, and more so, the seductive woman, for exceeding her allotted space, for asserting her sexuality and selfhood, and for speaking out.[135]

She argues that the transgressive individuality of her chosen characters (Evadne from *The Maid's Tragedy*, Vittoria from *The White Devil*, and Bianca from *Women Beware Women*) is what makes them exciting to the theatre audience, but that in the end patriarchal values reassert themselves. The response the audience is finally encouraged to take to these characters is in many ways comparable to the response the penitent Frances elicited. She may, in pursuing her love, have been earlier prepared to confront male attitudes; she may have felt able to be rude to Coke when he called; but in the public arena of her trial she knew too well the penalty of stepping outside the convention of modest silence. From the men, Elwes or Carr himself, a defence might have been expected; for a woman to offer such a defence was to enter the trap that if she spoke against her condemnation that speech itself would be held to violate the modest norms of her sex and confirm her guilt anyway (as happens to Vittoria in *The White Devil* – and still to women in the modern court-room). Such penitence may, of itself, have helped to make her seem a 'convincing' character, for as Lisa Jardine remarks 'A convincing representation of the developing psychology of the female hero is apparently the conversion of lascivious waywardness into emblematic chaste resignation'.[136]

We cannot know why Frances Howard finally decided to confess her guilt. According to Gondomar she admitted

> the part which she had taken in desiring and aiding the death of Overbury, as being a girl aggrieved and offended by the most unworthy things which he had said about her person; but that the Earl of Somerset, who at that time was not yet her husband, neither knew anything about it, nor took any part in it. She had rather guarded herself and kept the secret from him, because she held him to be a very true friend of Overbury. This was the truth, though it was the greater blame to her that she had been alone in the matter.[137]

She must certainly have recognised by this time that she had no chance whatsoever of escaping condemnation. The sequence of earlier trials had insisted repeatedly on her complicity, and she must have known that the King himself was already convinced of her guilt, as appears from a message he had transmitted to Somerset at the end of December through the new Lieutenant of the Tower, Sir George More, in which he said:

> if it shall plainly appear that she is very fowle, as is generally conceaved and reported that she is, as being the author and procurer of that murder, then I thinck justice may not be stayed, and he shold have just cause to be glad that he is freed from so wicked a woman.[138]

It is likely, in view of the promises of reprieve that were dangled in front of Robert Carr if only he would confess his guilt, that some such offer was made to Frances Howard. One need invoke no theories of confession to explain her capitulation (though this does not mean that she was not subject to the whole range of internal and external pressures that could be brought to bear).

Frances Howard might have made a morally edifying spectacle at her trial, but unlike Anne Turner and the others, her story was not completed by execution. Franklin had alleged that after Weston's trial Frances had ordered him not to confess having brought poisons, and told him 'the lord who was to examine him would promise him a pardon to confess; but believe him not, for they will hang thee when all is done' (ST, 947). Of Franklin's fate she was an accurate prophet; for herself the rules were different. One justification for her reprieve was that she alone of all those accused had confessed *before* coming to trial (even in the modern courtroom a 'guilty' plea is likely to dispose a judge to leniency); much less worthy were two of the other 'motives to mercy' that Bacon proffered – 'the respect of her father, friends, and family' and, especially, 'that the crime was not of a principal, but of an accessary before the fact, by the instigation of base persons' (ST, 1007).

Frances Howard's social standing was transparently the reason for her pardon – a terrible confirmation of Lear's bitter cry: 'Through tattered rags great vices do appear; / Robes and furred gowns hide all'.[139] As late as October 1616, about three months after the pardon was granted, Charles Richardson was arguing:

> As the sinne is no other to a rich man than to a poore man, but indifferent to all, parching or refreshing all alike: So must the Magistrate cary himselfe equally and indifferent to all men in the execution of justice. The rich must not be more favoured then the poore, nor the poore more severely dealt withall then the rich.

On the following page he invoked the Overbury case, taking the opportunity to celebrate the

> great care of his Majesty, to have the land purged from blood, wherewith it hath been polluted, and that there is so strict and just proceeding against all that were confederate in so wicked a fact. And the Lord strengthen the hart and hand of that most worthy Lord Chiefe Justice that he may stil go forward unpartially to cut off al those that had any hand in so foul a murder.[140]

The bridge between the two statements is the assertion that 'the lawes must not be like unto cobwebs which catch and hold the little flies, but the great ones break through them'. Richardson here pointedly echoes the remark attributed to Weston after he had consented to stand trial, that he hoped they 'would not make a net to catch little birds, and let the great ones go' (ST, 927). To modern eyes, as perhaps to Richardson's, Weston's fear that there was one law for him, another for the powerful, was entirely justified.

The question of whether or not the Countess should, or would be executed seems to have been for a while a matter for public debate.

Gondomar said: 'As to the execution of the sentences there are now
various opinions, because the pitifulness of the Countess's case and the
favour she is in give great hope that her life will be spared'.[141] An
anonymous versifier presented both sides of the case, in a verse hitherto
unpublished, which deserves quoting in full:

Petitio.
Looke, and lament, behould a face of Earth,
In bewtie heavenly, great in place, and birth.
Nor is her soule in bewtie less excellinge,
In whome so manie vertues have their dwellinge.
Much Noble Nature, bewtie, Charitie,
Much in goodnes, witt, and pietie,
Nor is the fayrest peece without a staine,
In fayrest peeces spotts appeare most plaine.
Sence of dishonor, in best myndes most stronge,
Made her desire, t'avenge soe vile a wronge
By meanes unlawfull, which have given offence,
To Lawe, to God to Kinge; In recompence
of one Soule lost, the Lawe hath taken fowre,
And this hath suffer'd much by Legall Powre.
   God doth shew mercie for the fowlest thinge
   to penitents. Doe thou soe Mightie Kinge.

Respontio.
It's strange to se a face soe highe in birth,
And heavenly, to converse soe much with earth,
Naye more with hell; her soule noe less excellinge
In what? In Vice where all these had their dwellinge.
Much brybinge, breakinge, Pride, and Infamie,
Much of her Mother, new adulterie,
This ugly soule hath yet a fouler staine;
Though in foule soules, greate synns appeare least plaine.
Murther a Cryinge sin, in her more stronge,
For drawinge bosome frends, into the wronge.
Then blame not God, nor Kinge to take offence,
Nor yet our Lawes to take in recompence
For one soule lost, soe lost, wer't foure tymes foure,
And this of all deserves strickt Legall power.
   The Livinge Lorde still suffers in this thinge
   Were't but for that. Proceede in Justice Kinge.[142]

The first stanza of the lyric does at least suggest that Frances Howard was revenging a real insult to her honour, but the proposition that she should be let off because enough had already been executed must sound appalling to a modern sensibility. The weight of the poem falls on the side of condemnation, an opinion which seems to have been widespread. Holles reported of the people that 'day by day they watch the Tower, least the execution should be stollen from them: so desirous be we of novelty, as we care not who be hanged to feed that humour'.[143] Chamberlain noted that the pardon, when it came, was not well received:

> yt seemes the common people take not this for goode payment, for on Saterday last the Quene with the Countesse of Darbie, the Lady Ruthen and the Lord Carew comming privatly in coach to see somwhat here in towne, there grew a whispering that yt was the Lady somerset and her mother, wherupon people flocked together and followed the coach in great numbers rayling and reviling, and abusing the footmen, and putting them all in feare.[144]

But the people were not merely resenting the loss 'of their ghoulish pleasures' as White characterises them;[145] there was, apart from anything else, a just anger that the rich had got away with it yet again. At another level, however, the absence of any drama in the court-room, and the lack of an execution meant that the populace was cheated of a satisfactory narrative conclusion to the most scandalous story of their times.

But though at least for the moment narrative completion was denied, there were, in addition to the other narrative schemata that have already been considered, two particularly powerful story-types that were appropriate to explain and shape the history of Frances Howard. The first derived from the motto 'Veritas filia Temporis' (Truth the daughter of Time). Fritz Saxl and D.J. Gordon have demonstrated the potency of this motto in the sectarian religious politics of the period;[146] but it was a commonplace also deployed in other kinds of narrative, and especially in stories to do with crime. Thomas Beard, in *The Theatre of Gods Judgements*, for example, writes of God's 'miraculous and supernaturall detecting of such murderers from time to time, who have carried their villainies so closely as the eye of man could not espy them'; John Rainolds noted similarly that 'God will in due time detect and discover [murder]; for he will make inquisition for blood, and will severely and sharpely revenge the death of his children'.[147] In the accounts of 'real-life' murders, too, the topos was frequently invoked.[148] It is not surprising, therefore, that the motif should have been so often recalled both in the trials themselves and in the subsequent narratives of the Overbury murder. The striking visual image at the head of 'Sir Thomas Overbury, or The Poysoned Knights Complaint' (Plate 12), with the figure of Time on the left, his scythe wrapped round with the motto 'Time revealeth Truth', will stand for them all.

This motto was enormously consolatory in giving hope of a purposeful direction to Time's whirligig; it was also very convenient for the prosecution in this case, since it masked the question of why no action was taken immediately upon Overbury's death. The appeal of the motto also helped to ensure a climate of opinion in which the guilt of the accused could be more readily assumed. If God had seen fit to reveal it, and the King to prosecute it, how could it not be the case that those who came before the court were guilty?

But perhaps the most potent of all the story-patterns to which the events could be accommodated was that of the female siren. The suggestion during the trial hearings that the Somersets had been conducting an adulterous affair allowed the assumptions which underlay the earlier hostility to the divorce to be retrospectively validated. As John Castle wrote, 'You will see by them [Frances's letters] how abusively her lust wronged those great judgements that spake for her separation from that noble Essex'.[149] But much more than that, it permitted the progress of their affair to be represented as the seduction of a worthy man by the wickedness of female vice. The motif is pithily expressed in one widely circulated epigram:

> Heere lyes hee that once was poore
> Then Ritch, then great, then wedded to a whore
> Hee woo'd, hee wedd, and in conclusion
> his loue, and whore, was his confusion[150]

In a much more extended poem, surviving to my knowledge only in one manuscript, this narrative is amplified. It begins 'Why how now Robine? discontented quite', and laments the lust that led him to 'thy wronge stylde Countess Englands Cokeatryce':

> What franticke humor haunted thee, what fitte?
> that thou to launch noe other place could fynde
> but there where thou wert shewer thy barke to splytt;
>
> . . .
>
> did Englands fruitfull bosome yeald such scope
> of vertuous plantes, and trulye noble stemmes
> and yett must thou neades coople with a whore

> to gaine base dross, despicinge pretiouse Jemmes
> loosinge thy share in heaven and earth and all
> to tast a bitt which tasted was with galle.[151]

A more self-consciously literary variation is offered in a poem in the commonplace-book of the second Earl of Clare:

> Me thinks I see a lady sitt and mourne
> like Hellen, whose hott lust sett fyer on Troy,
> Paris lyes wounded, Menelaus doth scorne
> his amorous spouse, and makes her griefe his joy,
> ould Lindarus sitts mourning all in black,
> Castor and Pollux hide their heads with shame
> on every side her Troians go to wrack
> and the wide world exclaimes on Hellenes name;
> eache drunken Greeke makes her his tale of mirth,
> and with her shame fills every strumpets eares,
> Whylst shee poore soule sitts cursing of her birth
> seasoning each word with sighs, each sighe with teares,
> and to oblivious grave would gladly fly,
> to steale away from the worlds calumny.[152]

For all its condemnation, this poem at least seems to express some kind of sympathy for Frances in giving her transgression an epic flavour. It is rare to see.

The picture of Robert Carr as a Verdant to Frances Howard's Acrasia, a Mars to her Venus, is supplemented by lament at the fact that he preferred the love of a woman to the true affection of his male friend, Overbury. This extra, familiar ingredient served to fix Frances Howard ever more firmly within the stereotype of deceitful and dangerous womankind. And it is in this form that their story was subsequently often represented. The author of *Truth Brought to Light* wrote:

> the Viscount caught in the net of adulation, the more he striveth to be loose, is caught the faster, so that lust, having by this means got liberty, being covered with greatness, like a fire concealed in a pile of rotten wood, burst forth in all looseness and licentiousness.[153]

William Loe offered a similar reading in rather more extreme language. Dedicating his *Vox Clamantis* to Buckingham he says that it would have been happy for Carr if:

> it had pleased the Almightie his soule might have been awakened out of that fearefull slumber, wherein hee then lay, bewitched with the

Circean Cups of ambition, Wantonnesse, and sensuall securitie. Then had not his fingers, nor the hands of others, his Agents in evill, dropped with the cruell bloud-guiltenesse, neyther had their consciences been tortured, and tormented with the Hellish horrour of heart-bleeding wickednesse.[154]

Wilson characterised Carr as

In his own nature, of a gentle mind, and affable disposition, having publick affections, till they were all swallowed up in this gulf of beauty, which did precipitate him into these dangerous Contrivances. For that which made his friendship false, diverted his publick affection to his private interest . . . And if he had not met with such a Woman he might have been a good man.[155]

And so the tale has persisted of poor Robert and his lustful quean.

In the course of this chapter we have seen how important these stereotypes of character and of plot were in persuading contemporaries of the guilt of Frances Howard. The murder of Overbury could be represented as a warning of the dangers of the court, the illusion of the pursuit of place and the untrustworthiness of the great. At the same time the fact of its discovery revealed the everlasting justice of God, and, most potently of all, it could be held up as an example of the dangers of lust and the menace of womankind. It is precisely because the narrative could be made so tidy, so rounded, and be simultaneously accommodated into so many satisfying narrative frames that it has retained its appeal down to the present day.

The only blemish on the narrative's completeness was that there was no execution of Frances Howard. The Somersets lived in some comfort in the Tower before they were finally released.[156] Of their later life virtually nothing is known, though the gossips were ready to believe that they existed in a state of mutual loathing. Frances Howard died in 1632 of uterine cancer – as is revealed by the post-mortem report that survives amongst the papers of her first husband.[157] What morbid motives of revenge prompted Essex to secure this report must be a matter of speculation. What is not in doubt is the opportunity the manner of her death gave to her enemies to have their belated execution. Wilson wrote:

Her death was infamous . . . And though she died (as it were) in a corner (in so private a condition) the loathsomeness of her death made it as conspicuous as on the house top: For that part of her Body which had been the receptacle of most of her sin, grown rotten (though she never had but one Child) the ligaments failing, it fell down, and was cut away in flakes, with a most nauseous and putrid savour; which to augment, she would roul her self in her own ordure in her bed, took delight in it. Thus her affections varied; For nothing could be found sweet enough to augment her Beauties at first, and nothing stinking enough to decipher her loathsomeness at last: Pardon the sharpness of these expressions, for they are for the Glory of God, who often makes his punishments (in the ballance of his Justice) of equal weight with our sins.[158]

In an early chapter there was cause to notice the way in which historians have tended to avert their eyes from the 'disgusting particulars' of Frances Howard's story. They have also shied away from quoting this extract in full. But its very specificity and the gleeful satisfaction it derives from the dying body of Frances Howard accord with the images of justice and of God's revenges that characterise the theory and practice of execution. It is the final retribution exacted by a servant of Essex on the woman who had exposed his master to ridicule. But much more than that, it echoes the language found, for example, in Spenser's description of the stripped Duessa:

> Her teeth out of her rotten gummes were feld,
> and her sowre breath abhominably smeld;
> Her dried dugs, like bladders lacking wind,
> Hong downe, and filthy matter from them weld;
>
> . . .
>
> Her neather parts, the shame of all her kind,
> My chaster Muse for shame doth blush to write;
> But at her rompe she growing had behind
> A foxes taile, with dong all fowly dight.[159]

In her death, as so often in her life, Frances Howard is subsumed into the stereotypes of misogyny. If this final assault is the most unpleasant, it is nonetheless continuous with her characterisation throughout the history of her representation.

Epilogue

The final chapter did not speculate on the 'truth' of Frances Howard's guilt or innocence in the matter of the murder of Thomas Overbury. There are many gaps in the evidence – notably the absence of any examination of the doctors who tended Overbury during his imprisonment. There is a strong presumption that these were political show-trials. There can be no doubt at all that the thin-spun tissue of evidence, founded on hearsay, double-hearsay, doctored examinations of witnesses and the rest would not stand up for a moment in a modern court. S.R. Gardiner trenchantly observed that:

> Those who take an interest in observing the progress which has been made in our judicial institutions since the reign of James I, can hardly find a more characteristic specimen of the injustice which once prevailed universally in criminal courts than is to be found in this trial of Weston . . . If Coke had lived in our own day he would have directed the jury to find a verdict of Not Guilty.[1]

We may be less confident of the progress of justice than the Victorian historian – which would cast even stronger doubt upon the proceedings – but his conclusion is undeniable.

It may be that Overbury died from natural causes. There is a good case, made at the time and subsequently often repeated, that Robert Carr was implicated in the scheme to imprison Overbury, but not in any murderous plot. (Though even here the readiness to acquit Carr, contrasted with the ready vilification of his wife might seem to say something about the gendered perception of criminality.) It would be hard, however, to deny that Frances Howard had an intention to kill. The one writer who has produced an argument for Frances Howard's innocence, Lorie Jerrell Leininger, makes some telling points about the contradictory and fragile evidence, but in the end she is forced to rely very heavily on the hypothesis that all the accused, and especially Elwes, were coerced and bullied into producing their witness against her.[2] I would tend to believe that she did want at least to incapacitate Overbury. Whether or not she continued with the plot, whether or not there were any poisoned tarts and jellies, or whether Elwes diverted them, it is difficult to explain away that first phial of liquid that Elwes maintained he saw Weston carrying. To do so seems to me to require a hypothesis of conspiracy and narrative inventiveness on Coke's part almost as extreme as the Lord Chief Justice's own paranoid speculations about papistical poisoners.

The question of guilt is not a trivial one. I have argued strongly that the factual misrepresentation of the early part of Frances Howard's life makes a significant difference to the way one responds to the narrative of her conduct and the literature that surrounds her second marriage. But in the case of the Overbury murder it becomes important to elucidate the ways that Frances Howard was prosecuted, condemned, and subsequently reviled by a continuous process of accommodation of the narrative to stereotypical frames and misogynist character types.

During the course of writing this book I have frequently been aware of the way current events seem to reduplicate so many of the concerns that the trials of Frances Howard raise. We have seen the processes of criminal justice fiercely questioned and judgements overturned on an unprecedented scale; in particular we have been made aware of the fragility of confession evidence, and the power of national, racial and gender stereotyping to influence police and jurors alike. A succession of sexual scandals affecting politicians on both sides of the Atlantic have focused attention on the relationship between public and private morality. In Britain we have witnessed in the stories of the collapse of royal marriages the emotional investment we make in our own fairy-tales, and at the same time have been made sharply conscious of the power of scandal and gossip.

True it is that the story of Frances Howard seems 'relevant' to these and other contemporary events. (Or, to put it the other way round, perhaps these events have helped to supply me with the particular focus I have brought to her story.) But attractive though these coincidences are, they seem rather like the kind of coincidence beloved of modern directors of Shakespeare, or of teachers in the classroom desperate to waken some response in their pupils. Their very persuasiveness entices us to neglect the substantial differences between the culture of Shakespeare, or James I, or Frances Howard and our own. Yet it is through contemplation of those differences that we come to a richer understanding both of our own cultural situation and that of the past. To underline some of those differences has been one of the main aims of this book. But, as we have continually had cause to remark, one of the striking things about the story of Frances Howard is the way in which modern retellings seem to bring with them so readily and so unproblematically assumptions and responses that seem curiously out of place in the late twentieth century.

And herein lies the relevance of the story of Frances Howard to a modern audience. In a newspaper article entitled 'Why the Moors Murders are kept alive', David Astor writes of the way in which the terrible murders of five young people in 1966 are still constantly referred to in the tabloid press, whereas other serial murders have more quickly faded from view. He points out that as time passes Ian Brady, whose idea the murders plainly were, features much less prominently than Myra Hindley, his associate in the killings. And then he asks:

> So, how did these newspapers reach their apparent certainty that it is the woman who is diabolically wicked? They certainly can have had almost no first-hand information. It seems that they developed their picture of her simply by assuming that she was at the centre of the drama and then creating a character to fit the role ... The woman is usually referred to as "evil" or "monster" or "moors monster" and is ritually abused in the most unrestrained terms, as if she had lost her human status.

He continues:

> Why, in fact, does the public continue reading about the Moors Murders? It cannot be to discover who committed the crimes, because everyone has known that for over 20 years. Could it be the vengeful excitement of feeling that no fate is bad enough for that women [sic] ... It is a thought that belongs to the witch-hunting of the 17th century.[3]

This is the real significance of retelling the trials of Frances Howard. So long as she is demonised, so long as publishers find it worth their while to produce books entitled *Infamous Women* with no parallel volume on 'Wicked Men', just so long will such attitudes persist in our courts of law and in society at large.

Joan Wallach Scott wrote that: 'Sexual difference ... is a variable social organisation that itself must be explained. History figures in this approach not exclusively as the record of changes in the social organisation of the sexes but also crucially as a participant in the production of knowledge about sexual difference. I assume that history's representations of the past help construct gender for the present'.[4]

Exactly.

Notes

INTRODUCTION

1 For example: Andrew Amos, *The Great Oyer of Poisoning* (London: Richard Bentley, 1846); Sir E. Parry, *The Overbury Mystery* (London: Fisher Unwin, 1925); William McElwee, *The Murder of Sir Thomas Overbury* (London: Faber & Faber, 1952); Miriam Allen deFord, *The Overbury Affair: The Murder Trial that Rocked the Court of King James I* (Philadelphia: Chilton, 1960); Beatrice White, *Cast of Ravens* (London: John Murray, 1965); Joseph Allen Matter, *My Lords and Lady of Essex: Their State Trials* (Chicago: Henry Regnery, 1969); Edward LeComte, *The Notorious Lady Essex* (London: Robert Hale, 1969).

2 Arthur Wilson, *The History of Great Britain, Being the Life and Reign of James I* (1653). The works of Weldon and Sanderson are both reprinted in Sir Walter Scott, ed., *Secret History of the Court of James* (2 vols, Edinburgh: John Ballantyne and Co.; London: Longman, 1811). Godfrey Goodman, *The Court of King James I*, ed. J.S. Brewer, 2 vols (London: 1839).

3 Hayden White, *Tropics of Discourse: Essays in Cultural Criticism* (Baltimore and London: Johns Hopkins University Press, 1979) pp. 84–5.

4 See, for example, G.R. Elton, *Return to Essentials: Some Reflections on the Present State of Historical Study* (Cambridge: Cambridge University Press, 1991). For a more sympathetic survey of attitudes to this question see Peter Burke, ed., *New Perspectives on Historical Writing* (Cambridge: Polity Press, 1991).

5 Jean E. Howard, 'The New Historicism in Renaissance Studies', in Arthur F. Kinney and Dan S. Collins, eds, *Renaissance Historicism: Selections from English Literary Renaissance* (Amherst: University of Massachusetts Press, 1987) p. 15.

6 W. Lance Bennett and Martha S. Feldman, *Reconstructing Reality in the Courtroom* (London: Tavistock Publications; New Brunswick: Rutgers University Press, 1981) p. 4. See also Bernard S. Jackson, *Law, Fact and Narrative Coherence* (Merseyside: Deborah Charles Publications, 1988).

7 David Riggs, *Ben Jonson: A Life* (Cambridge, Mass., and London: Harvard University Press, 1989) p. 201.

8 G.P.V. Akrigg, *Jacobean Pageant, or The Court of King James I* (London: Hamish Hamilton, 1962) p. 182.

9 Aileen Ribiero, *Dress and Morality* (London: B.T. Batsford, 1986) p. 77.

10 See Joan Smith, *Misogynies* (London: Faber & Faber, 1989) pp. 1–2.

11 See Roy Strong, *The English Icon* (issued by the Paul Mellon Foundation; London: Routledge & Kegan Paul, 1969) especially pls 205, 232, 292, 312, 345, 352.
12 *CSP (Venetian)*, XV p. 80.
13 Quoted in Louis A. Montrose, '*A Midsummer Night's Dream* and the Shaping Fantasies of Elizabethan Culture: Gender, Power Form', in Margaret W. Ferguson, Maureen Quilligan and Nancy J. Vickers, eds, *Rewriting the Renaissance: The Discourses of Sexual Difference in Early Modern Europe* (Chicago and London: University of Chicago Press, 1986) pp. 66–7.
14 Nathanael Richards, *The Celestial Publican* (1631) sig. H2^r.
15 Margaret R. Miles, 'The Virgin's One Bare Breast: Female Nudity and Religious Meaning in Tuscan Early Renaissance Culture', in Susan Rubin Suleiman, ed., *The Female Body in Western Culture* (Cambridge, Mass., and London: Harvard University Press, 1986) pp. 193–205. See also Anne Hollander, *Seeing Through Clothes* (New York: Viking Press, 1978) ch. 3.
16 Ellen Chirelstein, 'Lady Elizabeth Pope: The Heraldic Body', in Lucy Gent and Nigel Llewellyn, eds, *Renaissance Bodies: The Human Figure in English Culture c. 1540–1660* (London: Reaktion Books, 1990) pp. 57–9.
17 C.H. Herford, Percy and Evelyn Simpson, eds, *Ben Jonson* (Oxford: Clarendon Press) vol. X (1950) p. 449.
18 Strong, *English Icon*, pp. 326–48.
19 See Arthur M. Hind, *Engraving in England in the Sixteenth and Seventeenth Centuries, Part II: The Reign of James I* (Cambridge: Cambridge University Press, 1955) pp. 362–4.
20 R.S. White, *The Merry Wives of Windsor*, Harvester New Critical Introductions to Shakespeare (New York and London: Harvester Wheatsheaf, 1991).

1   THE FIRST TRIAL: AN ARRANGED MARRIAGE

1 Though it was stated that Frances Howard was thirteen at the time of the marriage in the petition for divorce, there is some uncertainty about her age. In two Bodleian MSS, Ashmole 174 and 243, horoscopes of Frances Howard disagree about her date of birth, the first giving 26 August 1591, the second 31 May 1590. Some commentators have suggested that she was as old as seventeen at the time of her marriage (J. M. Robinson, *The Dukes of Norfolk: A Quincentennial History* (Oxford and New York: Oxford University Press, 1982) p. 90). But though the arithmetic of the divorce petition in the form printed in *State Trials* is self-evidently nonsense, since it claims that she was thirteen in 1606 but twenty-two or three by 1613, the weight of evidence is that she was indeed about thirteen years old.
2 Lawrence Stone, *Family and Fortune: Studies in Aristocratic Finance in the Sixteenth and Seventeenth Centuries* (Oxford: Clarendon Press, 1973) pp. 268–9.
3 Richard Griffin [Baron Braybrooke], *The History of Audley End* (London: S. Bentley, 1835) pp. 42–3.
4 Lawrence Stone, *The Family, Sex and Marriage* (London: Weidenfeld & Nicolson, 1977) p. 652.
5 In the event this last marriage was also to run into difficulties. When Elizabeth conceived children in the last years of her husband's life (and he was by then in his eighties) it was assumed that they were begotten by her lover, Lord Vaux

(whom she married five weeks after her husband's death), and their right to the Earldom of Banbury was disputed for several centuries.

6 See Ann Jennalie Cook, *Making a Match: Courtship in Shakespeare and his Society* (Princeton: Princeton University Press, 1991) pp. 265–6.

7 Lawrence Stone, *The Crisis of the Aristocracy, 1558–1641* (Oxford: Clarendon Press, 1965) p. 653.

8 Stone, *Family and Fortune*, p. 217.

9 Mervyn James, 'At a Crossroads of the Political Culture: The Essex Revolt, 1601', in *Society, Politics and Culture: Studies in Early Modern England* (Cambridge: Cambridge University Press, 1986) p. 416.

10 Neil Cuddy, 'Anglo-Scottish Union and the Court of James, 1603–1625', *Transactions of the Royal Historical Society*, 5th series, 39 (1989) p. 114.

11 Vernon F. Snow, *Essex the Rebel: The Life of Robert Devereux, the Third Earl of Essex, 1591–1646* (Lincoln, Nebr.: University of Nebraska Press, 1970) p. 21.

12 Arthur Wilson, *The History of Great Britain* (1653) p. 55.

13 *CSP (Venetian)*, X, p. 308.

14 Snow, *Essex the Rebel*, p. 25.

15 *SP* 14/15/98.

16 See Martin Butler, 'Private and Occasional Drama', in A.R. Braunmuller and Michael Hattaway, eds, *The Cambridge Companion to English Renaissance Drama* (Cambridge: Cambridge University Press, 1990); Jonathan Goldberg, *James I and the Politics of Literature* (Baltimore and London: Johns Hopkins University Press, 1983); David Lindley, ed., *The Court Masque* (Manchester: Manchester University Press, 1984); Stephen Orgel, *The Illusion of Power* (Berkeley, Los Angeles and London: University of California Press, 1975).

17 Thomas Campion in his *Lords' Masque* of 1613 and Chapman in the preface to *The Memorable Masque* of the same year are similarly preoccupied with the inability of the ignorant to understand their work.

18 D.J. Gordon '*Hymenaei*: Jonson's Masque of Union', reprinted in *The Renaissance Imagination: Essays and Lectures by D.J. Gordon*, ed. Stephen Orgel (Berkeley and Los Angeles: University of California Press, 1975) pp. 157–84.

19 Alan MacFarlane, *Marriage and Love in England, 1300–1840* (Oxford: Basil Blackwell, 1986) pp. 211–12. See also Cook, *Making a Match*, ch. 2.

20 See Alan Young, *Tudor and Jacobean Tournaments* (London: George Philip, 1987) for description and analysis of the genre.

21 A.B. Grosart, ed., *The Life and Complete Works of Robert Greene* (London: The Huth Library, 1881–3) 12 vols; V, p. 163.

22 See Lawrence Stone, *Crisis*, pp. 72–3, for an account of the activity of Essex in knighting followers, and the derision that this provoked.

23 William Gataker, *Marriage Duties* (1620) pp. 38–9.

24 Joseph Swetnam, *The Araignment* (1615) pp. 51–2.

25 Thomas Middleton, *A Chaste Maid in Cheapside*, ed. R.B. Parker, The Revels Plays (London: Methuen, 1969) IV.iv.20.

26 David Atkinson, 'Marriage under Compulsion in English Renaissance Drama', *English Studies*, 67 (1986) pp. 497–8.

27 *History of the World*, Book V, in Gerald Hammond, ed., *Sir Walter Raleigh: Selected Writings* (Manchester: Carcanet, 1984) p. 226.

28 Atkinson, 'Marriage under Compulsion', p. 490.

29 Cyril Tourneur, *The Atheist's Tragedy*, ed. Brian Morris and Roma Gill, New Mermaids (London: Ernest Benn, 1976) I.iv.116, 119–20.

30 John Webster, *The Devils' Law Case*, ed. Frances A. Shirley, Regents Renaissance Drama (London: Edward Arnold, 1972) I.ii.214–22.

31 Stone, *Crisis*, p. 596.

32 Sidney, *Astrophil and Stella*, Sonnet 69, ll.9–11, ed. Katherine Duncan-Jones (Oxford and New York: Oxford University Press, 1989).

33 *The Essays of Montaigne Done into English by John Florio*, ed. George Saintsbury (London: David Nutt, 1893) 3 vols, I, p. 72.

34 MacFarlane, *Marriage and Love*, pp. 128–9. Cook, *Making a Match*, ch. 4, gives an account more weighted towards the power of parents.

35 Stone, *Crisis*, p. 611.

36 Kathleen M. Davies, 'Continuity and Change in Literary Advice on Marriage', in R.B. Outhwaite, ed., *Marriage and Society* (London: Europa, 1981) pp. 58–80.

37 MacFarlane, *Marriage and Love*, p. 183.

38 John Marston, *The Wonder of Women or The Tragedy of Sophonisba*, in Peter Corbin and Douglas Sedge, eds, *Three Jacobean Witchcraft Plays*, The Revels Plays (Manchester: Manchester University Press, 1986) IV.i.32–41.

39 See Caroline Lucas, *Writing for Women: The Example of Woman as Reader in Elizabethan Romance* (Milton Keynes: Open University Press, 1989).

40 Shelley, *A Defence of Poetry*, ed. H.F. B. Brett-Smith (Oxford: Basil Blackwell, 1972) p. 46.

41 Robert Anton, *Vices Anotimie Scourged* (1617) pp. 46–7.

42 William Heale, *An Apologie for Women* (1609) p. 10.

43 For many parallel insistences on the need to satisfy both requirements see Cook, *Making a Match*, ch. 4; Keith Wrightson, *English Society 1580–1680* (London: Hutchinson, 1982) ch. 3.

44 *CSP (Venetian)*, X, p. 365.

45 Chamberlain, I, p. 381.

46 Alison D. Wall, ed., *Two Elizabethan Women: Correspondence of Joan and Maria Thynne 1575–1611* (Devizes: Wiltshire Record Society, 1983) pp. xxv–xxvi. It has been suggested that this episode may have influenced Shakespeare's treatment of the Romeo and Juliet story.

47 William Painter, *The Palace of Pleasure*, ed. Joseph Jacobs (London: David Nutt, 1890) 3 vols, I, pp. 130–7.

48 Martin Ingram, *Church Courts, Sex and Marriage in England, 1570–1640* (Cambridge: Cambridge University Press, 1987) pp. 212–18.

49 Painter, *The Palace of Pleasure*, II, p. 321.

2   INTERLUDE: FILLING IN THE BLANKS

1 Chamberlain, I, p. 328.

2 *HMC Downshire MSS*, II, p. 328.

3 *HMC Salisbury* MSS, XXI, p. 368.

4 Beatrice White, *Cast of Ravens* (London: John Murray, 1965) pp. 18–19.

5 William McElwee, *The Murder of Sir Thomas Overbury* (London: Faber & Faber, 1952) pp. 36–7.

6 See Lawrence Stone, *Family and Fortune: Studies in Aristocratic Finance in the*

Sixteenth and Seventeenth Centuries (Oxford: Clarendon Press, 1973) ch. 9.

7 Lawrence Stone, *The Crisis of the Aristocracy 1558–1641* (Oxford: Oxford University Press, 1965) p. 492.

8 Barbara K. Lewalski, 'Lucy, Countess of Bedford', in Kevin Sharpe and Steven N. Zwicker, eds, *Politics of Discourse: The Literature and History of Seventeenth-century England* (Berkeley, Los Angeles and London: University of California Press, 1987) p. 55.

9 Mary Siraut, ed., *The Trevelyan Letters to 1840* (Taunton: Somerset Record Society, 1990) p. 103.

10 'The Owle', in *Poems of Michael Drayton*, ed. John Buxton (London: Routledge & Kegan Paul, 1953) 2 vols, I, p. 100, ll. 705–10.

11 See Leeds Barroll, 'The Court of the First Stuart Queen', in Linda Levy Peck, ed., *The Mental World of the Jacobean Court* (Cambridge: Cambridge University Press, 1991) pp. 191–208, and Linda Levy Peck, *Court Patronage and Corruption in Early Stuart England* (Boston: Unwin Hyman, 1990) pp. 68–74.

12 *SP* 14/84/12.

13 *SP* 14/84/27, 29.

14 A.L. Rowse, 'Bishop Thornborough: A Clerical Careerist', in *For Veronica Wedgwood These*, ed. Richard Ollard and Pamela Tudor-Craig (London: Collins, 1986) pp. 95–6.

15 Ian Donaldson, ed., *The Oxford Authors: Ben Jonson*, (Oxford: Oxford University Press, 1985) p. 604. All subsequent references to Jonson's poetry are to this edition.

16 See Keith Thomas, *Religion and the Decline of Magic* (London: Weidenfeld & Nicolson, 1971; Harmondsworth: Penguin, 1973) pp. 209–300, 335–82.

17 Thomas, *Religion*, p. 379.

18 Chamberlain, I, p. 449.

19 *SP* 14/72/53.

20 *SP* 14/51/133.

21 Charles Richardson, *A Sermon Concerning the Punishing of Malefactors* (1616) p. 15.

22 White, *Cast of Ravens*, pp. 37–8.

23 Jonson, *Epicoene or the Silent Woman*, ed. R.V. Holdsworth, New Mermaids (London: Ernest Benn, 1979) II.ii.121–8.

24 *A Warning for Fair Women*, Old English Drama Facsimile (London, 1912) sig. C^r-v.

25 Thomas, *Religion*, p. 375.

26 Linda Woodbridge, *Women and the English Renaissance* (Urbana and Chicago: University of Illinois Press, 1984) ch. 9.

27 William Goddard, *Satyricall Dialogue* (Low Countries: 1616?) sig. C.

28 In *Jyl of Breyntford's Testament*, ed. F. J. Furnivall (London: privately printed, 1871).

29 Wilson, *History*, p. 57.

30 Quoted in Stone, *Crisis*, p. 665.

31 Robert Niccols, *The Cuckow* (1607) p. 43.

32 Beaumont and Fletcher, *The Maid's Tragedy*, ed. T.W. Craik, Revels Plays (Manchester: Manchester University Press, 1988) II.i.8–18.

33 Kathleen McLuskie, *Renaissance Dramatists* (New York and London: Harvester Wheatsheaf, 1989) p. 193.

34 *The Plays and Poems of Philip Massinger*, ed. Philip Edwards and Colin Gibson (Oxford: Clarendon Press, 1976) 5 vols, II, III.i.8–12.

35 Chamberlain, I, p. 487.

36 Francis Osborne, *The True Tragicomedy Formerly Acted at Court*, ed. John Pitcher and Lois Potter (New York and London: Garland, 1983) p. 54.

37 Francis Mason, *Two Sermons* (1621) sig. A2ᵛ.

38 John Dod and Robert Cleaver, *A Plaine and Familiar Exposition of the Ten Commandments* (18th edn 1630) p. 259.

39 William Whately, *A Bride-Bush* (1617) p. 10.

40 Thomas Beard, *The Theatre of Gods Judgements* (2nd edn 1612) pp. 431, 435.

41 *Ben Jonson*, ed. C.H. Herford, Percy and Evelyn Simpson (Oxford: Clarendon Press) vol. X (1950) p. 449.

42 *Divine Catastrophe of the House of Stuarts*, in Sir Walter Scott, ed., *Secret History of the Court of James the First* (Edinburgh: John Ballantyne, 1811) 2 vols, II, p. 369.

43 Tourneur, *The Revenger's Tragedy*, ed. R.A. Foakes, The Revels Plays (London: Methuen, 1966) I.iv.26–44. (The play is now more generally ascribed to Middleton.)

44 Chamberlain, I, p. 438.

45 University College London, MS Ogden 4, fol. 29.

46 Thomas Beard, *The Theatre of Gods Judgements* (2nd edn London, 1612) p. 4.

47 Stone, *Crisis*, p. 391.

48 Alexander Niccholes, *Discourse of Marriage and Wiving* (1620) sig. E2ᵛ.

49 Lawrence Manley, 'From Matron to Monster: Tudor-Stuart London and the Languages of Urban Description', in Heather Dubrow and Richard Strier, eds, *The Historical Renaissance: New Essays on Tudor and Stuart Literature and Culture* (Chicago and London: University of Chicago Press, 1988) pp. 348, 355.

50 Peter R. Seddon, ed., *Letters of John Holles* (Nottingham: Thoroton Society, 1975–86) 3 vols, II, p. 314.

51 Chamberlain, I, p. 54.

52 'To the World a Farewell for a Gentlewoman, Vertuous and Noble', ll. 65–8.

53 Linda Pollock, ' "Teach her to live under obedience": The making of women in the upper ranks of early modern England', *Continuity and Change*, 4 (1989) p. 245.

54 Ibid. pp. 250–1.

55 *HMC Salisbury MSS*, XXI, p. 157.

56 *CSP Venetian (1610–1613)*, p. 412.

57 *CSP Venetian (1615–1617)*, p. 61.

58 J.O. Halliwell, ed., *The Autobiography and Correspondence of Sir Simonds D'Ewes* (London: Richard Bentley, 1845) 2 vols, I, pp. 90–1.

59 J.W. Williamson, *The Myth of the Conqueror: Prince Henry Stuart: A Study of 17th Century Personation* (New York: AMS Press, 1978) p. 130.

60 Stone, *Crisis*, p. 667.

61 Weldon, *Court and Character of King James*, in *Secret History*, I, pp. 388–9.

62 Coppélia Kahn, 'Whores and Wives in Jacobean Drama', in Dorothea Kehler and Susan Baker, eds, *In Another Country: Feminist Perspectives on Renaissance Drama* (Metuchen, NJ, and London: The Scarecrow Press, 1991) p. 252.

63 BL MS Additional 35832, fol. 5.

64 *HMC Salisbury MSS*, XXII p. 29. (A much fuller account than that in the *State Trials*.)
65 CUL MS Dd.3.63, p. 23.
66 *SP* 14/83/20.
67 Berkshire Record Office MS D/EN/F6/1/17.
68 Chamberlain, I, p. 510–11.
69 CUL MS Dd.3. 63, fols 28, 21.
70 Ibid., fols 31, 35, 54.
71 Bodleian MS Willis 58, fol. 229.
72 Thomas Birch, *Court and Times of James I* (1848) 2 vols, I, p. 381.
73 Ibid., p. 380.
74 Massinger, *The Plays and Poems*, vol. I.
75 Massinger, *The Plays and Poems*, vol. II.
76 Alexander Niccholes, *Discourse of Marriage and Wiving* (1615), quoted in Roderick Phillips, *Putting Asunder: A History of Divorce in Western Society* (Cambridge: Cambridge University Press, 1988) p. 106.
77 Walter Bouchier Devereux, *Lives and Letters of the Devereux, Earls of Essex* (London: John Murray, 1853) 2 vols, I, pp. 243–4.
78 Edward Le Comte, *The Notorious Lady Essex* (London: Robert Hale, 1969).

3   THE SECOND TRIAL: SEEKING AN ANNULMENT

1 See William A. McClung and Rodney Simard, 'Donne's Somerset Epithalamion and the Erotics of Criticism', *Huntington Library Quarterly*, 50 (1987) pp. 95–106.
2 Heather Dubrow, *A Happier Eden: The Politics of Marriage in the Stuart Epithalamium* (Ithaca and London: Cornell University Press, 1990) pp. 132–3.
3 BL MS Additional 15476, p. 1. Many other MS accounts begin with summaries of the divorce hearings.
4 Middleton and Rowley, *The Changeling*, ed. N.W. Bawcutt, Revels Plays (London: Methuen, 1958) III.iv.135–9.
5 T.S. Eliot, 'Thomas Middleton', in *Selected Essays* (London: Faber & Faber, 3rd edn 1951) p. 163.
6 Godfrey Goodman, *The Court of King James the First*, ed. John S. Brewer (London: Richard Bentley, 1839) 2 vols, I, p. 221.
7 Robert Abbot, *A Wedding Sermon Preached at Bentley in Darbyshire* (1608), quoted in Roderick Phillips, *Putting Asunder: A History of Divorce in Western Society* (Cambridge: Cambridge University Press, 1988) pp. 98–9.
8 Lawrence Stone, *The Crisis of the Aristocracy 1558–1641* (Oxford: Oxford University Press, 1965) p. 661
9 CUL MS Dd. 3. 63, fol. 31.
10 R. Winwood, *Memorials of Affairs of State*, ed. E. Sawyer (1725) 3 vols, II, p. 463.
11 I have used that in BL MS Harley 39, fols 416–31.
12 Samuel R. Gardiner, *History of England, 1603–1642* (London: Longmans, Green and Co., 1883) II, p. 211. To Kenneth Parker, however, I owe the information that the good citizens of Guildford have recently objected to the erection of a statue to Abbot, on the grounds of 'an accidental killing and a number of sexual misdemeanours'. The defence offered by Dr Edward Norman

is, in the context of my story, a chilling one: 'as for stories of young women, we in today's world take such things more grievously. Just because of a few indiscretions, we should not strike him off the historical record' (*London Evening Standard*, 10 March 1992, p. 8).

13 Neil Cuddy, 'The revival of the entourage: The Bedchamber of James I 1603–1625', in David Starkey, ed., *The English Court from the Wars of the Roses to the Civil War* (London: Longman, 1987) p. 173.

14 For a thorough survey of Carr's shifting allegiances during his career, see Peter R. Seddon, 'Robert Carr, Earl of Somerset', *Renaissance and Modern Studies*, 14 (1970) pp. 46–68.

15 *HMC Mar & Kellie MSS*, II, pp. 52–3. Much later, at the time of Abbot's death, Holles, in rather ambiguous terms says he 'was a timorous weake man, yet was he orthodoxe, and hindered much ill, only the Court ill was too strong for him, the Nullity excepted, wherin he was backt by that Queene, and the hope of the then favorits fall, through that kings mutability' (*Letters*, p. 452).

16 Leeds Barroll, 'The Court of the First Stuart Queen', in Linda Levy Peck, ed., *The Mental World of the Jacobean Court* (Cambridge: Cambridge University Press, 1991) pp. 191–208, is mainly concerned with her artistic patronage, but has some points to make more generally.

17 *HMC Portland MSS*, IX, p. 31. The letter is dated 17 February 1613 – but surely refers to February 1614, and to the marriage of Lord Roxborough. Seddon in his edition refers to this letter, corrects the date, but suggests wrongly that it refers to the Carr/Howard wedding. Apparently on this occasion Essex once again became involved in a public quarrel and threatened a duel; see Vernon F. Snow, *Essex the Rebel: The Life of Robert Devereux, the Third Earl of Essex, 1591–1646* (Lincoln, Nebr.: University of Nebraska Press, 1970) p. 73.

18 CUL MS Dd. 3.63, fol. 39. The Queen was particularly hostile to North-ampton at this time, since she was engaged with him in a fierce quarrel over the stewardship of Greenwich Park; see Linda Levy Peck, *Northampton: Patronage and Policy at the Court of James I* (London: George Allen and Unwin, 1982) pp. 73–4.

19 See *HMC Downshire MSS*, III, p. 83.

20 Sir Walter Scott, ed., *Secret History of the Court of James the First* (Edinburgh: John Ballantyne, 1811) 2 vols, I, pp. 377–8.

21 *The Works of John Ford*, ed. Alexander Dyce (1895; reprinted New York: Russell and Russell, 1965) 3 vols, II, p. 228.

22 CUL MS Dd. 3. 63, fol. 44.

23 The Revd Thomas Lorkin, writing in June, is still convinced that the 'great places of the court are not yet disposed' because of 'the faction which is between the family of the Howards on the one side, and the Earl of Southampton and Viscount Rochester on the other' (Birch, *The Court and Times of James I* (1848) I, p. 248).

24 Roderick Phillips, *Putting Asunder*, p. 71.

25 See Phillips, *Putting Asunder*, ch. 2. I am much indebted to this work throughout these and subsequent comments.

26 Ibid., p. 69.

27 A.R. Winnett, *Divorce and Remarriage in Anglicanism* (London, 1958) pp. 32–3. The fear of poison here ties in with Calvert's letter, and with Lancelot Andrewes's worry that putting Frances Howard and her husband back together

would be to run the risk of prompting them to poison. The implications of this will be dealt with in the next chapter.

28 Phillips, *Putting Asunder*, p. 113.

29 George Calvert, in *HMC Buccleugh MSS*, I, p. 63.

30 Lambeth Palace MS 943, p. 48. Winnett (p. 103–8) discusses this divorce, and points out that this letter, though headed in the MS 'A discourse written by the Earl of Devonshire' is but the prelude to a longer treatise. That treatise, which Winnett thinks lost, can be found in the British Library (MS Stowe 423, fols 81–103); the prefatory letter is in MS Lansdowne 885, fols 86^r–87^v. I have used the MS of the treatise in Northamptonshire Record Office, Finch-Hatton MS 90.

31 Northamptonshire Record Office, Finch-Hatton MS 90, fol. 8^{r-v}.

32 Lawrence Stone, *Road to Divorce: England 1530–1987* (Oxford: Oxford University Press, 1990) p. 307.

33 Quoted in Sylvia Freedman, '*The White Devil* and the Fair Woman with a Black Soul', in Clive Bloom, ed., *Jacobean Poetry and Prose* (London: Macmillan, 1988) p. 151.

34 Milton, *Doctrine and Discipline of Divorce* (1643), ed. Ernest Sirluck, *Complete Prose Works of John Milton*, II (New Haven: Yale University Press; Oxford: Oxford University Press, 1959) p. 345.

35 For a discussion of Milton's tracts see James Grantham Turner, *One Flesh: Paradisal Marriage and Sexual Relations in the Age of Milton* (Oxford: Clarendon Press, 1987) especially ch. 6.

36 Anon., *Truth Brought to Light and Discovered by Time* (1651) p. 31.

37 Pierre Darmon, *Trial by Impotence: Virility and Marriage in Pre-Revolutionary France*, trans. Paul Keegan (London: Chatto, 1985) p. 95.

38 Robert Snawsel, *A Looking Glass for Married Folks* (1610) pp. 39–40.

39 I quote from a modern-spelling text prepared by Stephanie Wright. There is an old-spelling edition of the play, ed. A.C. Dunstan (London: Malone Society, 1914) and the lineation follows this text; a new edition by Diana Purkiss is in preparation (Pickering and Chatto, 1993).

40 William Terracae, 'A Plenarie Satisfaction, oute of the holie Scriptures, Cannons, and Civill Lawes authorised'. Northamptonshire Record Office, Finch-Hatton MS 319 fol. 11^v. I am deeply grateful to Jeremy Maule for drawing this poem to my attention. The identity of the author is a mystery.

41 John Dove, *Of Divorcement: A Sermon Preached at Pauls Crosse the 10 of May 1601*, p. 51.

42 Catherine Belsey, *The Subject of Tragedy* (London: Methuen, 1985) p. 174.

43 Betty S. Travitsky, 'Husband-murder and Petty Treason in English Renaissance Tragedy', *Renaissance Drama*, new series, 21 (1990) p. 187.

44 D. Harris Willson, *King James VI and I* (London: Jonathan Cape, 1956) p. 339.

45 R.H. Helmholz, *Marriage Litigation in Medieval England* (Cambridge: Cambridge University Press, 1974) pp. 87–8.

46 This, of course, has been the case throughout the history of marriage litigation. See Stone, *Road to Divorce*, pp. 18–19.

47 Darmon, *Trial by Impotence*, p. 76. Opponents were aware of this, but chose to take their stand on English practice (*ST*, 852).

48 Chamberlain, I, p. 444.

49 BL MS Harley 39, fol. 427^r.

50 Goodman, *Court of King James*, I, p. 222.
51 CUL MS Dd.3.63, fol. 37.
52 Anon., *Truth Brought to Light*, p. 31.
53 William Sanderson, *Aulicus Coquinariae*, in Walter Scott, ed., *Secret History*, II, pp. 199–200.
54 Freud, 'On the Universal Tendency to Debasement in the Sphere of Love', in *Freud on Sexuality*, Pelican Freud Library, vol. 7 (Harmondsworth: Penguin, 1977) p. 247.
55 Reginald Scot, *The Discoverie of Witchcraft* (1584) p. 77.
56 The play may well have been alluding to the divorce case. The possibility was first suggested by R.C. Bald, 'The Chronology of Middleton's Plays', *Modern Language Review*, 32 (1937) p. 41. The allusion has been suggested by Anne Lancashire as the reason why the play seems not to have been frequently performed, in 'The Witch: Stage Flop or Political Mistake?' in Kenneth Friedereich, ed., *'Accompaninge the players': Essays in Celebration of Thomas Middleton, 1580–1980* (New York, 1983) pp. 161–81. While it is indeed possible that the play seemed indiscreet after 1613, the annulment hearings are not a necessary condition of its writing. It is more usefully considered as a sign of patterns of belief than specific commentary.
57 University of Leeds MS Trv.q.3, p. 92. Michael Brennan, ed., *The Travel Diary (1611–1612) of an English Catholic, Sir Charles Somerset* (Leeds: Leeds Philosophical and Literary Society, 1993) pp. 163–4.
58 See Kenneth Fincham, 'Prelacy and Politics: Archbishop Abbot's Defence of Protestant Orthodoxy', *Historical Research*, 61 (1988) pp. 37–64.
59 In the speech he had hoped to give before the final judgement Abbot still maintained his belief that *maleficium* was a Romish device, though he puts it much more cautiously (*ST*, 847).
60 In the fifteenth century such examinations were carried out. Helmholtz recounts a case in York where women attempted to excite a man's sexual desire in very direct fashion, without success, but suggests that the practice terminated by 1450 (*Marriage Litigation*, p. 79).
61 Chester City Record Office, MS CR 63.2.19, fol. 14.
62 BL MS Cotton Vitellius C. XVI, fol. 119. This MS is fire-damaged, and possibly imperfectly assembled. It seems to contain the materials from which Dunne wrote his treatise, and a number of other revealing notes on the hearings.
63 Northamptonshire Record Office, Finch-Hatton MS 319, fol. 20[r].
64 Ben Jonson, *Epicoene*, ed. R.V. Holdsworth, New Mermaids (London: Ernest Benn, 1979) V.iv.51–3.
65 W.R. Davis, ed., *The Works of Thomas Campion* (London: Faber & Faber, 1969) p. 189.
66 Marlowe, *Elegies*, III.vi.27–36, in *The Poems of Christopher Marlowe*, ed. Millar MacLure, The Revels Plays (London: Methuen, 1968).
67 Thomas Nashe, 'The Choice of Valentines', in *The Unfortunate Traveller and Other Works*, ed. J.B. Steane (Harmondsworth: Penguin, 1972) p. 462.
68 Wilson, *History*, p. 58.
69 Ibid., p. 59.
70 Darmon, *Trial by Impotence*, p. 91.
71 T.I. [or T.J.], *The Haven of Pleasure* (1597) pp. 147, 158. This author blames

women's unreason on what might now be called pre-menstrual tension; it's the need to disperse the noxious humours of the menses that gives women their raging natures.

72 This is the version in BL MS Additional 24665, fol. 20; In Bodleian MS Ashmole 38 it is subscribed 'My Lady Somerset'. Arthur Marotti points out to me that this version is in a commonplace-book collected by a royalist soldier – who may therefore have seen it as part of an attack on Essex.

73 Stephen Greenblatt, 'Fiction and Friction', in *Shakespearean Negotiation: The Circulation of Social Energy in Renaissance England* (Oxford: Clarendon Press, 1988) pp. 66–93; Thomas Laqueur, *Making Sex: Body and Gender from the Greeks to Freud* (Cambridge, Mass., and London: Harvard University Press, 1990), especially chs. 1–3.

74 *Niobe* (1611) sig. C2^v–3. The nervousness about women's sexual excitement is part of a more general anxiety affecting both male and female alike. Christian morality, and medical science, which claimed that sex shortened your life, combined to produce advice that married couples should not have sex too often, or enjoy it too much.

75 Peter Stallybrass, 'Patriarchal Territories: The Body Enclosed', in Margaret W. Ferguson, Maureen Quilligan and Nancy J. Vickers, eds, *Rewriting the Renaissance: The Discourses of Sexual Difference in Early Modern Europe* (Chicago and London: University of Chicago Press, 1986) pp. 126–7.

76 BL MS Harley 6578, fol. 44.

77 Peter Corbin and Douglas Sedge, eds, *Three Jacobean Witchcraft Plays* (Manchester: Manchester University Press, 1986).

78 Dympna Callaghan, *Women and Gender in Renaissance Tragedy* (New York and London: Harvester Wheatsheaf, 1989) p. 143.

79 Alison D. Wall, ed., *Two Elizabethan Women: Correspondence of Joan and Maria Thynne, 1575–1611* (Devizes: Wiltshire Record Society, 1983) pp. 37–8. This letter is conjecturally dated 1607.

80 Ibid., p. 48.

81 Lisa Jardine, *Still Harping on Daughters: Women and Drama in the Age of Shakespeare* (Hemel Hempstead: Harvester, 1983; 2nd edn Harvester Wheatsheaf, 1989) p. 72.

82 See Keith Thomas, 'The Double Standard', *Journal of the History of Ideas*, 20 (1959) pp. 195–216.

83 George C. Potter and Evelyn M. Simpson, eds, *The Sermons of John Donne* (Berkeley and Los Angeles: University of California Press, 1957) III, p. 248.

84 William Heale, *An Apology for Women* (1609) p. 15.

85 BL MS Harley 39, fol. 420^{r-v}.

86 BL MS Cotton Vitellius C. XVI, fols 98, 124^{r-v}.

87 Chamberlain, I, p. 461.

88 Laurent Joubert, *Popular Errors*, trans. Gregory David de Rocher (Tuscaloosa and London: University of Alabama Press, 1989) pp. 208–22.

89 Darmon, *Trial by Impotence*, p. 140.

90 Ibid., p. 171.

91 *Secret History*, pp. 389–90. Others were equally confident that it was a daughter of Thomas Monson.

92 *Aulicus Coquinariae*, in *Secret History*, II, p. 210.

93 For the 'muffled resentment' of the female rituals of childbirth see Adrian

Wilson, 'The ceremony of childbirth and its interpretation', in Valerie Fildes, ed., *Women as Mothers in Pre-Industrial England: Essays in Memory of Dorothy McLaren* (London and New York: Routledge, 1990) pp. 81–3.

94 See James C. Oldham, 'On Pleading the Belly: A History of the Jury of Matrons', *Criminal Justice History*, 6 (1985) pp. 1–64. Their other responsibilities included determining whether female convicts were pregnant, and decisions as to whether a widow was pregnant before her husband's death. I am grateful to A.R. Braunmuller for drawing this article to my attention.

95 John Gaule, quoted in Karen Newman, *Fashioning Femininity and English Renaissance Drama* (Chicago and London: University of Chicago Press, 1991) p. 60.

96 Newman, *Fashioning Femininity*, pp. 56–7.

97 Joubert, *Popular Errors*, p. 211. The Revels editors of *The Changeling* also cite Burton's contempt for such tests in *The Anatomy of Melancholy*, III.iii.2.

98 Sir Philip Sidney, *Arcadia*, ed. Maurice Evans (Harmondsworth: Penguin, 1977) p. 725.

99 Margot Heinemann, *Puritanism and Theatre: Thomas Middleton and Opposition Drama under the Early Stuarts* (Cambridge: Cambridge University Press, 1980) p. 179. Two readings of the play dealing with its absorption of material from the Overbury case are J.L. Simmons, 'Diabolical Realism in Middleton and Rowley's *The Changeling*', *Renaissance Drama*, new series, 11 (1980) pp. 135–70, and Christina Malcolmson, ' "As Tame as the Ladies": Politics and Gender in *The Changeling*', *English Literary Renaissance*, 20 (1990) pp. 320–39.

100 Northamptonshire Record Office, Finch-Hatton MS 319, fol. 21^v.

101 BL MS Additional 15476, fol. 91^v.

102 Bodleian MS Malone 23, p. 65. This is the most usual form of the poem, though in a Folger Library MS the last four lines are separated off as a distinct verse (see James L. Sanderson, 'Poems on an Affair of State', *Review of English Studies*, 17 (1966) p. 60). This poem is widely distributed, and is to be found among the MSS at Hatfield House (see *HMC Salisbury MSS*, XXIV, p. 231), where it could have been read by Frances's sister.

103 Bodleian MS Malone 19, p. 74.

104 BL MS Sloane 2023, fol. 60^v. Its likely dating before the Overbury murder trials is supported by several pieces of evidence. One MS collection has a sequence of poems on the Carr/Howard affair and this lyric comes before a heading 'Theis ensuing were sithence the discoverie of theis poysonings'. After the division is another widely circulated poem, 'Pilot or Pirate, thou hast lost this Pincke', which seems to be an answer to this verse, and, uniquely to my present knowledge, a rewriting of this lyric largely in pentameters, which takes events down to the Overbury trials. (Norman K. Farmer, Jr, 'Poems from a Seventeenth-century Manuscript with the Hand of *Robert Herrick*', *Texas Quarterly*, supplement to 16(4) (Winter 1973) pp. 1–185. The transcriptions of many of the poems, reproduced in facsimile, are faulty. See Peter Croft, 'Errata in "Poems from a Seventeenth-century Manuscript" ', *Texas Quarterly*, 19(1) (Spring 1976) pp. 160–73.)

105 Gail Kern Paster, 'Leaky Vessels: The Incontinent Women of City Comedy', *Renaissance Drama*, new series, 18 (1987) pp. 43–65.

106 Bodleian MS Rawlinson D, 1048, fol. 64.

107 *HMC Downshire MSS*, IV, p. 107.

108 Ibid., pp. 190–1.
109 Birch, *The Court and Times of James I*, I, p. 254.
110 *HMC Mar and Kellie MSS*, II, p. 51 (20 May 1613).
111 Winwood, *Memorials*, III, p. 475.
112 Chamberlain, I, p. 458.
113 Malcolmson, ' "As Tame as the Ladies" ', p. 324.
114 A.H. Manchester, *A Modern Legal History of England and Wales, 1750–1950* (London: Butterworth, 1980) p. 382.

4   INTERLUDE: CELEBRATION

1 Chamberlain, I, p. 496.
2 Ibid., I, p. 498; *HMC Cowper MSS*, I, p. 87. See also, e.g., *HMC Rutland (Belvoir) MSS*, IV, p. 500, and William McElwee, *The Murder of Sir Thomas Overbury* (London: Faber & Faber, 1952) p. 148.
3 Walter R. Davis, ed., *The Works of Thomas Campion* (London: Faber & Faber, 1969) pp. 263–86; subsequent page references in the text.
4 E.A.J. Honigmann, ed., *Masque of Flowers*, in *A Book of Masques* (Cambridge: Cambridge University Press, 1967) pp.149–78.
5 Ian Donaldson, ed., *Ben Jonson* (Oxford: Oxford University Press, 1985) p. 449.
6 BL MS Royal 12A xxxv.
7 Phyllis Brooks Bartlett, ed., *The Poems of George Chapman* (Oxford: Oxford University Press; New York: Modern Language Association of America, 1941) pp. 301–36. Quotations are from this edition, but Chapman's punctuation is so idiosyncratic that I have modified it where necessary to produce a more readable text.
8 See, for example, Guy Fitch Lytle and Stephen Orgel, eds, *Patronage in the Renaissance* (Princeton: Princeton University Press, 1981), and Linda Levy Peck, *Court Patronage and Corruption in Early Stuart England* (Boston: Unwin Hyman, 1990).
9 See, for example, Richard S. Peterson, *Imitation and Praise in the Poems of Ben Jonson* (New Haven and London: Yale University Press, 1981); Arthur F. Marotti, *John Donne, Coterie Poet* (Madison: University of Wisconsin Press, 1986).
10 William McClung and Rodney Simard, 'Donne's Somerset Epithalamium and the Erotics of Criticism', *Huntington Library Quarterly*, 50 (1987) p. 95.
11 Heather Dubrow, *A Happier Eden: The Politics of Marriage in the Stuart Epithalamium* (Ithaca and London: Cornell University Press, 1990) p. 178.
12 Annabel Patterson, 'All Done', in Elizabeth D. Harvey and Katharine Eisaman Maus, eds, *Soliciting Interpretation* (Chicago and London: University of Chicago Press, 1990) p. 51.
13 See, for example, Raymond B. Waddington, *The Mind's Empire: Myth and Form in George Chapman's Narrative Poems* (Baltimore and London: Johns Hopkins University Press, 1974) pp. 196–214; Heather Dubrow, *A Happier Eden*, pp. 178–200; and David Lindley, *Thomas Campion* (Leiden: E.J. Brill, 1986) pp. 216–34.
14 Ian Donaldson, ed., *Ben Jonson*, The Oxford Authors (Oxford: Oxford Uni-

versity Press, 1985) p. 449. All subsequent references to Jonson's poems are to this edition.

15 Chamberlain, I, p. 499.

16 It is, however, tempting to speculate that the masque which brings *Women Beware Women* to its bloody end might gesture towards this earlier performance. As we have seen already, the events of the divorce seem to have etched themselves in Middleton's mind.

17 Chamberlain, I, p. 485.

18 The *Irish Masque* contains some unflattering parodies of Campion's work performed the previous night, but these, too, could have been added later, and might reflect Jonson's pique at his piece being displaced from the prime spot in the Christmas feasts. On the Irish background see David Lindley, 'Embarrassing Ben: The Masques for Frances Howard', in Arthur F. Kinney and Dan S. Collins, eds, *Renaissance Historicism: Selections from ELR* (1987), pp. 248–64.

19 R.C. Bald, *John Donne: A Life* (Oxford: Clarendon Press, 1970) p. 278.

20 *A Book of Masques in Honour of Allardyce Nicoll* (Cambridge: Cambridge University Press, 1967) p. 159.

21 For biography see G.M. Story and Helen Gardner, eds, *The Sonnets of William Alabaster* (Oxford: Oxford University Press, 1959).

22 David Riggs, *Ben Jonson: A Life* (Cambridge, Mass.: Harvard University Press, 1989) pp. 203–4.

23 See Bald, *Donne*, ch. 11.

24 David Norbrook, 'The Monarchy of Wit and the Republic of Letters: Donne's Politics', and Annabel Patterson, 'All Done', in *Soliciting Interpretation*, pp. 16–19, 51–3.

25 A.R. Braunmuller, *Natural Fictions: George Chapman's Major Tragedies* (Newark: University of Delaware Press; London and Toronto: Associated University Presses, 1992) p. 141.

26 Arthur Wilson, *The History of Great Britain* (1653) p. 72.

27 Northamptonshire Record Office, Finch-Hatton MS 319, fol. 6^v.

28 BL MS Royal 12.A.xxxv, fol. 12^v.

29 Dubrow, *A Happier Eden*, pp. 189–90.

30 BL MS Royal 12.A.xxxv, fol. 5^v. The Latin reads: 'Non vos casta fidem turtur, non grata columbae / Murmura, non luctas hederae, non oscula conchae / Edoicant: sit uterque utrique exemplar amoris. / Vt cito te faciat coniux de virgine matrem: / Et cito suscipias illum de coniuge patrem.'

31 See Braunmuller, *Natural Fictions*, p. 135.

32 For extended discussion of the masque see Lindley, *Campion*, pp. 217–34.

33 Spenser, *The Faerie Queene*, ed. A.C. Hamilton (London and New York: Longman, 1977) VI.xii.27–8.

34 Norma Dobie Solvie, *Stuart Politics in Chapman's Tragedy of Chabot* (Ann Arbor: Michigan University Press, 1928).

35 *The Plays of George Chapman, The Tragedies*, general editor Allan Holaday (Woodbridge: D.S. Brewer, 1987). *The Tragedy of Chabot*, ed. G. Blakemore Evans, I.i.68–80.

36 *HMC Downshire MSS*, IV, p. 252.

37 John Orrell, 'The London Court Stage in the Savoy Correspondence, 1613–1675', *Theatre Research International*, 4 (1979), p. 80.

5   THE THIRD TRIAL: MURDER

1 Harold Spencer Scott, ed., *Journal of Sir Roger Wilbraham, Camden Miscellany*, X (London: Royal Historical Society, 1902) p. 115.
2 BL MS Harley 7002, fol. 286ᵛ.
3 Ibid., fol. 201.
4 Chamberlain, I, p. 478.
5 *SP* 14/81/86 (a copy of the original which is recorded in *HMC Buccleugh MSS*, I, p. 160).
6 Astonishingly enough, there were those who endured this awful end rather than face trial. The usual motivation was that their families would not be deprived of their goods as would happen if they were found guilty.
7 Northamptonshire Record Office, Isham-Lamporte MS 3395, fol. 2ʳ.
8 *HMC Salisbury MSS*, XXII, p. 21.
9 BL Additional MS 28640, fol. 153; quoted in White, *Cast of Ravens* (London: John Murray, 1965) p. 127.
10 Bodleian MS Willis, 58, fol. 241ᵛ.
11 The speech seems to have made a strong impression, for a large number of MSS include versions of it.
12 James Spedding, ed., *The Letters and Life of Francis Bacon* (London: Longmans, Green, Reader and Dyer, 1869) vol. V, p. 338.
13 J. Payne Collier, ed., *The Egerton Papers, Camden Society*, 12 (London, 1840) p. 474.
14 Bodleian MS Smith, 17, fol. 30; and BL MS Cotton Titus C. VII, fol. 28.
15 *SP* 14/82/96.
16 *SP* 14/82/122; 14/83/1.
17 *SP* 14/82/98.
18 *SP* 14/83/20.
19 *SP* 14/83/20.
20 Coke to the King, 30 November 1615. BL MS Additional 32092, fol. 226ᵛ.
21 *SP* 14/82/73.
22 Andrew Amos, *The Great Oyer of Poisoning: The Trial of the Earl of Somerset* (London: Richard Bentley, 1846) p. 333.
23 Webster, *The Devil's Law Case*, ed. Frances A. Shirley, Regents Renaissance Drama Series (London: Edward Arnold, 1972) IV.ii.28–35.
24 BL MS Additional 35832, fol. 6.
25 Chester City Record Office MS CR 63.2.19, fol. 15ᵛ.
26 The enormous interest that the events generated made possession of such records highly desirable. So, at least, thought a 'poore cuntrie man' who dedicated his collection of 'the whole processe of this disastrous tragedie' to Sir Thomas Bromley as a token of his love and duty (CUL MS Dd.12.36).
27 It is interesting to speculate on the questions that would be raised by an attempt to produce a fresh modern edition of the trials. In many ways the problems would overlap with and illuminate current controversies in the literary field. Editors of literary texts agonise over the theoretical possibility of an 'auth-oritative' text, partly at least because different surviving states might reflect different originals – as in the case of the two surviving texts of *King Lear*, for example. In the case of these trials, however, we know that Coke's words were spoken only once, and that there *is* therefore a single 'origin' for the diverse

reports, however impossible it might be to recover it. The complementarity of the problems for textual editor and historian in dealing with the traces that survive are symptomatic of the underlying problems that this book attempts to address in understanding the construction placed upon the career of Frances Howard.

28 According to the account in Bodleian MS Willis 58, fol. 227.

29 Bodleian MS Tanner 299, fol. 198ᵛ (a fuller version than that in *ST*).

30 Quaratesi, the Florentine, called it 'a very strange way of judging', clearly appalled at the absence of defence witnesses. Anna Maria Crinò, 'Il processo a Lord e Lady Somerset per l'assassinio di Sir Thomas Overbury nelle relazioni di francesco Quaratesi e di Pompilio Gaetani', *English Miscellany* (1951) p. 284. I am grateful to Matilde Coletta for providing me with a translation of this important article.

31 Anne Worrall, *Offending Women: Female Lawbreakers and the Criminal Justice System* (London and New York: Routledge, 1990) p. 22.

32 W. Lance Bennett and Martha S. Feldman, *Reconstructing Reality in the Court-room* (New Brunswick: Rutgers University Press; London: Tavistock Publications, 1981) p. 60.

33 Spedding, *Bacon*, V, pp. 312–14.

34 The degree of calculation which went into Bacon's characterisation can be seen from the summary he sent to the King of the course he proposed to adopt in Carr's trial, in Spedding, *Bacon*, V, pp. 287–8.

35 Even a handy guide for trainee lawyers like Michael Hyam, *Advocacy Skills* (London: Blackstone Press, 1990) makes repeated reference to Cicero and Quintilian.

36 G.P.V. Akrigg, ed., *Letters of King James VI & I* (Berkeley, Los Angeles and London: University of California Press, 1984) pp. 335–45.

37 Anna Maria Crinò, 'Il processo a Lord e Lady Somerset', p. 261. The impli-cation of Frances's father and mother is interesting; when Elwes tried to make the same insinuation at his trial he was quickly stamped on by Coke.

38 Holles, *Letters*, I, pp. 73, 93–4.

39 *HMC De L'Isle and Dudley MSS*, V, pp. 340, 344.

40 S.R. Gardiner, 'On certain Letters of Diego Sarmiento de Acuña, Count of Gondomar, giving an account of the affair of the Earl of Somerset, with Remarks on the career of Somerset as a public man', *Archeologia*, 41 (1867) p. 165.

41 Ibid., pp. 169–70.

42 BL Additional MS 35832, fol. 4ᵛ.

43 *SP* 14/82/72.

44 Lambeth Palace MS 663, fol. 184ᵛ.

45 *HMC Buccleugh MSS*, I, p. 248.

46 Chamberlain, II, p. 1.

47 Ibid., p. 5.

48 Spedding, *Bacon*, V, p. 214.

49 Bodleian MS Malone 19, p. 157.

50 *HMC De L'Isle and Dudley MSS*, V, pp. 331–2.

51 BL MS 2194, fol. 77, contains this note on Carr: 'He was a great favorite: neither pierce Gaveston nor the Spensers with Edward 2nd nor the Earle of

Warwicke with Henry the 6 nor the Duke of Suffolk with Henry the eigth as this man was with King James'.

52 Marlowe, *Edward II*, ed. W. Moelwyn Merchant, New Mermaids (London: Ernest Benn, 1967) I.iv. 390–3, 402–4.

53 Bodleian MS Malone 23, fol. 6ʳ. Two lines derived from another epigram are tacked on to the end of this version.

54 Herford and Simpson in their edition of Jonson's works suggested that this masque was performed in 1614/5. John Orrell has demonstrated their hypothesis to be wrong in 'The London Stage in the Florentine Correspondence, 1604–18', *Theatre Research International*, 3 (1978) p. 174.

55 Anna Maria Crinò, 'Il processo a Lord e Lady Somerset', p. 275. Martin Butler and I are preparing a fuller study of the politics of this masque.

56 Bodleian MS Willis, 58, fol. 240.

57 *HMC Salisbury MSS*, XXI, p. 215. In her confession to Dr Whiting Turner alleged that Frances never took communion.

58 Robert Niccols, *Sir Thomas Overburies Vision* (1616) sig. C4ᵛ.

59 Bodleian MS Tanner, 299, fol. 196.

60 Chester City Record Office MS CR 63.2.19, fol. 5.

61 John Webster, *The Duchess of Malfi*, ed. John Russell Brown, The Revels Plays (London: Methuen, 1964) I.i.5–15.

62 Chester City Record Office MS CR 63.2.19, fol. 9ᵛ. A much more prosaic account was offered by Sanderson, who said that these effigies were nothing but 'babies' or dolls used by dressmakers to model clothes.

63 Reginald Scot, *The Discoverie of Witchcraft* (1584) p. 116.

64 Nathanael Richards, *The Celestiall Publican* (1631) sig. G8ᵛ.

65 Lambeth Palace MS 663, fol. 184.

66 Bodleian MS Willis 58, fol. 224.

67 John Dod and Robert Cleaver, *A Plaine and Familiar Exposition of the Ten Commandments* (18th edn 1630) p. 260.

68 William Whately, *A Bride-Bush* (1619) p. 6.

69 *The Araignement and burning of Margaret Ferne-seede for the Murther of her late Husband* (1608); Gilbert Dugdale, *A true Discourse of the practises of Elizabeth Caldwell, Ma: Ieffrey Bownd, Isabel Hall widdow, and George Fernely, on the parson of Ma: Thomas Caldwell* (1604).

70 Catherine Belsey, *The Subject of Tragedy: Identity and Difference in Renaissance Drama* (London and New York: Methuen, 1985) ch. 5.

71 John Rainolds, *Defence of the Judgement of the Reformed Churches that a man may lawfullie not onelie put awaie his wife for her adulterie but also marrie another* (1609), p. 88.

72 See Linda Woodbridge, *Women and the English Renaissance* (Urbana and Chicago: University of Illinois Press, 1984) pp. 177–8, 255–61. Plays could, of course, challenge the stereotype, as *The Duchess of Malfi* conspicuously does.

73 John Rainolds, *The Triumphs of Gods revenge against the cryinge and execrable sinne of wilful and premeditated Murther* (edn of 1634) p. 354.

74 BL MS Additional 35832, fol. 5ʳ.

75 Bodleian MS Willis 58, fol. 193ʳ.

76 Bodleian MS Willis 58, fol. 234. The exact wording of this letter is a matter of some controversy; Amos uses the difference between the various texts as indication of the deviousness of the prosecution.

77 Bodleian MS Tanner 299, fol. 199.
78 J.L. Vives, *The Education of a Christian Woman*, trans. R. Hyrd (1529) p. 126.
79 *The Civile Conversation of M. Stephen Guazzo*, trans. George Pettie (1581) (London: Constable, 1925) 2 vols, II, pp. 30–1.
80 Jonson 'To Celia', a version of Catullus, 'Vivamus mea Lesbia, atque amemus' (Donaldson, ed., p. 289).
81 Folger MS V.c. 89, fols 7ᵛ, 9. I am grateful to Bruce R. Smith for telling me of this poem, and generously supplying the transcript of the MS. He points out that, rather like the poem 'Why should we maids' already cited, in one MS it is a poem supposed to be written *to* rather than *by* a woman (Bodleian MS Rawlinson Poet. 85, fol. 116).
82 John Day, *Law Tricks* (1608), Malone Society Reprints (Oxford: Malone Society, 1950), ll. 257–63.
83 Painter, *The Palace of Pleasure*, II, p. 42.
84 See Joan Smith, 'M'Learned Friends', in *Misogynies* (London: Faber & Faber, 1989) pp. 1–9; Helena Kennedy, *Eve Was Framed*, ch. 5 'Asking for It'.
85 Thomas Middleton and Thomas Dekker, *The Roaring Girl*, ed. Paul Mullholland, The Revels Plays (Manchester: Manchester University Press, 1987) III.i.81–7.
86 J.A. Sharpe, *Defamation and Sexual Slander in Early Modern England: The Church Courts at York* (York: Borthwick Papers, no. 58, 1982); Martin Ingram, *Church Courts, Sex and Marriage in England, 1570–1640* (Cambridge: Cambridge University Press, 1987) ch. 10.
87 Sharpe, *Defamation and Sexual Slander*, p. 27.
88 Martin Ingram, 'Ridings, Rough Music and Mocking Rhymes in Early Modern England', in Barry Reay, ed., *Popular Culture in Seventeenth-century England* (London and Sydney: Croom Helm, 1985) p. 181. Of course actions for slander were brought by men, and men too suffered libels accusing them of cuckoldry, for example. Nonetheless, specifically sexual slander is the basis for a far higher percentage of the female actions than those of men.
89 Francis Mason, *Two Sermons* (1621) p. 55.
90 Painter, *The Palace of Pleasure*, I, p. 310.
91 Anna Maria Crinò, 'Il processo a Lord e Lady Somerset', p. 272.
92 Ibid., pp. 264–5.
93 *SP* 14/82/68.
94 *SP* 14/82/84. At his trial Robert Carr was also confronted with this evidence, and said 'it was once resolved somebody in court should fall out with Overbury, and offer him some affront; but that was not followed' (*ST*, 982).
95 Stone, *Crisis*, p. 247.
96 Bodleian MS Willis 58, fol. 212.
97 Sampson Price, *Ephesus Warning before her Woe* (1616) p. 18.
98 Rainolds, *The Triumphs*, pp. 1, 4, 26.
99 Painter, *The Palace of Pleasure*, III, p. 54.
100 Worrall, *Offending Women*, p. 31.
101 Ann Jones, *Women who Kill* (2nd edn London: Gollancz, 1991) ch. 2.
102 Thomas Beard, *The Theatre of Gods Judgements* (2nd edn 1612) p. 339.
103 Painter, *The Palace of Pleasure*, I, pp. 218–39.
104 See, for example, Helena Kennedy, *Eve Was Framed*, ch. 8.

105 Wilson, *History*, p. 67.
106 J.O. Halliwell. ed., *The Autobiography and Correspondence of Sir Simonds D'Ewes* (London: Richard Bentley, 1845) 2 vols, I, pp. 74–5.
107 *Secret History*, I, p. 381.
108 Amos, *The Great Oyer*, p. 57.
109 Bodleian MS Malone 23, fol. 6ʳ. Many other examples can be found. The last line frequently reads 'a wife, a witch, a murderess and a whore', and Frances is variously characterised as a 'saucy' or a 'scurvy' girl.
110 Bodleian MS Rawlinson D 1048, fol. 64.
111 Spedding, *Bacon*, p. 297. (Significantly different from the version printed in *State Trials*.)
112 Ibid., p. 313.
113 Northamptonshire Record Office, Isham-Lamporte MS 3396.
114 BL MS Cotton Titus B.vii, fol. 476 (printed in Birch, *The Court and Times of James I*, I, p. 333).
115 *SP* 14/33/32, 33.
116 Thomas Tuke, *A Treatise against Painting* (1616) p. 52.
117 Bodleian MS Willis 58, fol. 226.
118 Belsey, *The Subject of Tragedy*, pp. 160–4.
119 This is not to deny that a more modern notion of self was coming into being, and that in the drama of the period in particular the representation of character was undergoing a radical shift.
120 The two key works are *Discipline and Punish*, trans. Alan Sheridan (London: Allen Lane, 1977) and *The History of Sexuality*, I, trans. Robert Hurley (London: Allen Lane, 1979).
121 BL MS Additional 34218, fol. 226ᵛ. There are many variant versions of Elwes's speech, some of which seem fairly obviously to have been smartened up by the reporters. The general drift of his remarks is constant, but the exact sequence and the rhetorical polish differ.
122 *SP* 14/83/20.
123 *SP* 14/83/33 (my italics).
124 Thomas W. Laqueur, 'Crowds, carnival and the state in English executions, 1604–1868', in A.L. Beier, David Cannadine and James M. Rosenheim, eds, *The First Modern Society: Essays in English History in Honour of Lawrence Stone* (Cambridge: Cambridge University Press, 1989) pp. 305–56.
125 J.A. Sharpe has drawn attention to the significance of religion; but even he, it seems to me, is too ready to place religion entirely in the service of the state. See ' "Last Dying Speeches": Religion, Ideology and Public Execution in Seventeenth-century England', *Past and Present*, 107 (1985) pp. 144–67.
126 Thomas Cooper, *The Cry and Revenge of Blood* (1620) p. 52.
127 Foucault, *Discipline and Punish*, p. 67.
128 See, for example, Richard Wilson, 'The Quality of Mercy: Discipline and Punishment in Shakespearian Comedy', *The Seventeenth Century*, 5 (1990) pp. 1–42; Jonathan Dollimore, 'Transgression and surveillance in *Measure for Measure*', in *Political Shakespeare*, ed. Jonathan Dollimore and Alan Sinfield (Manchester: Manchester University Press, 1985) pp. 72–88.
129 BL MS Additional 34218, fol. 227ᵛ.
130 Niccols, *Sir Thomas Overburies Vision*, sig. D1ᵛ.
131 BL MS Additional 34218, fol. 226ᵛ.

132 Linda Levy Peck, *Court Patronage and Corruption*, pp. 174–9.
133 Martin Wiggins, *Journeymen in Murder: The Assassin in English Renaissance Drama* (Oxford: The Clarendon Press, 1991).
134 *SP* 14/83/20.
135 Anne M. Haselkorn, 'Sin and the Politics of Penitence: Three Jacobean Adulteresses', in Anne Haselkorn and Betty S. Travitsky, eds, *The Renaissance Englishwoman in Print: Counterbalancing the Canon* (Amherst: University of Massachusetts Press, 1990) p. 126.
136 Lisa Jardine, *Still Harping on Daughters*, pp. 71–2.
137 S.R. Gardiner, 'On certain Letters of Diego Sarmiento de Acuña', *Archeologia*, 41 (1867) p. 178.
138 James More Molyneux, 'Message from King James I to the Earl of Somerset, in the case of Sir Thomas Overbury, sent on the 29th of December, 1615, through Sir George More, Lieutenant of the Tower', *Archeologia*, 41 (1867) p. 77.
139 This is the Folio text; Quarto reads 'small vices'.
140 Charles Richardson, *A Sermon Concerning the Punishment of Malefactors* (1616) pp. 27–8.
141 S.R. Gardiner, 'On certain Letters of Diego Sarmiento de Acuña', p. 185.
142 BL MS Additional 25707, fol. 46^r. This lyric was brought to my attention by Arthur F. Marotti in a lecture at the Reading Literature and History Conference, 1992.
143 Holles, *Letters*, I, p. 129 (2 June 1616).
144 Chamberlain, II, p. 17.
145 White, *Cast of Ravens*, p. 177.
146 Fritz Saxl, 'Veritas Filia Temporis', *Philosophy and History: Essays presented to Ernst Cassirer* (Oxford: Oxford University Press, 1936) p. 203ff; D.J. Gordon, 'Veritas Filia Temporis: Hadrianus Junius and Geoffrey Whitney', reprinted in *The Renaissance Imagination*, ed. Stephen Orgel (Berkeley, Los Angeles and London: University of California Press, 1975) pp. 220–32.
147 Thomas Beard, *Gods Judgements*, p. 295; John Rainolds, *The Triumphs*, p. 14.
148 See, for example, Thomas Cooper, *The Cry and Revenge of Blood* (1620), and *The Araignement and Burning of Margaret Ferne-seede* (1608).
149 Birch, *The Court and Times of James I*, I, p. 380.
150 Bodleian MS Malone 23, fol. 7.
151 Chester City Record Office MS CR 63.2.19, fol. 12^r.
152 BL Harley MS 6383, fol. 78. I am extremely grateful to Alastair Bellany for bringing this poem to my attention.
153 *Truth Brought to Light*, pp. 21–2.
154 William Loe, *Vox Clamantis* (1621).
155 Wilson, *History*, p. 88.
156 On 2 September 1619, for example, Peter Edney was paid 'for the dyett, lodging, apparell and teaching in musicke of one of the Pages belonging to the Countesse of Somersett'. A. Ashbee, ed., *Records of English Court Music*, IV (Snodland, 1991) p. 104. Lynn Hulse kindly drew this item to my attention.
157 Snow, *Essex*, p. 191.
158 Wilson, *History*, p. 88.
159 Spenser, *The Faerie Queene*, I.viii.47–8.

EPILOGUE

1 S.R. Gardiner, *History of England from the Accession of James I to the Outbreak of the Civil War, 1603–42* (London: Longmans, Green & Co, 1883) 10 vols, II, p. 338.

2 Lorie Jerrell Leininger, 'Exploding the Myth of the Lustful Murderess: A Reinterpretation of Frances Howard's Role in the Death of Sir Thomas Overbury', *Topic*, 36 (1982) pp. 38–53. I am very grateful to Lois Potter for drawing this article to my attention at the very last stage of the writing of this book.

3 *Guardian*, 2 January 1990.

4 Joan Wallach Scott, *Gender and the Politics of History* (New York: Columbia University Press, 1988) p. 2.

Index